TRANSITION
A STORY OF CHANGE

Peacock Press

TRANSITION - A STORY OF CHANGE © ANNE FALLAS

ISBN 978-1-912271-6-03

Published by Peacock Press, 2020
Scout Bottom Farm
Mytholmroyd
Hebden Bridge HX7 5JS (UK)

Design and artwork by DM Design and Print

TRANSITION
A STORY OF CHANGE

ANNE FALLAS

With a special thanks to Leon.

A foreword by Maddy Harland
Editor of Permaculture Magazine...

"This is a very rare animal, an eco-novel written well. Set in France at time when the Earth's climate is unravelling, it tells the story of a group of people who are struggling to make sense of their lives, build a small, self-sufficient community and prepare for a posttechnological world. Rather than being gloomy, it treats the exploration of a new way of living with optimism and joy. Encoded in the tale are metaphors about human and planetary evolution that would be familiar to students of esoteric psychology. The novel works. I read it cover to cover and enjoyed its style and structure and I didn't find it obvious or preachy. Worth seeking out."

Maddy Harland, Editor, Permaculture Magazine

CHAPTER 1

'That's it. I've bloody well had enough!' Steve shouted as he took off his work gloves and threw them at Charlie.

The two men had hit another knot in the log. Frustrated, Steve went to sit on the makeshift bench outside Templar House, Charlie followed.

'Come on, Steve, or we'll never get finished,' Charlie pleaded as he sat down on the bench.

'We are not going to cut all those logs with that saw. Charlie, face it, it's not working. Three days we've been at it and look at the miserly pile of cut logs. Get real!' Steve leant back against the wall and inspected the blisters on his hands.

'Well, what do you suggest?' Charlie asked.

'I suggest you buy a chainsaw. It's the only way we'll get together four months supply of cut logs,' Steve replied.

'That doesn't seem right to me. Years ago they used to cut all their logs by hand. I don't know if I can justify going and buying a machine. It seems a cop-out.'

'Charlie the Luddite.'

'Maybe!' Charlie answered and shrugged.

'You'll have to decide on what to do. There's no way we are going to be able to cut our winter fuel by hand. That monstrous fireplace in there will eat what we've cut in next to no time and we'll freeze,' Steve frowned.

Charlie became serious. Deep in thought, he weighed up the advantages and disadvantages of buying a chainsaw. In his mind he imagined the huge pile of uncut logs being easily transformed into logs of the correct dimension, all neatly filling the woodshed.

'Labour-saving,' Steve whispered into Charlie's ear. Charlie did not respond, instead his thoughts moved into the realm of plumbing. The necessity of this modern convenience was becoming increasingly apparent. 'Maybe you're right. A chainsaw would do the job in next to no time. The time it would save we could spend on doing the plumbing.'

'Or installing a woodburner,' Steve suggested. 'The fireplace isn't economical. A good woodburner would heat the room and use much less fuel. Fewer logs to cut,' Steve said as he brushed the sawdust from his trousers.

The following day the two men found themselves installing a woodburner in Templar House.

'What a bloody mess. There's soot everywhere,' said Steve, looking around.

Some of the soot had begun to settle around the fireplace, but clouds of drifting soot moved further into the room.

'That's the bad news,' Charlie gave a white-toothed grin.

'What's the good news?' Steve asked.

'The flue pipe is in place. Look!' Charlie pointed up the chimney.

Steve switched on his torch and checked the flue pipe. 'It's in a perfect position,' he sounded amazed.

'It just happened, it wasn't intentional!' Charlie replied. Steve slotted the pipe into the back of the fire and sealed it with fire cement. Charlie attempted to clean up the soot without making too much mess. 'Hell, it's everywhere. The table, the piano, the window ledge, the floor, they're all covered in it.'

'You are making it worse by trying to sweep it up. Use the hoover,' advised Steve.

'We haven't got one.'

'Have we not?'

'No, and have you only just realised? We've been here a month!' Charlie carried on sweeping the soot into a pile. He was annoyed, and flashed Steve an angry look.

When he had finished sweeping he said, 'It's going to get too cold to have a shower outside, we really need to get on with the plumbing.'

'I agree, but we can't do everything,' said Steve, filling the shower bag. 'I thought you wanted to prepare some land for planting potatoes?'

'Maybe we could do a bit of both each day,' Charlie shrugged.

'The plumbing should come first. How long do you think it will take us to dig the field over?' Steve asked.

'I've made a good start,' Charlie felt annoyed again.

'A good start! You've barely scratched the surface!' Steve responded.

'Then what do you suggest?' Charlie snatched the shower bag from Steve and made his way to the door.

'Buy a rotavator or employ a plumber.'

'My dream of a simple life is being shattered.'

'Face up to reality. That simple life was a hard life for thousands of people. They suffered, Charlie. It was a battle to survive. That's the reality,' Steve spoke calmly.

Charlie leant back against the door. 'Well we'll make a compromise then, we'll take the middle road. The path between the dream and the reality. What do you think?'

'We can try, but I'm not sure how we can do it,' Steve replied and passed Charlie a towel. 'Here, scrub up and I'll make us something to eat.'

Charlie moved their chairs closer to the woodburner and poured glasses of scotch. When Steve returned, Charlie was deep in thought. A pained expression marked his face. Steve sat down quietly and left Charlie to his thoughts.

He was reliving his final visit to his parents. He had parked the VW at a discreet distance from their house and had walked the rest of the way. He strode up the driveway and rang the doorbell. Gina answered, she had been surprised to see him. He walked to his father's study, knocked, waited and then walked in. His father was sitting at his desk, a copy of the financial paper open in front of him. Charlie's father looked over the top of his glasses, his expressionless face spoke realms. It said, 'Hurry up, get on with it, you are disturbing me.'

'Hello. To what do I owe this visit?'

'Hello Father!' Charlie explained to him clearly the nature of his visit. He told him he had bought a house in France and was going to live there.

'What will you do for money?'

Charlie blurted out the rehearsed answer. He explained that he wanted to try to be self-sufficient, grow food, keep hens and goats.

His father had picked up the phone. 'Mother, your son has gone insane, get in here now, speak to him and then get a doctor to see him.'

Charlie saw red. The anger which had built up and been locked away for years began to explode. 'I am NOT insane, you stupid old fool. How dare you even think that?' Charlie's fist smashed down on his father's desk and he saw the look of hatred in his father's eyes. 'Why did you have a child? Why did you not get a new foal or a pup, something you could train, dominate and control!'

'Don't you speak to Daddy like that. Have you taken drugs? Or are you drunk?' his mother had asked.

'Neither. I am in full control of my faculties but father is not happy about that.'

'This son of yours has bought a hovel in France of all places and wants to keep goats, bloody goats.'

'I want to be self-sufficient,' Charlie told his mother.

'You'll have to be self-sufficient from now on because you are not getting another penny from me, that's for sure,' his father raged. 'All I have done for you and you have the audacity to flush it down the pan.'

'I think you had better leave,' his mother said as she went to comfort her husband.

Charlie walked to the door. His father's voice boomed after him, 'Not another penny, I don't invest in lame dogs!'

'Perhaps you should start,' Charlie replied.

'And never come back, you waste of space!'

Those final words, spoken by his father, replayed and hit another body blow.

Charlie grimaced.

'What's the matter?' asked Steve quietly.

'I was thinking back to when I last saw my parents. I made a final visit just before we moved here,' Charlie explained, and passed Steve a glass of scotch.

'Did it not go well?' Steve asked.

'No. My father's last words informed me that I was a waste of space.'

Steve took a sip of scotch and said, 'Prove him wrong.'

'How?' asked Charlie, shaking his head.

'Get organised here and then invite them both to stay. Your father will have cooled down by then and he'd be a fool not to be impressed by this place.'

'That man stay here? He wouldn't settle for anything less than a four-star hotel with a luxury en-suite bedroom,' Charlie explained, and took a gulp of scotch.

'Then we'll rig something up,' said Steve seriously.

'What do you suggest? A spot of dusting, some new sheets and a chamber pot under the bed?' Charlie laughed cynically.

The following morning Charlie had left in the VW before Steve had got out of bed. Steve read the note Charlie had left, informing him that he would be back around eleven.

'That's just Charlie, no explanation,' Steve said to himself, and went to get some breakfast.

While Charlie was away, Steve finished filling the logstore with the cut logs. He had just finished when Charlie pulled up outside the house.

'Lots of good news, but first open up the VW, there are things in there.'

Steve opened up the door of the van and found inside a vacuum cleaner, a set of kitchen scales and a bag of shopping.

'I thought you didn't want to buy anything else?' Steve laughed as he lifted the cleaner out of the van.

'I think you're right, we need to get organised, and some things are a necessity. My other purchase is being delivered this afternoon,' Charlie explained, as he helped Steve to carry the things into the house.

'And what is this other purchase?' Steve asked.

'You'll see. Let's have a coffee outside and I'll tell you my news.'

The men sat on the bench together in the early winter sun. Charlie opened a packet of biscuits and began to tell Steve his news. 'When I was in town I bumped into Anita, she helped me to buy the hoover and the scales. Giles will be with us next week to help do the plumbing. And they have a cooker we can have. It's a bit like an Aga or a Rayburn, it will heat water, keep the kitchen warm and you can do the cooking with it. Anita says it's brilliant for baking bread and she even told me where we can buy a sack of organic bread flour, there's a mill not far from here.'

'The cooker sounds perfect for us, but I have absolutely no idea how to make bread,' Steve said.

'Don't worry, Giles will show us the next time he makes a batch. And for my final bit of news, Anita knows of a mobile piano teacher in the area and what's more, he's bi-lingual,' Charlie grinned.

The delivery van arrived late in the afternoon. By this time Charlie had hoovered every room in the house and Steve had rearranged the kitchen. The van pulled up in front of the house and before Charlie or Steve could help, the delivery man unloaded a rotavator onto the path.

As the van drove away Charlie inspected his purchase. The brand new green machine shone. As he inspected the plough attachment, Steve sat on the bench and studied the instruction manual. 'Bit of bad news, the manual is in French,' called Steve.

'Damn!'

'But hang on, there are some diagrams.'

Charlie walked over. 'Does it show how to attach the plough?'

Steve flicked through the manual. 'Here this looks like it.' He showed Charlie the diagram on the open page.

'It looks complicated and it's starting to go dark,' Charlie complained. 'It's too late to try it out now. We'll put it under cover and try it out in the morning.'

Charlie pushed the rotavator into the barn and Steve carried the plough attachment. Charlie closed and padlocked the door.

'Come on, they'll be safe in there,' Steve said. 'I want to show you something in the kitchen.'

The two men went into the house together. 'My, you certainly have had a change around,' Charlie exclaimed as he went into the kitchen. 'And what on earth is that door doing there?' he asked in amazement, as he walked over to the once hidden door.

'It was hidden behind the big cupboard,' Steve opened the door. 'Have a look inside.'

Charlie went inside. 'My God, it's an old larder.'

'A larder complete with marble slab and pine shelves,' Steve added.

'It's freezing in here,' Charlie noted. 'Perfect for storing your bread flour.'

The next day Charlie and Steve felt the sharpness of early winter as they stood on the edge of the field with the rotavator.

'Come on Charlie, start it up, it's freezing just standing here,' Steve rubbed his hands together.

Charlie pulled the starter for the fifth time, but still the engine would not start. 'You have a go, it's as dead as a dodo,' Charlie moved to one side and held up his hands.

Steve walked over and tugged hard and sharp on the starter. The engine came to life. Charlie grinned, took hold of the handlebars and released the clutch.

'Which gear is it in?' Steve asked.

'First,' replied Charlie as he walked behind the machine. As the machine moved, the plough attachment neatly turned over a slice of earth.

'Keep it straight,' shouted Steve as he walked behind.

'I'm trying!' shouted Charlie, 'But it's hard work!'

Charlie carried on until he reached the far end of the field. He called to Steve, 'You have a go!'

Steve turned over the plough attachment and then walked behind the machine as it made a second line. 'Is it straight?' he asked Charlie.

'Straight enough. It's hard work though, isn't it?' Charlie was shouting above the din of the machine.

'It's because we're starting from scratch, it's uncultivated land.'

'It'll be easier next year!' said Charlie, examining the neatly ploughed strip of land.

Steve led him to a patch of land next to the vegetable plot and pointed. 'A possible problem. Rabbit droppings, and rabbit droppings mean rabbits, and rabbits eat veg. We need to fence the patch.'

'Surely not,' Charlie objected.

'Charlie, do you want to do hours of backbreaking work just to provide food for God knows how many rabbits?'

'It's more expense!' Charlie exclaimed.

'Giles is bound to have some fence posts kicking around, so with a bit of luck we'd only need to buy a roll or two of fencing. It would save expense in the long run,' Steve explained.

Charlie stared glumly at the plot.

CHAPTER 2

By lunchtime the storm had died out, leaving many fallen branches in its wake. The ditches at the side of the roads were struggling to cope with the amount of rainfall and in places small streams formed and ran across the road.

The van and VW, avoiding the fallen branches, travelled slowly and eventually pulled up outside the house.

'We'll unload and then I'll get off for lunch,' said Giles as he opened up the van.

'Where the hell is Steve when you need him?' Charlie was struggling to get a toilet out of the VW.

'I'm here, hold your horses,' Steve said as he appeared from around the back of the house.

'Where did you disappear to?' Charlie asked.

'I thought I saw someone go around the back of the house as we were pulling up,' Steve said as he helped to unload the VW.

'And was there anyone?' Charlie asked.

'He'd scarpered.'

Giles overheard the conversation and came over. 'A number of folk in the area have been spotting a stranger wandering about. Make sure you lock things up, just in case. You never know.'

'That's me finished, I'll be back around two,' Giles said as he started up the van.

When he had gone, Charlie and Steve went into the house.

'What did this stranger look like?' Charlie asked.

'Tall, unkempt and very thin. But he could certainly move quickly. I was wondering if he was the intruder who came into the camper van.' Steve began to make the sandwiches.

'Why didn't you get a better look at him that night? Surely it wasn't completely pitch black.' Charlie unpacked the carrier bag and put the bottles of scotch into the cupboard.

'I didn't want to draw any attention to myself in case he was dangerous,' Steve replied.

'So you admit to seeing a person that night?' Charlie stopped what he was doing.

'I think so,' Steve admitted.

'Why didn't you say so at the time?' Charlie asked.

'I didn't want it to upset our holiday. I figured it was best to keep it to myself.'

As he looked in the cupboard he asked, 'Why four bottles of scotch?'

'We both like a nip in the evening so I thought I'd stock up, and before you start giving me one of your lectures, I am not turning into an alcoholic!'

'Just be careful, that's all,' Steve said.

The morning's storm gave way to a beautiful afternoon. A blue sky complete with a golden sun appeared.

The three men took their coffee break in the afternoon sun.

'With the water heater in place in the cellar, we can now run some pipes under the kitchen floor without having to lift a floorboard!' Giles said as he took a piece of cake from the plate.

'We will need to lift floorboards upstairs though, won't we?' asked Charlie.

'Not many, the plumbing is all more or less in one area,' Giles replied. 'This cake is first class, where did you get it from?'

'Steve made it,' said Charlie, keeping his eye on the last piece.

'You want to get yourself over to see Martha and Michael. Last year they were desperately searching for a cook or a chef to make evening meals and had to give up the idea in the end, they couldn't find anyone.'

'Really?' Steve sounded interested.

Giles nodded and then added, 'It would be a bit of cash for you.'

'Sounds like a good idea,' said Charlie as he helped himself to the last piece of cake.

'Will you sit down or go and take another shower, you are driving me mad!' Steve said as he made his way into the kitchen.

Charlie heard PJ's car pull up in front of the house and he rushed to open the door. Steve stayed in the kitchen and discreetly closed the kitchen door.

Charlie, expecting to see a flamboyant eccentric musician, was slightly disappointed as a small unassuming figure walked up to him.

'Hello Mr Charles, I'm PJ,' he said, holding out his hand.

'Charles is my Christian name, please call me Charlie - everyone else does,' said Charlie shaking his hand.

He led PJ into the house and without wasting any time PJ walked over to the piano and sat down.

'The piano came with the house,' Charlie explained, as PJ adjusted the tuning.

From his briefcase he pulled out a thin booklet which he placed on the music stand. He explained to Charlie, 'This is where we will begin. The book is really for children but it will teach you the basics and then we can move on.'

Charlie sat at the piano and PJ sat down on the chair next to him, and for the next thirty minutes he taught Charlie how to play the scale of C major and how to recognise the notes of the scale written in the booklet.

'You will need to practise this every day. Loosen up those fingers, Charlie. Play it first with the right hand and then with the left. Practise well and then you will be able to play with both hands together. There's also a short piece of music for you to practise too.' PJ opened the page and with his pencil ticked the piece.

Charlie felt his heart sink as he read the title.

'Try it now if you will,' PJ instructed, and tapped the piece with his pencil.

With no obvious escape route, Charlie took a deep breath and began to play the simple piece of music. In the kitchen Steve attempted to fight back hysteria as he heard Charlie playing 'Baa Baa Black Sheep'.

PJ stopped Charlie's hands from playing and asked, 'What on earth is that awful wailing sound?'

Charlie turned his head to listen. 'It sounds like my lodger having a bout of hysteria.'

Leo lay unable to sleep. He could hear Martha and Michael going to bed, Martha was speaking in a low voice. Leo got up and went over to the window. A sharp crescent moon gave little light and only a few stars were visible, most were hidden behind unseen cloud.

He opened the window and breathed in the November night air. It reminded him of Bonfire Night back home. Aware of Leo's presence, two bats flew close to him. He wondered why they hadn't settled down somewhere for the winter. As Leo's eyes tried to follow the bats, he thought for one moment that he could see a light in the distance. He tried to focus on the light but it had gone. He kept his eyes fixed on the spot where the light had been and waited.

A few minutes later the light flashed again and there was no doubt in Leo's mind that someone was out there with a torch. His eyes followed the intermittent torch light and he realised that it was going along the path to Studio Cottage.

He closed the window, dressed hurriedly and, unable to find his shoes, put on his slippers. Quietly he made his way down the stairs to the front door. He unlocked the door and went outside.

Leo had heard the rumours. He had heard about the stranger who had triggered off local concern and who had caused most folks to lock their doors at night. He knew Maddy and Steve had seen someone on the night of the party. Nobody knew who the man was.

Leo pushed through the last clump of brambles and made his way out of the trees to the side of Studio Cottage. He crouched down by the side of the cottage and waited.

As he lifted his eyes from the ground around him, the torchlight appeared. It was only three or four yards away, approaching quickly. As the footsteps came closer, Leo could barely make out the figure.

The figure paused at Sylvie's gate. Leo felt that the stranger was aware of him, not just aware, but Leo felt sure that he was saying something, without using spoken words.

'We didn't meet this time but we will,' were the unspoken words.

Steve borrowed the VW and went to see Martha and Michael. Martha answered the door. 'Hello, what a lovely surprise, but I'm afraid you won't find Sylvie here.'

'I know, it's actually you I have come to see.'

In the kitchen, Michael was sitting at the table reading a newspaper, he looked up when he heard Steve walking in.

'Hello Boyo. How's it going?'

'Brilliant. Giles has worked wonders. We have hot water, showers and flushing loos!' Steve replied, sitting down at the table.

Michael laughed, 'When you have had to manage without these things you certainly appreciate them. Isn't it wonderful to see the loo flush?'

Steve began to explain, 'Charlie mentioned to Giles that I love to cook and that I'm not a bad cook. Giles suggested that I came to see you, he thought you might still be considering doing evening meals.'

'What a strange coincidence,' Martha sat back in her chair.

'Only yesterday I had a call from Sissy Pirton. She asked if it would be possible to book in here for two weeks in the new year. She wanted bed, breakfast and dinner for eight people. Sissy is one of our regulars and comes to stay a couple of times each year. I really didn't want to let her down, but I don't want to cook dinner for eight people for two weeks!'

'We are still trying to semi-retire!' Michael chipped in with a smile, 'And I think you have just landed yourself a job!'

Martha broke Steve's thoughts. 'Don't look so worried. I'd be there to help, and so would Sylvie. We could have a dummy run, us three, Giles and Anita, Leo, Sylvie and Charlie, that's eight.'

'It sounds terrifying,' Steve admitted.

'Think it over and get back to me when you've made a decision. If it went well and you were interested, there would be work for you from the end of April, as we're constantly being asked to provide dinner.'

'We might even pay you a wage,' Michael added.

That evening Steve went to see Sylvie. As he pulled up outside the house she rushed outside to meet him.

'You're going to be the chef!' she squealed, as Steve got out of the van.

'How did you find out so quickly?' he asked, wrapping his arms around her.

'The storm knocked the electricity off, so Michael brought me some candles. Come in,' she said, grabbing hold of his arm.

'I'm considering it but I haven't made a decision yet. I'm not sure I'm capable.'

'Of course you are capable! And we could work as a team, we'd make a brilliant team.'

'I thought about that, but it's the responsibility, I don't know if I'm up to it.'

'We can share the responsibility. It would be a wonderful opportunity for us both. How do you think I felt with the prospect of running the B&B on my own?' Sylvie frowned at him.

He drove slowly home and parked outside the house. The light downstairs was still on.

Inside, Charlie lay slumped at the table. Next to him was the empty whisky bottle. Steve knew the bottle had been full when he left the house earlier. The room felt cold. Steve touched the top of the woodburner, it had gone out hours ago.

He shook Charlie, and when he did not respond, he shook him harder. Charlie woke from his drunken slumber with a start.

'What the...' he slurred. 'I'm pissed and I'm cold.'

'You let the fire go out. But I wouldn't worry, with all that whisky inside you it's unlikely that you will freeze.'

'I'm so cold,' Charlie repeated.

'Come on, let's get you to bed,' Steve helped Charlie to his feet.

'I'm so sorry, so sorry,' he mumbled as they climbed the stairs.

When they got to the landing, Charlie turned to Steve and said clearly, 'I've started writing poetry.'

'I know. Your notebook was open on the table the other night.'

Charlie stood still. 'Did you read anything?'

'Only a couple of lines, something about some blue tits.'

'That's one of mine, but the last one isn't.'

'What do you mean?'

'The last poem, it isn't mine,' Charlie sounded anxious.

'It's freezing on this landing, let's get into the bedroom and then you can explain,' Steve said as he supported Charlie.

Charlie sat down on the end of the bed as Steve stood next to the heater. Charlie began to explain, 'I know I'm pissed but I know what I am telling you. The last poem, I didn't write it, someone else did. It's not my handwriting and I knew you hadn't written it, you wouldn't have known some of the words.'

'Thanks.'

'I'm not insulting you, the words are not ones we would use. Would you write about the apocalypse?'

'The apocalypse?'

'Steve, there's someone else in this house apart from me and you. Go get the notebook and I'll prove it to you.'

'Look Charlie, you are pissed, maybe tomorrow things will seem different.'

'Tomorrow my notebook will only contain my poems?'

'I'm not saying that. Let's talk about it tomorrow when we are both clear-headed, but not now, Charlie. Come on, get into bed where it's warm.' Steve helped Charlie into bed.

He was about to leave the room when Charlie called to him,

'Steve, you are the only person I have ever really been close to.'

CHAPTER 3

Over the next couple of days, the weather changed abruptly. Wet and stormy weather gave way to a severe drop in temperature. Hard frosts penetrated the valley.

Michael replenished Sylvie's log pile and Anita and Giles laid insulation in their loft. Charlie and Steve spent their days cutting and stacking logs and Steve, who had been feeding the birds with the left-over stale bread, had decided to make a bird table.

When Charlie went to do the weekly shop, Steve found some pieces of old wood in the barn and began to construct the table. Making the platform and the stand was easy, but constructing a roof section was proving difficult.

He persevered, and eventually a simple roof began to take shape. As he stood back to admire his handiwork a strange feeling came over him. He not only felt that he was being watched but he was aware of words entering his mind. The words were not spoken. The words, 'Do not be afraid of me,' were repeated. Steve turned around and found himself face to face with the stranger.

The two men stared at each other. Eventually the stranger spoke. In perfect English he asked, 'I need help. Please will you help me? Steve, please.'

'How do you know my name?'

'I heard you in the orchard on the night of the party.'

'What did you hear?' Steve asked.

'Everything you said,' the stranger replied and then added,

'I know you are the only one who can help me.'

Steve stared at the thin, gaunt and unkempt figure in front of him. 'Where do you live?' he asked.

'In the woods. I have shelter there and I survive there.'

'How? How can I help you?' Steve asked.

'I need warm clothes and perhaps a blanket.'

Steve took a quick mental stock of the situation. This weak and fragile figure was not a threat. He needed some help. Charlie was out of the house. Eventually he said, 'Come into the house with me, it's OK, I am on my own, and I will find you some clothes.'

Steve pointed to the chair by the fire. 'Sit down and get warm while I go upstairs and see what I can find.'

The stranger gingerly sat down. The experience seemed strange. To sit in a house and to sit by the fire provoked memories which had seemed lost and forgotten and now came flooding back.

As Steve came back into the room, the stranger nervously stood up and moved away from the chair. 'It's OK, it's only me.' Steve placed an armful of things on the table. Two woollen jumpers, a pair of thick cord trousers, socks and two blankets. 'Oh! and I found these shoes as well, but I don't know if they'll fit you.' Steve passed the shoes to the stranger.

'They are too small!' he said.

'Hang on then.' Steve ran back upstairs and moments later he reappeared carrying a pair of black brogues. 'What about these?' he asked, passing the shoes over.

The brogues were the right size. Steve passed the stranger a pair of socks. 'Here, you might as well put them on now.'

Sitting back down in the chair, the man took off his sandals as Steve looked on in horror. His feet were covered in raw open sores.

'Wait!' Steve looked at the feet. 'Those sores look infected and if you don't do something about them soon you'll risk getting gangrene or blood poisoning.'

'Not now!' he replied, putting on the socks and the brogues.

'Why don't you come here once a week when Charlie is out and take a shower?' Steve suggested.

The stranger ignored him.

'Well it's up to you. Charlie goes shopping the same morning each week and he's gone for about two hours.'

'I know,' the stranger replied.

Steve smiled as he packed the clothes and blankets into a bin bag. 'Here, put this on,' he said, as he passed a jumper to the man.

The stranger put on the warm jumper and picked up the bin bag. He was making his way out of the door when Steve stopped him. 'Here, you'll need this far more than me,' he said as he gave the man his waterproof jacket. 'It even has a hood.'

'Pack it in! I can't take anymore.' As Giles spoke, his face hardened and his eyes became cold.

'You started it.' Anita's voice was filled with anger. She threw the cup she was holding against the wall. It smashed and sent tiny coloured fragments of pot into the room. She slumped back into the chair. The atmosphere closed in and Anita felt trapped, almost encased.

Giles broke the silence. 'I'm going out!' His voice was punctuated by the slam of the door.

Anita got up from the chair and ran after him. 'Wait!' she called.

'Leave me alone!' he answered without turning around, and he continued to march down the path.

Anita caught up with him and grabbed his arm. Giles stopped and turned to her, the anger in his eyes flashed. 'Let go!' His voice was cold.

'I will not until you listen to me.' Anita's voice sounded weak.

'Get your hand off my arm.' Giles snatched his arm away and continued to march down the path. His body language spoke anger.

Anita ran after him and again grabbed his arm. This time he did not stop, he marched on, snatching his arm from Anita's grip and leaving her standing alone. All she could do was to stand and watch as Giles got into the van, slammed the door and drove away.

Giles did not know where he was going, all he knew was that he had to get away.

He pulled the van over and switched off the engine as the anguish he felt inside became too much.

'I can't take anymore!' he cried out loud. The anguish tightened its grip and as he rested his forehead on the steering wheel, he cried out again, 'I cannot take anymore!'

The river, still swollen by the recent storms, roared by. Giles turned his head to listen. The volatile energy of the river mirrored the energy within him. But the river was going somewhere, it had a destination. Giles felt he was going nowhere.

Anita anxiously waited by the kitchen window. She had picked up the pieces of the broken cup and had let the little cat come inside. The cat, unaware of anything wrong, wound itself around her legs.

Anita dragged a chair from the table and put it next to the window. Outside the trees were only just visible in the darkness. As usual the row had begun out of the blue, initially it had been about nothing. A difference of opinion had rapidly escalated into a clash of character. Anita could see this but she knew Giles could not. Her stomach sank. She knew Giles was on the brink of leaving her.

Anita sat and waited by the window until the early hours of the morning, then gave up her vigil and went to bed.

As she lay in the double bed her thoughts slowly headed into the realm of despair. That realm was a cold, stark and lonely place, it was empty.

With ears alert, she heard the sound of the van making its way up the track. The engine stopped and footsteps made their way to the house. Anita dived out of bed, pulled on a jumper and ran downstairs. She entered the kitchen at the same time as

Giles.

Giles closed the door and turned to face Anita. 'Go back to bed.' His voice was not angry anymore. The anger had been replaced by something quiet. The voice continued, 'Please just go back to bed.' Giles closed his eyes as he spoke.

Anita turned and walked back upstairs and got into bed, it was still warm. She pulled the covers up around her face. She tried to blot everything out but the image of Giles looking so small and defeated would not go away.

A long hour passed and eventually Giles came into the bedroom. He walked over to the bed and sat down. Anita pulled down the covers from her face.

Giles was the first to speak. 'We cannot go on like this, it's crippling both of us. We need to find peace or we will really damage each other.' His face bore sadness as he continued to speak, 'I'm going to move out for a while.'

Anita sat bolt upright. 'You want to leave, is that what you are telling me?'

'I don't "want" to leave but we both need some space. I feel if I don't...' his voice tailed off. Words jumbled in his mind and desperately he sorted through them, 'I may one day hurt you.'

Anita turned away and nervously she began to smooth a crease in the sheet. Giles continued to speak, 'Over the edge is a person who you really would not want to know.'

Anita looked at him. His eyes stared back at her as he said,

'If I am pushed any further, the person that I keep a tight rein on will break loose and I do not know what he is capable of.' Giles looked away. 'All I know is that earlier when you followed me outside, I felt so angry, I was angry at you. When you grabbed me and wouldn't let go, do you really want to know what I wanted to do?'

Anita shook her head. Tears had begun to form in her eyes.

'I don't want to know,' she said.

'I wanted to break your bloody arm. That's what I have become, a bastard who can seriously think about hurting and damaging the person he is supposed to love.'

Anita objected, 'Giles you are not a violent person, you are not.'

'But I could be. I can be pushed to the point where I could be and I cannot...' his voice disappeared.

Anita moved closer to him. Giles moved away and continued, 'I know it's in all of us, but I feel I am coming closer and closer to it, closer to being the beast.' He stopped speaking and put his head in his hands.

'We all have petty rows and that's all they are. We are very different people and different people have different points of view, different opinions. That's all it is, a clash of personalities,' Anita explained.

'To you maybe, but not to me. It's gone much further than that.' Giles rubbed his eyes. He felt drained and the lack of sleep wasn't helping. 'I'm wiped out. I don't want to talk anymore. I'm going to pack a few things and go over to Charlie's,' he added as he got up from the bed. He walked over to the chest of drawers and began to pull out some clothes.

'Damn you!' Anita angrily got out of bed, walked out of the room and slammed the door behind her.

The days passed painfully slowly. Anita found that she missed so much about Giles. She missed his smile, his laughter, the tender way he would hold her, she missed the sound of him coming home, but most of all she missed the safe, secure warmth of their love.

She put away some of the things belonging to him, things lying around which she could no longer bear to see. There was a book, half read, its bookmark stating the point in time when Giles had left. She opened it up and touched the words with her finger and remembered the last time they had sat and read together, they had huddled close and shared a blanket to keep out the draughts.

Anita threw the book into a box, snatched up her gardening gloves from the table and went outside. She made her way to a patch of thin winter sunlight and began to pull up the weeds furiously. Anger had replaced grief.

She tugged at an obstinate clump of brambles. The brambles would not budge. 'Well damn you, stay there!' she said aloud.

'Do you always speak to brambles like that?' a voice asked. Anita jumped, then turned and saw Charlie standing at the gate with a huge bright smile.

'I can't get it open,' he said as he pulled on the gate.

'Charlie!' she exclaimed, rushing over to the gate and letting him in. 'There's a knack to it!' she explained.

'I was out for a walk and wondered if there was any chance of a cup of tea?'

'I'm trying to clear some space for spring planting.' She pointed to the area where she had been working. 'But it's taking some doing.' She took off her gloves and led Charlie into the kitchen.

Charlie pointed to the cat. 'Does that thing ever move?'

'Sometimes!' Anita replied as she put the kettle onto the hotplate.

Charlie bent down and stroked the cat.

'Has he sent you here?' Anita asked.

'Kind of.'

'Why did he not come here himself?'

'I think he's afraid of the response.' Charlie sat down at the table.

'Charlie, it's been over a week, and the longer he leaves it the more difficult it will become, surely he can see that?'

'Can I suggest that you go to him? Steve and I would keep out of the way.'

'Do you know, Charlie, I would never have taken you for the counselling type!'

'I'm not! Hell! I can't even sort my own life out, let alone someone else's,' Charlie held up his hands.

'I'll give it serious thought.'

'Steve and I will be out tomorrow evening,' Charlie grinned.

'You old fox!' Anita laughed.

Together they walked back down the path and Anita opened the gate. 'How come you haven't been snapped up?'

Charlie smiled, 'I'm waiting for the right woman and the right time!'

'For God's sake Giles, will you sit down, you're doing my head in. You are worse than him when old PJ is due!' Steve pointed to Charlie.

'At least I don't go ranting and raving when I can't find something in the kitchen!' Charlie retaliated.

'That's because you rarely look for anything in the kitchen apart from the next bottle of scotch!'

'Will you two pack it in!' Giles snapped. 'Anyway I thought you were going over to Sylvie's?'

'We are,' Steve got up from the table. 'Come on, let's go.' Charlie walked over to Giles, and said, 'I hope it all works for both of you. We'll be back about eleven.'

Anita's arrival was marked by a tiny quiet knock on the huge front door.

'I didn't hear the car,' Giles said as he opened the door and let Anita in.

'I walked here.'

'It's not safe to walk alone at night, you know there's a prowler around.'

'I got here safely. It was a beautiful starlit walk and I didn't even need my torch.' She took off her coat and draped it around a chair.

Giles stood and looked at her. 'Are you OK?' he asked.

'As well as the situation we are in permits.' She sat down.

'Would you like a glass of wine?' he asked as he walked over to the table. Anita nodded in reply. Giles poured two glasses of wine and as he passed one to Anita, he said, 'To us.' Anita took a sip of wine as Giles sat down opposite her.

'I don't want to beat about the bush,' she said. 'So let's be honest with each other and get to the point of it all.'

'As far as I can work out, it's a queer time to live. Everyone seems either mixed up, screwed up or fucked up. Including us,' Giles said seriously.

There was a silence. Anita, choosing her words carefully, broke the silence, 'If we stay together we need to be more tolerant, more sensitive.'

'I thought we already tried that one,' Giles said, 'and it didn't work.'

'I don't mean just being considerate, I mean being more aware, aware of the other person,' she explained.

'I can't see a difference.'

'It's subtle.'

'As you know I am not one of the most subtle of people!' Giles smiled.

'Sometimes you are and you can be.'

'Carry on,' he said, feeling slightly dubious.

'We teach our children to be thoughtful but we don't actually allow them to be sensitive.'

'That's because they would be constantly getting hurt. It's a big bad world out there,' Giles said.

'It doesn't have to be like that, things can be different, things can change. We can learn to become more sensitive, learn to become sensitive adults. That's all I am trying to say.'

'I'm not sure I can be the person you want, that super sensitive guy you obviously need,' Giles said honestly.

'We both need to be more sensitive, this isn't just about you, it's about both of us. You need me to be more sensitive too.'

'It seems like a lot of hard work,' he said.

'Nothing is easy, but surely it's worth having a go.'

Giles stared at the ceiling and eventually he said in a quiet voice as he looked at Anita, 'We could try. But this is the final time and if it doesn't work this time then for me it's over.'

Anita remained silent.

CHAPTER 4

'Charlie, will you get out of the van and come inside?'

'No, I'm not moving,' Charlie's words were slurred.

'Come on, Charlie, you can't sleep here. Come inside,' Steve held open the passenger door and waited.

'No!' was the response.

'You'd be warm and comfy in your own bed, come on,' Steve insisted.

'No!' Charlie closed his eyes.

With that final 'no', Steve slammed the van door and walked inside. He went into the kitchen, filled the kettle and then sat by the fire. As he sat there he heard the van door open. It was followed by the violent retching noises that he had become so used to hearing. Most nights would end with Charlie vomiting.

Steve knew what would come next. Charlie would stagger indoors and sheepishly apologise. The low opinion of himself would emerge, taking centre stage, and the display of self-pity would continue well into the early hours.

Steve got up from the chair, filled a hot water bottle and made his way upstairs. As he closed his bedroom door, he could hear Charlie calling for him.

'Fuck off!' he called back.

Anita was buttering toast when Giles came into the room.

'You know, it's so good to be home,' he said.

'It's good to have you home,' she replied.

'What are you doing today?' he asked as he sat at the table.

'I want to finish clearing the garden and then I thought I would go over and see Charlie.' Anita poured two cups of tea.

'I'm going over there myself. I have to drop off some fence posts for their veg garden. It seems they have a rabbit problem. I'll be going over after breakfast if that's any use to you?'

'I'll finish breakfast and then get a lift with you. I can do the garden this afternoon.'

Steve heard the van pull up. He opened the door and was surprised to see Anita standing there. 'I thought it was Giles.'

'He's dropping off your fence posts around the back. I cadged a lift to have a word with Charlie, is he about?'

'He's not up yet but he shouldn't be long. Come in where it's warm,' Steve said. 'So you and Giles are back together?' Anita warmed her hands in front of the fire and said,

'Thanks to Charlie's counselling.'

'That's what HE needs,' Steve said quietly as he sat by the fire. 'He's drinking scotch every night to the point where he loses it, and I've had enough of trying to persuade him to pack it in. Only he can sort himself out. I can't do it, I've tried.'

'What's caused this?' Anita asked as she sat opposite Steve. Steve shook his head. 'I don't really know, I can only guess, and my guess is that he needs a woman.'

'Maybe he needs to get out more and meet people,' Anita suggested.

'It's not so simple. He's in love with someone. He doesn't admit it but it's fairly obvious. The problem is she's a married woman,' Steve explained.

Anita raised an eyebrow. 'I wish I could help but I would hate to interfere, there's nothing worse than an interfering do- gooder.'

Steve leant forwards and said, 'Maybe you could give him the opportunity to talk. You wouldn't be interfering then would you?'

'I could try,' Anita agreed.

Charlie entered the room and walked over to Anita. 'I won't kiss you, I haven't had a shave yet,' he said, rubbing the dark stubble on his chin.

'Giles has dropped the fence posts off, so I'll go and take them into the garden,' Steve said as he walked over to his wellies. He kicked off his slippers and added, 'Anita hasn't had coffee yet.'

Charlie passed the mug of coffee to Anita and sat down opposite her. 'Everything OK with you and Giles?' he asked.

Anita smiled. 'You are really a good man. Honestly, how come you haven't been snapped up?'

Charlie took a drink of his coffee. 'The last time you asked me that I told you that I was waiting for the right person and the right time. I wasn't joking! It's the truth.'

'Have you met this person?' Anita asked.

Charlie stared into the distance and then nodded, 'I've met her but the right time hasn't arrived yet.'

'Do you think it will?'

Charlie slipped back into thought and then answered, 'This may sound wacky.' He grinned and then continued, 'I feel it is my destiny to be with this woman but that there are forces at work which may prevent it.'

'Then protect yourself.' Anita paused and then added, 'And don't destroy yourself.'

Charlie sat back in his chair and smiled at Anita, 'I know he's told you!'

'He's worried about you, that's all. There are forces at work out there, both good and bad ones. It's up to us to try and prevent the destructive ones from entering our lives.' As Anita explained, she looked at Charlie.

'I know that,' he gazed into the fire and then added, 'I've always known that.'

'Then do something about it,' Anita suggested.

'It's not easy!' Charlie said, forcing a smile.

'Is there anything I can do to help?' she asked.

Charlie sank into deep thought and after a few moments said, 'Teach me about herbs.'

'Herbs?' Anita was surprised by his answer.

'I know that herbs have a potency within them, a potency which can heal and protect, that's right isn't it?' he asked.

Anita nodded and then explained, 'Their principle can protect as well as heal. The ancient peoples knew about this power and used it in their daily lives, but for most of us it doesn't exist, we have forgotten or lost the knowledge.'

'I think the wisdom is within us all, we just haven't woken up yet! We are still asleep!' Charlie grinned.

'I'll teach you what I know about herbs,' she agreed.

'But it's not complete, the rest you will have to discover for yourself.'

'Perfect!' Charlie smiled.

'But... it's part of a deal,' Anita sounded sheepish.

Charlie laughed, 'Go on spill the beans, what is the deal?'

'I will pass on my knowledge of herbs to you, but you in return... have to quit drinking.' Anita looked away.

'Steve put you up to this.' Charlie was annoyed.

'No, he didn't,' Anita frowned. 'It's me being the person I didn't want to be. The interfering do-gooder!' She was upset.

'Like me the other afternoon?' he said, taking hold of her hand, and then adding, 'We have a deal.'

'You can't be serious?' Giles glanced at Leo.

'Well, I am!' Leo replied as he fidgeted around in the passenger seat.

'Keep still will you, you're putting me off driving,' Giles complained.

'This seat is knackered and how my poor mother sits in it I'll never know.'

'Your poor mother was the one who knackered it,' responded Giles. He then added seriously, 'Leo, you can't possibly walk up to his front door and then when he answers it, simply ask him to support you financially. It's not the done thing.'

'Well it's going to be the done thing today, because that's exactly what I'm going to do and if he tells me to clear off then I'll wish him a good day, turn around and go home.' Leo stared out of the window.

'How long have you been planning this?' Giles asked.

'A few weeks,' Leo answered and then continued, 'If I don't get a sponsorship then I can't finish the work for the exhibition and he can afford to help me.'

'You've got a bloody nerve, you really have!' Giles was taken aback.

'Thanks. What do you want to bet he'll help?'

'Nothing. But I'll bet 100 Euros that he'll tell you to shove off.'

'Let me out here,' said Leo taking off his seatbelt. 'I'll walk the rest of the way.'

Giles pulled over and stopped the van, and as Leo climbed out he said, 'Good luck!' and then quietly added, 'You'll need it.'

Chateau de Vallon, hidden from the road behind trees, was impressive. As Leo stood in the driveway he felt that he was witnessing not only a chateau which was lived in, but a chateau alive with purpose.

As he approached the huge front door Leo felt less confident and the tiny doubt in his mind grew larger with every step. As he reached the door, the doubt turned into full-blown fear and he wished he hadn't embarked on the idea.

He was about to turn around and go back home when something stopped him and made him take hold of the large iron doorknocker. Having firmly knocked on the door twice, Leo knew that there was no going back.

The door was opened by a tiny woman in her late sixties. Her pale face was almost translucent. Her two bright blue eyes were bead-like and matched the necklace she was wearing. Her smile was warm and friendly and as she led Leo into the grand hallway he found himself transported into another world.

A huge oval chandelier hung above and its glass droplets sent shafts of rainbow-coloured light into the hall.

The walls were home to a collection of paintings. Old Masters hung alongside modern oils and watercolours. Leo's eye was caught by a stark black and white watercolour. He was drawn to it and as he tried to work out why on earth an artist would dismiss such varied colour in favour of black and white, a voice addressed him.

'Leo, am I correct?' Leo spun around and found himself facing Sion Devallon. He was a well-known, charismatic and sometimes controversial figure. He was a man who was often misunderstood and more often the subject of gossip. Leo had wondered if anyone really knew him.

A man of grace and charm extended warmth as he offered his hand to Leo, and as Leo accepted the hand, he found himself strangely linked to Sion Devallon.

'Are you familiar with this artist?' he asked and then explained, 'He never uses colour. To him everything is black and white, everything he sees and everything he experiences, black and white. You shall meet him one day, him and others, your own kind. Come now and let's go into the study.'

Leo followed as Devallon led the way. The study was a long well-lit room. Piles of books littered a desk and a table, and more books littered the floor. A narrow strip had been left clear and Leo followed along this pathway to the far side of the room.

The space here was also limited. Stacks of unframed canvasses leant against the walls and a collection of sculptures fought for the remaining free space. Two armchairs had been squeezed in, facing the French windows. The view of the grounds beyond stretched for miles.

Sion explained, 'This is my den. The housekeeper does not stray into here, unless invited!' As Sion spoke he ran a finger across the dust resting on one of the books. 'She isn't invited in here very often, as you can tell.' He smiled at Leo and then pointed to one of the armchairs. 'Come and sit with me next to the window, we can see the lake from here and also the wilderness beyond. I favour the wilderness. Do you Leo? Do you love the wilderness?'

Leo, unable to express himself in words, nodded. He sat down in the armchair next to Sion and looked out across the lake. Beyond was the wild and untouched landscape.

'Leo, are you at ease?' Sion asked and then continued, 'The light is good here. Soothing. I sit here to take my siesta. You may take a nap if you wish.' He then said with a smile, 'I want to know how much money you need.'

Leo quickly turned away as the feeling of shock became a painful embarrassment.

'Do not turn away from me. Be honest with me,' Sion touched Leo's arm as he spoke.

Leo looked at Sion and quietly began to speak, and as he spoke he thought of his paintings. He thought of the ones completed and the ones only existing in his mind. 'I need finance for a project of twelve oils for the exhibition. I need a sponsor so that I can complete the work.'

'How many have you left to complete?' Sion asked.

'Six.'

'I will sponsor you. I will allow you three hundred Euros for the total completed works.' As Sion spoke, Leo's heart sank: the total was not enough. Sion continued to speak as he gazed out of the window. 'And I will allow you three thousand Euros for the next six paintings. A total offer of three thousand, three hundred Euros. In return Leo, I would hope to get a priority invitation to your exhibition and you must allow me to choose and keep one of the paintings.' Sion looked at Leo, who had become speechless again.

Leo opened his mouth to speak but the words would not come. Sion held his arm and said, 'Sometimes silence speaks realms.'

As Leo was about to leave, Sion called him back. 'Leo, I will send you an invitation to dinner, to meet other artists. Your own kind.'

CHAPTER 5

'You played that piece well. Very well. You would have played it perfectly but for one thing,' PJ looked seriously at Charlie.

'One thing?' Charlie asked.

'Your hands Charlie, it's your hands,' PJ replied.

Charlie looked down at his hands. They seemed no different from usual. 'What's wrong with them?'

'They were shaking all the way through that last piece. Shake, shake, shake. Why?' PJ asked.

Charlie knew the reason, he also knew that he didn't want anyone else to know, but as he looked at PJ he knew it would be difficult to lie. 'I have just quit drinking,' he admitted honestly.

'What was your tipple?' PJ asked.

'Scotch.'

'That's my tipple,' PJ admitted. 'In moderation. Each evening I enjoy a glass of a fine 8 or 1O-year-old malt, nicely chilled in the fridge.'

'Chilled?' said Charlie in surprise.

'Yes chilled, and it's delicious, but don't try it or you'll be back on the rocky road to ruin!' PJ raised his specs, looked at Charlie and then put them back down.

'That feels like where I have been,'Charlie said thoughtfully.

'I'll give you a new piece of music to practise. It's a little more complex than the others and will demand extra work. It will take your mind off other things.' PJ searched in his case. Eventually he pulled out the one he wanted. 'Beethoven!' he announced, and passed the music to Charlie.

Moments later PJ was reversing down the track at high speed, narrowly missing Steve who was walking up the track.

'That man drives like a maniac,' said Steve as he walked into the house, 'and what's more, I'm sure he gave me a little gesture!'

Charlie began to laugh. 'He is not what he appears to be!' and added proudly, 'He's moved me onto Beethoven.'

'Already?' Steve said, then explained, 'I've just seen Anita, she's coming this afternoon to help with the menus and she said she'll bring you some books.'

'What about?' Charlie asked as he closed the lid of the piano.

'Herbs. She was very elated, apparently Leo got his sponsorship,' Steve explained.

'You're joking?' Charlie couldn't believe the news. 'I thought it was a wild shot.'

'It seemed so.' Steve hung up his coat. 'But luck was with him.'

Charlie displayed the new sheet music and said, 'Beethoven!' Steve looked at the portrait on the front cover and said, 'So the lesson went well!'

'Apart from one very embarrassing thing,' Charlie admitted.

'What did you do?' Steve asked with a smirk.

'PJ noticed I had the DTs.' Charlie held out his hands and exaggerated their shaking.

'That's embarrassing,' Steve agreed.

'You want to be careful with that guy,' Giles said as he began to unload his tools from the van.

'And why's that?' Leo asked as he stood and watched.

'I've heard things about him,' Giles answered. He stopped what he was doing and looked Leo in the eye.

'From your cronies in the bar, no doubt. And what did these wise ones say?' Leo asked and then leant against the van while he waited for the reply.

'He's a shirt lifter,' Giles answered.

Leo looked puzzled and Giles continued to explain, 'A queer, a poof, a...'

Leo burst out, 'Stop it! For God's sake Giles I didn't think you were like that.'

'I'm not like that, but he is,' Giles sniggered.

'My God, I didn't think you were a bigot and I definitely didn't have you down as homophobic.' Leo stood and faced Giles. He stared at him in disbelief, turned and walked away.

Giles shouted after him, 'It's not normal.' Leo did not respond, he just carried on walking, fuming as he went.

Anita came out of the house carrying a large pile of books. She asked Giles, 'Where's Leo going?'

Giles held the books while Anita got into the passenger seat. 'I've no idea. He just took off.'

'He can be touchy,' Anita said, as Giles got into the van, 'and you wind him up.'

Giles nodded and as the van turned onto the main road, Anita exclaimed, 'Look there's Leo, slow down Giles, he may want a lift.'

As the van moved alongside Leo, Giles slowed down. 'He's waving us on,' Anita explained, and waved back at Leo.

It had been a normal day. It had been a normal evening. But in the early hours of the morning, both Steve and Charlie awoke, startled.

Charlie sat bolt upright in his bed and listened. Steve, being a little cautious, poked one ear out from under his bedding and listened. Both men heard the same thing.

Charlie jumped out of bed and put on his dressing gown. He opened the bedroom door, listened again and then hurried down the corridor and into Steve's room. Steve pulled his head back under the covers. 'It's only me,' said Charlie.

Steve sat upright. 'What the hell is that noise?' He switched on the bedside lamp.

Charlie shook his head, 'Get up and help me to find out.' Steve got out of bed and pulled on a jumper. 'It's freezing in here,' he complained.

'It's freezing everywhere,' Charlie answered. 'Much colder than usual. The house is like an icebox.'

Steve grabbed his torch and followed Charlie onto the landing. The sound ceased. Both Charlie and Steve looked at each other, puzzled. Steve shrugged and in complete silence took Charlie's arm and led him to the top of the stairs. The icy chill had ceased too. The men walked down the stairs and when they reached the bottom step, Steve noticed something.

The light from his torch fell upon a small mound of fresh mud. Charlie knelt down and inspected it. 'Let's get more light onto this.'

Steve walked over to the light switch and turned on the main light. 'There's more over here,' he said, pointing to the right of the stairs, 'and a few old leaves.'

Charlie walked around the corner to the recess at the back of the staircase. 'Pass the torch,' he asked. Steve passed Charlie the torch and watched as Charlie shone the beam onto the floor.

'Someone has opened the trap door. Look, the box of newspapers has been pushed against the wall and that's not where they were. And there's more mud here.' He pointed to another small pile of mud.

'There's only the cellar down there, isn't there?' Steve asked.

'The cellar and two tunnels,' Charlie explained.

'The tunnels are disused, sealed off?' Steve asked.

'Maybe not. Giles thought that they could be intact and usable.' Charlie kicked the mud to one side.

As the year began to wind down, the wet weather continued. The continual dampness weakened people and many succumbed to influenza. The strongest fought the bug, and after a few days returned to health. The weak and the vulnerable were not able.

Maurice lay perfectly still. His breathing was slow and laboured. The fever had taken its toll.

Very slowly he opened his eyes. In the corner of the semi- dark hut he could see the figure. It was still there. It was still patiently waiting.

As Maurice drifted in and out of consciousness, the figure silently observed. Eventually it turned and moved towards Maurice. Maurice was aware. He felt the heavy black hooded cape brush against him and he felt the closeness of death.

The figure left Maurice alone. It was not his time. Maurice closed his eyes and felt the relief wash over him. Death had come close but was leaving.

Emptying his thoughts and disconnecting from the sensations of his body, he listened. He heard the river. From the sound of the river he knew many things.

He knew where the river had been and he knew where it was going. He knew exactly where it had sprung from. His mind was carried back to that place, to the source. Here he entered the womb.

The mother spoke to him. She told him about the river. The river would rise and she, the mother, would wash her earth. Wash, cleanse and make new.

Maurice could see the rains that would come and as he saw them he knew what he had to do.

The fever had taken his strength and he knew that he would need every ounce of strength in order to complete his task. He must sleep. Before drifting back into sleep, he touched the ring on his finger. He cupped the bright blue stone and thanked God for his life.

Leo sat cross-legged on the floor with the handwritten invitation in front of him. The date of the invitation from Sion coincided with that of Steve's debut meal.

Leo got up from the floor. 'Bollocks!' he said, and made his way downstairs.

Outside Michael's office door, he called, 'Are you in there?'

'Come in.' Michael was seated at his desk in front of a pile of invoices, bills and other bits of paperwork. He took off his glasses and rubbed his eyes.

'You got a problem Boyo?' he asked.

Leo showed him the invitation from Sion and explained, 'It's my big opportunity to meet other artists but, at the same time I don't want to let Steve down.'

'It's unfortunate that they coincide, but Steve can make you a meal anytime. You may not get another invitation like this.' He passed the invitation back to Leo. 'I'd go to this one if it was me.'

Steve rested back against the side of the woodstore. 'Look, Leo,' He took his work gloves off. 'It's not a problem. In fact for me it's good news, one less person to cater for.'

Leo brushed the sawdust from the chopping block and sat down. 'I really wanted to come and then this invitation arrived out of the blue.'

'Stop worrying. You can try my food out when I cater for Sissy Pirton.'

'You must be joking!' exclaimed Leo, 'Sissy Pirton is a man-eater and would quite easily eat me alive. It wouldn't be your food she'd be interested in.'

Steve laughed, 'I'd heard she and her nurses could get a bit...' Steve paused.

'Wild,' Leo volunteered.

'So it seems like you could be on the road to success!'

'I don't know what it is, all I know is that it feels right. But to be honest with you, it hasn't gone down too well with Giles.'

Steve was surprised, 'I thought he'd have been pleased for you.'

'Apparently he's heard a rumour about Sion,' Leo looked at the ground and moved the sawdust with the edge of a twig,

'From his cronies.'

'He believes the rumour?' Steve asked.

'Yes!' Leo nodded and continued, 'It might be true for all I know, but even if it was true it wouldn't bother me.' After a pause Leo asked, 'Has Charlie got over the shock of having an intruder in the house?'

Steve sat on his haunches next to Leo. 'He settled back down after he'd secured the trap door with 6-inch nails!'

They both laughed and Leo said, 'I know how to get into that tunnel near the river.'

Steve was surprised. 'Do you?'

'Last summer I was messing around down by the river and I came across a stone hut in the woods. I went inside and there was the entrance to a tunnel. I walked down it for a little way but it was pitch black, damp and slippery, so I turned back. I think it might be the one that leads here.'

'Could you find it again?' Steve asked.

'Probably.'

'How do you fancy taking a walk over there sometime?' Steve asked.

'I'm for it, but let's wait until it's dried up a bit.' Leo burst out laughing. 'We could scare the hell out of Charlie!'

A few fine days arrived. The winter sun felt warm. It dried the air and the dampness began to disappear. Steve and Leo took advantage of the fine weather one afternoon and made their way down to the river in the hope of finding the tunnel entrance.

'I should have put new wellies on, these old ones have a hole in them.' Leo held up his foot and showed the hole to Steve.

Steve smiled and carried on walking. 'Hey, did you know your mum is passing on her knowledge of herbs to Charlie?'

'I pity you,' Leo replied as he walked behind Steve. 'You'll go into your kitchen and find huge pans of disgusting stuff bubbling away and then you'll have to drink it.'

'It doesn't appear to have done you any harm,' Steve replied, and turned to look at Leo.

'Seriously, the herbal medicines mum makes are good. I mean they work.'

'Have you ever wanted to learn about them?' Steve asked as he continued to walk down the track.

'Over the years I guess I've picked up bits of information. I can identify many of the plants, but I've never wanted to study it seriously.' Leo stopped in his tracks. 'Hey, look at this!' He pointed to a pathway where the vegetation had been flattened.

'Someone has been up and down here often and recently.' Steve followed Leo onto the path. 'It will make walking easier without having to fight through these brambles.'

'It kind of stops here,' said Leo. The short pathway had come to an abrupt end. Clumps of brambles made an impassable thicket. 'What do we do now?' Leo asked.

Steve looked around him. 'There's a clearing over there,' he said pointing to an area on his left, 'but we'll still have to get through this lot.'

'Here goes,' Leo carried on, walking with difficulty through the established bramble patch. 'That's my trousers ruined,' he complained with a frown as he inspected the tear in his trouser leg.

'Do you want to go back?' Steve asked.

'No, we might as well carry on, it's not much further.'

The two men battled their way through the growth and eventually came out in the clearing. Another well-used path appeared on the far side and they made their way over to it. The path sloped downwards and from the vantage-point of the edge of the clearing, they both spotted the stone hut.

Steve leant back against a tree and got his breath back. 'I didn't think you'd be able to remember where it was.'

'I wasn't sure that I would remember, that path led us to it,' Leo said and then balancing on one leg, he bent down and pulled off his wellie. He took off his wet sock and pushed it into his pocket and put his wellie back on.

The two men stood together outside the hut. Leo fumbled in his pocket and found his torch. Steve pushed the hut door open and went inside. Leo followed and shone his torch around the small hut. The place reeked of damp, and mildew had formed on the walls. The earth floor was wet.

The beam from the torch fell upon a makeshift bed of filled sacks with a single blanket thrown over it. Leo shone the torch onto an old large tin box. He opened the box and found inside a small piece of mouldy cheese and the remains of a loaf of bread.

Steve spotted the bin bag of clothes he had given to the stranger. Underneath the bag was an old suitcase. 'Do you want to look inside?' Leo asked.

'No, it's none of our business.'

'This stuff wasn't here last summer, the place was empty. That door there,' Leo said, pointing, 'is the door to your tunnel.' As Leo spoke he experienced a strange feeling which crept over him. It began in the base of his spine and travelled upwards. It felt familiar, it was the feeling he had experienced outside Sylvie's cottage. As the hairs on the back of his neck stood on end, he turned around sharply, let out a shriek and jumped backwards.

Standing in the doorway, silently observing, was the stranger. His hair was damp and matted, his face smeared with dirt. His two wild eyes stared at Leo. Leo felt he would never forget the sight he was witnessing. He could not work out if the eyes bore madness, malice or anger. Whatever it was, the stare made Leo feel sick.

Steve turned and was shocked to see the stranger. He looked gaunt and fragile and had lost considerable weight. He looked directly at Steve and said in anger, 'Why did you come here? Why? You have destroyed everything.'

'We haven't damaged anything. We only came here to check out the tunnel and I can assure you we had no idea you were here,' Steve explained.

'You,' said the stranger, pointing to both Steve and Leo, 'have destroyed our only chance of survival. We are all doomed.'

Steve looked at Leo and saw his confused expression. The stranger began to rant, 'How many people will now find out where I am, how many? And when they find out, my plan and my hopes will be destroyed and along with it our survival.' He began to pace anxiously.

Leo burst out, 'You're bloody weird, you are. I'm going home. Get out of my way.' As he spoke Leo pushed the man to one side and made his way out of the hut.

'Are you coming Steve?'

'Just give me five minutes,' Steve nodded.

'I'll be up in the clearing,' Leo answered as he marched away.

'You,' Steve said firmly, 'trusted me enough to come and ask for clothes, and I trusted you enough to let you into my home. So trust me now and trust Leo as well.' As the stranger turned his face Steve continued, 'My concern is that you look dreadfully ill. This place,' he said, pointing to the inside of the hut, 'is damp, cold and unhealthy, and if you carry on living like this YOU won't survive. YOU will be the one doomed.'

'I have been spared,' the man said quietly.

'Maybe you have, but maybe you won't be as lucky next time.'

'I can't leave here,' he said anxiously, 'I need to be here, it's the right place.'

Steve reached out and held the man's arm. 'Then let me help you to make it warm and dry. Tomorrow, with Leo's help, I'll bring you a paraffin heater, bedding and whatever else I can find that would be useful. Do you accept?'

The man moved away from Steve's grip and said, 'I have no choice.'

As Steve began to walk away he called back, 'What's your name?'

The gaunt, thin and haunted-looking figure turned and answered quietly, 'Maurice'.

Steve made his way up to the clearing and found Leo sitting on a fallen tree trunk.

'Come on Steve, the daylight is starting to go, we'd better get a move on.' He added bluntly, 'What the fuck was that all about?'

Steve explained as he walked alongside Leo, 'Firstly you are sworn to secrecy. No one must find out that he is here. OK?'

'For God's sake, he could be a killer or a madman on the run. He certainly acts like a madman.'

'Give him a chance. He feels he needs to be here for some reason and I have offered, with your help, to take him a paraffin heater and some bedding. Tomorrow.'

Leo stopped walking. 'I don't believe this. You could be roping us into something dodgy.'

As Leo began to walk off, Steve pulled him back by his arm and said, 'Give him a chance.'

They carried on walking and Steve said with concern, 'The difficult bit is smuggling the stuff to him without Charlie knowing.'

Leo was deep in thought. 'I have an army camp bed he can have, a sleeping bag, stove and kettle. He can have those, I never use them.' He then added, 'He smells.'

The following morning, just before daybreak cleared away the last of the darkness, Steve and Leo met up by the barn. Leo had brought all the things he had said he would. Apart from the camp bed everything had fitted into a large bin bag.

'Mum had this bottle of lavender oil spare.' Leo pulled from his pocket a small brown bottle and showed it to Steve.

'She won't notice it's missing. What have you got?' he asked.

'This paraffin heater, a canister of fuel, a bowl and a bucket and I've put some food in here.' Steve showed Leo the food he had stored inside the bucket. 'I hope we can get this lot through those brambles.'

'They should still be down where we walked yesterday. We'll just follow our tracks.' Leo pointed to the hammer poking out of Steve's pocket. 'What's that for?'

'He needs shelves in there to get stuff off the floor. Can you push those planks under my arm once I've picked this lot up?' Like a packhorse, Steve was loaded up. He and Leo then made their way quietly down to the river.

As the hut came into view, Leo said, 'I hope he doesn't start that "we are doomed" business.'

'It's just one of his things,' Steve said calmly.

'It's bloody weird,' Leo mumbled.

Later in the morning Maurice sat on the edge of the camp bed and waited for the kettle to boil. His old tin box doubled as a foodstore and a support for the camping stove.

Two shelves held his washing things, his clothes and the small collection of his belongings. In the corner of the hut by the door stood the heater which not only warmed the hut but with its gentle glow dissolved the stark gloom.

Before leaving, Steve had made Maurice promise to call for food each Thursday morning. He would also be able to refill the fuel canister.

Maurice poured the boiling water from the kettle into his old mug, waited and then removed the tea bag. He could remember the last time he had tasted tea, he could remember with clarity the china cup and saucer, and he would never forget the beautiful smile of the young woman with whom he had shared that final afternoon tea.

CHAPTER 6

The solstice, with its promise of longer days, was due. All around, preparations for Christmas were starting to take place.

Steve and Sylvie worked together in the kitchen doing all they could in readiness for the dinner party.

Charlie spent time fixing up the iron candelabra. He attached its hefty chains securely to the beams, placed the candles on the spikes and then hoisted it into position above the refectory table. The huge church candles he placed in the corners of the room alongside freshly cut bundles of holly.

With some time to spare he sat down at the piano, placed the sheet music on the stand and began to play the Beethoven piece he had spent so much time and effort practising.

The chords, as PJ had predicted, he could now play with ease and confidence. The sound filled the room. Charlie's mind drifted on the music's sweet mellow timbre and the haunting refrain.

With the haze of the Milky Way clearly visible, Leo walked down the drive towards the chateau, which was lit up both inside and out. Its tower was bathed in a soft golden light. Leo stopped walking and tried to imagine how the fortress would have been in the days of its Templar glory. Awesome then, but this evening it only radiated splendour.

As Leo continued walking he noticed a number of cars parked in the parking space. One was an MG sports car. He went over to it. The car was in pristine condition, its bodywork immaculate. Leo checked the number plate, its registration was Dutch.

As he approached the main door he could hear voices, laughter and music from within. The party had begun. Leo rang the bell, waited and was completely unprepared for what happened next. As the door swung open he was swiftly transported into wonderland, to the place where nothing is how it should be.

The person opening the door to him was a tall, well- built man, a man much taller and broader than Leo. He was wearing a full-length period dress, a rich tapestry of golds and ruby reds. He wore a white shoulder-length wig of curls and ringlets, which framed a white powdered face. His two bright blue eyes fluttered their lashes at Leo and his painted red lips parted, formed a smile and revealed yellow stained teeth.

Leo was about to introduce himself when the man-woman leant down towards him, his face only inches away from Leo's. He placed a finger on his lips and said, 'Sshh.' Taking Leo by the arm he led him inside.

Medieval music merged with voices and laughter. Leo felt his senses becoming suddenly overwhelmed. Shock and delight alternated as he was led into the banqueting hall. He had walked into a carnival, a masquerade.

The huge banquet table was laden with meats, salads of all description, pastries and fruits. The glistening centrepiece was a pig cooked and glazed with honey.

Guests in fancy dress smiled as the man-woman led Leo to the host. Sion, in medieval dress, was radiant. A loose-fitting, fine white cotton shirt gave him an ethereal air, mystical, almost magical.

'Leo!' he called out joyously, 'Come to me.' The man- woman tutted and walked off in a theatrical huff.

'Leo,' repeated Sion as he embraced him, 'I forgot to tell you that we are all wearing strange dress! But here, for you.' He passed Leo a parcel. 'Open it, wear it and keep it,' he said, smiling.

Leo opened the parcel and pulled out a silk smoking jacket. Sion took the jacket and helped Leo put it on. 'This is wonder- ful! I love it!' Leo exclaimed as he studied the delicate design on the silk.

'In the pocket you will find a cigarette holder and case, they are yours too,' Sion turned Leo around to face the hall. 'My guests will speak English to you, the ones who cannot will mime what they wish to say!' He spoke quietly into Leo's ear,

'The woman by the door,' he pointed to the woman dancing on a podium, wearing a gold bodysuit and surrounded by an ornamental disk, 'is Shiva. She is an artist, a Dutch painter. Her husband, Van Gogh, is standing next to her.'

'Van Gogh?' Leo sounded surprised.

'For this evening. He is wearing a false ear on his shoulder,' Sion explained, laughing, and then added seriously, 'He too is a fine Dutch artist. They both speak better English than you so do not be afraid to speak with them.' Leo nodded and Sion continued, 'See The Magpie over there? He sits at my table alone.' Sion pointed to the solitary figure dressed in black and white. He was also wearing a black mask. The mask covered the upper part of his face and ended with a long sharp nose. The nose resembled a beak. 'He is the artist we spoke of.'

'Black and white,' Leo spoke aloud.

'Do speak with him, you will find him interesting.' Sion turned to Leo and said, 'Please help yourself to food and to drink. Much later when you wish to retire and sleep, take a key from the board and find your bedroom.'

Leo smiled but found himself unable to speak. The words had dissolved before forming, feelings bombarded him. He felt alive, speechless but alive. Sion cupped his chin, tilted his face forward and kissed his forehead before leaving him alone with his thoughts.

When Leo realised that he was standing alone he walked over to the drinks trolley and helped himself to a glass of champagne. He spotted an empty seat and made his way over to it.

The seat was positioned close to a white satin-covered stool, on which sat a small woman dressed as a black cat. As Leo sat down the cat murmured, 'Stroke me.'

Leo turned to face the cat only to find that the man-woman had appeared. He bent down to Leo and the red mouth whispered, 'Are you stroking my pussy?'

Leo laughed, the black cat smiled and the man-woman tutted. He then produced a gold collar which he fastened around the cat's neck. The cat purred. He attached a leash to the collar and led the cat away. The cat turned once, looked at Leo and mouthed the words, 'Stroke me.'

Leo made himself comfortable. He put down his drink and pulled the cigarette case from his pocket. It was a small delicate silver case and inside he found some coloured cigarettes. In his pocket he found the cigarette holder. He chose a purple cigarette with a gold tip and placed it in the holder.

'Do you require a light for that? And may I sit on this stool?' Leo turned to find an elderly man sitting down beside him.

'I don't smoke,' Leo replied.

'Awful for the health.' The elderly man then produced a chesty and prolonged coughing fit. When the coughing had ceased, he wiped the spittle from his mouth and said, 'You are Sion's latest and newest prodigy. I am Lucien, his oldest. I am beyond anything now.' His eyes concentrated on an empty distant area of space and when his concentration returned to Leo, the elderly bent finger pointed in the direction of Sion.

'He will bring you a taste of everything. Good and bad. Light and dark. Everything. Prepare yourself.' Lucien then turned his face away.

Leo could imagine how the face had once been. It had seen youth. As if reading the words in Leo's mind, Lucien turned and said, 'Yes I am broken.'

Leo reached for his drink and took a mouthful. Lucien was silent and deep in thought. Leo rose from his seat and began to move away, and as he did Lucien called to him, 'But I am still here. Here with my people.' His eyes shone brightly as he held out his hand to Leo. 'Welcome,' he said.

Edging around the table, Leo made his way to where The Magpie sat. He walked past the dancing Shiva, her eyes closed as she concentrated on the precise movements of her body and her own inner music. Van Gogh was nowhere to be seen.

'May I?' asked Leo as he pointed to the empty seat next to The Magpie.

'You may,' nodded The Magpie. 'You are Leo. I would embrace you but I fear my nose would do you damage.' He pointed to the sharp beak-like protrusion. 'Everyone calls me The Magpie, but of course you know that, Sion will have told you.'

'He did,' Leo answered as he put down his drink and the cigarette holder.

'Here, you must eat.' The Magpie pushed a plate of cold meats and salad in front of Leo. 'And while you eat I shall speak with you.' He smiled and continued, 'I know that you have seen my work. It is true that I only paint in black and white. That is all I see.' As he spoke he gently lifted the mask to reveal his eyes. The skin around both eyes had been badly burnt, healed and had left scar tissue around the sockets.

Leo felt shocked and the meat he had just placed into his mouth did not taste good. He turned away.

The Magpie touched his arm and explained, 'My eyes, they are damaged but the damage has given me a unique sight and one for which I am truly grateful. It is my blessing. My work, I hope expresses this blessing.'

'Your work is unique,' Leo answered.

'And your work, Leo, what does it express?'

Leo thought for a while and then answered, 'Anger.' After a pause, he added, 'And peace.'

'I sometimes wonder how peace can exist in this distorted life.' As he spoke The Magpie helped himself to a piece of ham from Leo's plate. Leo pushed the plate between them.

'Maybe it's an illusion,' Leo shrugged.

'No, it is real. Peace does exist but it is very fragile. If you find it, Leo, you must handle it with great care or you will destroy it.' The Magpie continued to eat.

'Man seems to be able to do that so easily. He destroys so much without ever realising or being aware of what he is doing. I can't cope with that sometimes,' Leo admitted, and rested back in his chair. He added, 'Man destroys.'

The Magpie leaned forwards, looked Leo in the eye and then spoke, 'He also creates. Look at us, Leo. Look at us all in this room. We all create. We express creation, or an aspect of it. Everything is tied to its opposite.'

Leo nodded, 'Yes I know that, but it seems to be out of balance.'

The Magpie laughed, 'It is. But we must strive to compensate, make up the balance.'

Leo moved the food around on the plate. His appetite had diminished. 'It seems like war,' he said.

'That is a very strong word.'

Leo corrected himself, 'A fight for survival.'

The Magpie nodded and helped himself to the food left on the plate. 'Sion tells me you have a vision. A vision of a new world.'

'I see a different world, I don't know if it's new,' Leo explained.

'Perhaps then it is a part of the original plan?'

Leo nodded, 'Yes I think it is. I sometimes feel that I can think back to how it could have been, should have been.'

'All things are part of a circle, perhaps your world view will get a chance to fulfil itself when the circle completes its cycle.' The Magpie finished the food on the plate.

'That's an interesting...' Leo stopped speaking as a sudden loud announcement hailed from the end of the room.

'Now is the time!' shouted Sion.

Everyone became quiet. Shiva stopped her dance. The Magpie whispered to Leo, 'This is what we have been waiting for.'

At the far end of the room, people swung into action. A contraption was wheeled into the room. On the low trolley lay a figure wrapped in bandages. Leo and The Magpie stood to get a better look.

'It looks like his mummy,' laughed The Magpie, as Sion and the man-woman lifted up the figure.

The bandages fell slowly away revealing a bronze figure.

Sion walked around the figure. He touched it. He ran his hand down the smooth form and then stood back to look at it.

The face was a mask, its eyes two oval holes. Its open mouth was gaping. The perfect male body was a shell. Its back was completely missing, leaving enough space for a person to stand inside.

Sion stood inside the sculpture, aligned his eyes with the two holes and peered out. The sculpture fit him perfectly.

The man-woman stood to one side and began to speak,

'This is my final piece.' He waved his arm theatrically towards the sculpture. 'The piece has two titles. The first title is Mysterium Conjunctionis. The second title is Fusion. This work is my final offering to my benefactor.'

Sion came out from behind the sculpture. His face was that of someone who had experienced something precious. He walked over to the sculptor and wrapped his arms around him. The two men stood together for a very long time.

Eventually the music, the dancing and the laughter resumed. Leo and The

Magpie sat back down. 'That's an odd title,' remarked Leo.

'Mysterium Conjunctionis is an alchemical stage. Demeter is an alchemist,' The Magpie explained as he refilled both of their glasses. 'What are you working on at the moment?' he went on.

'It's a large piece, oil on wood. It resembles a waterfall flowing into a turbulent spiral at the bottom,' Leo answered as he picked up his glass.

'But it isn't a waterfall?'

'No, it's the downward movement of energy,' Leo answered.

'Is there anger in it?' The Magpie leaned back in his chair.

'Some. It's in the turbulent spiral,' Leo explained.

'And peace?'

'That's within the energy flowing downwards.'

'And what does it represent?' asked The Magpie.

'That's for you to work out!' laughed Leo.

'I already have!' The Magpie smiled. 'But please describe the colours to me.'

Leo turned his chair to face The Magpie and began to explain, 'Mostly milky, opaque, gentle and soothing colours reaching an intensity with vivid colours at the bottom of the painting.'

The Magpie smiled and nodded as he retrieved the colours from his memory. After a pause he then asked with a smile,

'Where have you put the bee?'

'It's in there!' Leo laughed. 'But I used a magnifying lens and worked with a very fine brush. To the naked eye the bee is a droplet of water.'

'Is the bee in every one of your paintings?' The Magpie was curious and amused.

'So far,' Leo answered. After taking another sip of his drink he asked, 'What kind of work do the others do?'

The Magpie rested back and collected his thoughts, 'The work of Demeter you have seen.' Both men looked towards the sculpture. As it caught the light, its form shimmered. The light illuminated the curves of the outer shell whilst the shadows of darkness hid in the interior. It was a harmonious balance of light and dark captured by one man.

The Magpie looked towards the dancing Shiva. Her body movements had slowed down almost to the point of stillness, but in that space she moved. Leo watched as she generated movement in slow motion. 'A living sculpture,' whispered The Magpie. 'But she also paints. She paints worlds within a world. Abstract, almost tactile, startling,' The Magpie smiled at Leo. 'Her husband, Hubert, paints the nude. Each painting is taken from a different angle. The foreground will focus on one particular site, say an elbow, and the background will contain the rest of the body. He calls his work "a journey".' The Magpie smiled.

'What about Lucien?' Leo asked, 'I can't imagine what he would paint.'

The Magpie's expression became serious, 'Lucien doesn't paint anymore. He can't. He suffers with bad health. His work has been amazing, quite astounding,' after a pause he continued, 'Leo, if you can try to imagine every piece of work from every artist in this room and combine that work, then you would have created something very unique. You would have created a small taste of Lucien's work.' The Magpie sat upright and then said seriously, 'He is the Master.'

Leo looked across at Lucien. The frail old man had not moved from his seat. Alone, he sat with his deep thoughts as the party went on around him.

The Magpie looked at his watch. 'Leo, you must excuse me, I must go. I promised to help Lucien navigate the stairs on his way to bed and it is past his bedtime!' The Magpie laughed as he pointed to his watch.

Leo smiled as The Magpie rose from his seat. 'Visit me and let us continue our discourse,' he said as he felt inside his pocket. Pulling out a small card, he handed it to Leo. 'Phone me, for there are things I wish to show you.' In a low voice he added, 'They are the reason why I am called The Magpie.'

The morning after the party, the house was quiet. Leo made his way downstairs and noticed Van Gogh leaning against the open front door. He exhaled smoke from his pipe and turned when he heard Leo approach.

'Do you know where I might find Sion?' Leo asked.

'No idea. But I doubt you will find him. He'll be in bed until after lunch,' Van Gogh replied.

Leo felt disappointed, 'I wanted to thank him before I left.'

The Dutchman continued to smoke his pipe. 'You leaving already?'

'It's going to start raining so I thought I'd better start walking,' Leo explained.

'I'll give you a lift,' the Dutchman said as he tapped his pipe against the wall. A lump of spent tobacco fell onto the ground, he trod on it, put the empty pipe into his pocket and said, 'Come on.'

The MG came to life with a throaty growl.

'What a beast!' exclaimed Leo.

'Not a beast, a beauty,' Hubert corrected.

With the car in gear, Hubert set off slowly down the drive.

'I can't go any faster than this,' he explained. 'These bloody stones on the drive play hell with the bodywork. I keep complaining to him but he takes no notice. You mention it to him.'

'He wouldn't listen to me, we hardly know each other,' Leo said.

'He'll listen to you,' Hubert said with confidence.

As the car came to the end of the drive, Leo pointed to the right. Hubert took the right turn and pushed down hard on the accelerator. The car responded and quickly picked up speed. Hubert threw back his head, laughed and shouted above the sound of the engine, 'NOW IT'S A BEAST!'

'Let's have a quick coffee, I've got some news for you.' Sylvie led Leo into the kitchen. 'But first, how did your night go?'

'Fantastic, wonderful, brilliant!' Leo passed the cups to Sylvie. 'How was Steve's meal?' he asked.

'First class, everything was perfect,' Sylvie smiled.

'So I missed a treat,' Leo said as he sat down.

'More than that, you missed some very interesting news.' Sylvie began to drink her coffee.

'Spill the beans!' Leo said as he moved closer to Sylvie.

'After we had finished our meal, Martha announced that she had some news for us all, Maddy and David have split up. He won't be coming home from India.'

'Oh, no!' Leo said quietly and with sadness.

'As you can imagine, Maddy is devastated, torn to pieces is how Martha put it.'

'What will she do?' Leo asked with concern.

Sylvie shrugged her shoulders. 'Martha has suggested that she comes here, well, to your mum's old house to be exact.'

'I thought Martha and Michael were moving into that?'

'Do you honestly think they'd ever leave this place? It's who they are, isn't it?'

Leo nodded in agreement and asked, 'Where does that leave you?'

'I'll still run this place with Steve as chef. Martha and Michael will oversee things and find some time for their retirement. I'll carry on living in Studio Cottage and you'll still be up in the attic,' Sylvie explained.

'I did wonder where I'd be,' Leo grinned and then added in a serious tone, 'Poor Maddy, I hope she'll be OK.'

'She'll be OK, she is a very strong and self-reliant person. To be honest with you, it could be the best thing that could have happened.' Sylvie looked at her watch and got up from the table. She bent and kissed Leo on the forehead and made her way to the door.

'Hey, Sylvie,' Leo said, 'wouldn't it be great to have Maddy around all the time?'

Sylvie paused and said, 'I think we all agree on that,' in a whisper she added, 'especially Charlie.'

CHAPTER 7

Giles dragged his stool over to his workbench and sat down. He opened up the plan sheets in front of him and began to study the plans for Charlie's furniture. Rough sketches drawn by Charlie had been transformed into accurate and workable joinery plans. Giles checked that they were all there.

The plan for the four-poster bed with its turned corner posts and high-backed headboard lay on top of the pile. Underneath it Giles found the plans for the chest of drawers, the blanket box and the small writing table. Pinned to each plan was Charlie's original sketch and his notes.

Giles studied the plan for the writing table and then read the note attached, it read: 'For my father's use'. Next Giles made an assessment of the wood required for the table.

He walked over to his stock of timber. Over the years he had collected together a large amount of mixed timbers. Well- seasoned planks of oak, chestnut, pine and beech filled the far end of the barn.

He pulled out the boards from the stack and rested them against the wall. He ran the palm of his hand down them, feeling and following the grain. He carefully checked both sides of each plank and when he was satisfied that the boards were the right ones, he carried them over to the workbench. As he propped them up against the bench, Anita came hurrying in.

'That was Michael on the phone, can you get over there? He's got serious problems with the boiler.'

'Damn! Why does he not just buy a new one? His boiler is defunct,' he said angrily pulling off his apron and putting on his jacket. 'I'll never get the time to start Charlie's furniture, let alone finish it!' he said as he made his way to the door.

On the Thursday morning, as Steve was busy in the kitchen, he suddenly remembered something. He looked at his watch and realised that Maurice's weekly food visit would be in approximately seven minutes. He tore off his apron and rushed upstairs in search of Leo.

'Leo, open up, it's me,' he called as he knocked on Leo's bedroom door.

Leo, obviously rudely awakened, grunted, 'What?'

'Lend me your car. The keys, quick. My bike's too slow and Maurice is about to turn up and I'm not sure Charlie has left.'

'I knew this would happen,' said Leo as he went to get his car keys.

'Hurry up,' Steve said anxiously.

'Here,' said Leo, passing him the keys, 'I don't know if you'll get there, she's playing up.'

'Great!' Steve rushed downstairs.

Eventually the car started, but Steve, unused to the position of the gear knob, found it difficult to put the car into gear.

'Bloody Noddy car,' he complained as he drove out of Les Lavandes.

The roll-back sun roof had been leaking, and Steve soon discovered that the driver's seat was soaking wet. 'This gets better,' he said sarcastically to himself.

Things got worse. As he drove close to Templar House he could see Charlie's camper van parked at the side of the house. Steve parked Leo's 2CV next to it and went in search of Charlie or Maurice.

As he opened the main door of the house, he found them both. Charlie was wearing an expression of amused disbelief. Maurice wore the same expression minus the amusement. They both turned and looked at Steve.

Steve walked over to Maurice and gently guided him towards his chair. 'Sit down Maurice. It's OK!' Maurice perched himself on the edge of the seat.

Charlie sat down in his own seat and as he did, he noticed Maurice's shoes. His own shoes. His old faithfuls.

'I owe you an explanation,' Steve began.

'NO!' cried Maurice as he got up from the chair. 'You made a promise,' he said, looking at Steve.

'Sit back down and listen to what I have to say to Charlie.' Steve turned and then said to Charlie, 'Maurice turned up here one day in the middle of winter. He hadn't any warm clothing or winter shoes and he was hungry. He trusted me. He trusted me enough to turn up here and ask for my help. I helped him, Charlie, because I felt I had to.' Steve turned and looked at Maurice. He had sat back on Steve's chair and had his head in his hands. Steve continued, 'He was suffering.'

Charlie looked at Steve and then at Maurice. Eventually he broke the silence, 'Where do you live, Maurice?'

After a long and painful silence, Maurice turned and said to Charlie, 'I live in the woods, your woods. I live in the hut at the entrance to your tunnel.'

'How on earth have you survived?' Charlie asked with concern.

'I have lived and survived like an animal,' Maurice replied and then added, 'until he helped me.'

Charlie moved his chair closer to Maurice and spoke gently to him, 'I own the woods and the hut where you live and you have my permission to stay there,' as

Charlie spoke Maurice lifted his head and listened, 'I can put it in writing for you and sign it in front of two witnesses, Steve and ...' Charlie paused.

'Leo,' Steve added.

'What do you do for food?' Charlie asked.

'He gives me food each Thursday and paraffin for the heater.'

'I've been taking it from the tank in the barn,' Steve admitted.

'I thought it was going down,' Charlie laughed, and then asked, 'And those shoes, Maurice, are they comfortable?'

'Very, I never take them off,' Maurice replied as he looked down at the brogues.

On the final evening of the stay of Sissy Pirton and the nurses, Steve worked especially hard. He had been working from early morning preparing what was to be his 'last supper'. He continued into the evening, perfecting as much as he could, getting everything just right. Sylvie and Martha worked around him, taking care not to disturb his intense concentration.

For Martha it was a joy to watch, for she knew she was seeing an extremely talented chef at work. Mostly self-taught, except for the foundation stones laid down by his mum, his talent came from within. His experiments and his ideas worked. His sensitive and delicate presentation was a delight to the eye.

Martha knew that good food not only satisfied the taste buds but also the other senses. As Steve put the finishing touches to a wonderful chocolate dessert, Martha knew that many people to come would have the experience of fine gastronomy through the work of Steve. She recognised that he was gifted.

'Your face is bright red,' Steve noticed as Michael came into the kitchen.

'It was hot in there,' he replied, and then asked Sylvie,

'Have you finished at the sink?'

'Nearly,' she said.

'Hurry up, we've got champagne on ice and it's ready to drink.' Michael went into the utility room and came back with the champagne.

Martha brought the glasses over to the table and said, 'This is to celebrate Steve's achievement.'

'A brilliant achievement,' added Michael as he opened the bottle.

'You are very talented. Very talented indeed,' Martha said to him.

Steve relaxed in his seat and Sylvie moved close to him. He wrapped an arm around her. 'I'm just relieved it went well,' he said.

'It was perfect,' Martha said.

Michael took a sip of his drink and said, 'You'd be happy if I advertised you as our chef?' Steve nodded and Michael continued, 'I thought about sending details to all our existing guests, an introduction and sample menu, what do you think?'

'That sounds fine to me,' Steve replied.

'I'll include it on our website, maybe you could help with that?'

Steve was about to reply when Martha said, 'Are you sure you want to take all this on board? Being chef I mean.'

'I feel ready for the challenge. I didn't before but I do now.' As he spoke Sylvie grabbed hold of his hand and squeezed it gently.

'We'll all help,' said Martha. 'We'll help both of you.' She looked across the table at both Steve and Sylvie.

'Before I forget,' said Michael, passing a small brown envelope to Steve, 'your wages.'

'Thanks,' said Steve with a smile, 'it will go towards a moped. The pushbike is OK, but cycling is the last thing you want to do after having been on your feet for hours!'

'You do look tired,' remarked Martha.

'I'm knackered,' Steve admitted.

'Borrow the car.' Michael passed the keys to Steve. 'You can bring it back in the morning. I'll see that Sylvie gets home safely when we've finished here.'

'You don't mind, do you?' Steve asked Sylvie as he got up from the table.

'No. I'll come and say goodnight at the car.' She got up from the table.

Outside the night air was chilly. The sky was perfectly clear and as Steve and Sylvie stood at the car they both looked up at the stars.

Steve wrapped his arms around her and said, 'We are going to be OK you know.'

CHAPTER 8

Charlie sat with eyes closed and enjoyed the solitude and the peace.

The house was still and quiet. Opening his eyes he focused on the huge beams of the ceiling. One in particular fascinated him. It was far from being straight, it was still in its original tree shape and its curve stretched across the room.

In the centre of the beam, neither obvious nor hidden, was a Templar cross. As Charlie looked up at the cross he imagined the knights finding safety within the house.

Charlie's peace and distant thoughts disintegrated as PJ pulled up outside. Charlie got up from his chair and went to open the door.

'Morning!' PJ announced as he walked in.

'Good morning!' replied Charlie as he made his way over to the piano.

PJ followed. 'How have you got on with the Bach?' he asked.

'Not good,' answered Charlie as he placed the music on the stand. 'I can't get the timing right.'

'Let me show you.' PJ sat at the piano, straightened the music and began to play the piece.

'It doesn't sound like that when I play it.'

'You really love music, don't you?' Charlie said when the lesson had finished.

'It was my first love,' PJ admitted as he got up from the chair, 'and it has brought me much joy and comfort, and it has got me through some difficult times.'

'It's helping me to give up the drink,' Charlie admitted.

'I thought it would. You aren't married are you Charlie?'

'No, I don't have a woman at the moment.' Charlie opened the door.

'Then let music become your love,' PJ suggested as he was leaving.

Steve burst into the room, unable to speak and breathe. He rested against the table and tried to catch his breath. 'I cycled here as fast as I could and it's winded me,' he explained in between deep breaths.

Charlie walked over to him and asked, 'Is there a problem?'

'Not a problem, I've got some news for you.' When he finally had his breath back he began to explain, 'Martha has just had a phone call from Maddy, she's moving over here in a month's time.'

Charlie stared at Steve in disbelief but did not speak.

'Aren't you going to say anything? I've just cycled over here like a maniac to bring you that news.' He shook his head at Charlie.

'It's come as a shock, that's all,' Charlie replied.

Steve sat down. 'But why?' he said.

'I'm not ready for it.' Charlie looked at Steve. 'I'm really not ready for that.'

'Not ready for what?' Steve asked, feeling confused.

'For Maddy,' was all that Charlie said. He walked over to the window and looked outside. He felt completely unprepared for the arrival of the person he was so deeply in love with.

'Slow down,' said Steve, reading between the lines, 'she's only just split up from her husband.'

Charlie turned around and said, 'Steve I'm not a fool and I understand how she must be feeling. What you don't understand is how I am feeling.'

'Then tell me,' Steve leant back against the chair and waited.

Eventually Charlie began to unwrap his feelings. 'You may think I'm crazy or whatever, that's up to you, but I feel that Maddy is not only the right person for me, she's the only person. I knew from the moment I set eyes on her that she was the only person in this lifetime that I would ever want. I've felt that ever since.'

Steve let out a long sigh and then said, 'That's heavy stuff, Charlie.'

Charlie shrugged. 'That's how it is. And this place,' he said, pointing around him, 'is not ready for her. The house and the garden are not finished.' After a silence he continued, 'And me, I'm not sorted out either.'

'Hey,' said Steve, 'you're doing OK, you've packed in drinking.'

'But I haven't resolved the things which pushed me there in the first place.' Charlie's face grew serious.

Steve got up and walked over to him. 'Take things slowly and let things happen naturally. If it's meant to be, then it will be. You're working through your problems but you can't expect a miracle.'

Charlie looked at him, 'It feels like one has just happened.'

'Perhaps it has.' Steve looked at his watch. 'I'm going to have to get back, I promised Michael I'd help with his website.'

'I didn't know you were computer literate?' Charlie said.

'I'm not. He's including some information about me and I want to make sure he tells the truth!' Steve walked over to the door. 'I won't be home tonight but I'll be back in time to make Sunday lunch.'

'Thank God for that!' said Charlie with a grin. 'Will you be able to help me in the afternoon? I want to finish the fence.'

'I'll help as long as it's not pouring down. We were knee- deep in mud the last time,' Steve said as he went outside.

'Ankle-deep!' corrected Charlie as he closed the door.

Leo placed the bottle of wine carefully on the passenger seat. He got into the driver's seat and pulled out of his pocket the note. Underneath The Magpie's address were the directions for how to get there.

The Magpie lived fifty kilometres away, in an area of high altitude. It was an area known for its rare wild flowers. Leo had visited the area before and had seen carpets of the rare plants in flower but he knew he would not see the plants on this trip, he was more likely to see snow on the mountains.

The Magpie had informed him that the roads to his home were clear of snow. A light lunch had been planned and Leo would then set off back in the late afternoon, avoiding the evening's bad road conditions.

As he drove closer to his destination he felt himself being almost lifted. The 2CV wound and climbed the mountain roads. To one side Leo could see a sheer drop. The edge of the drop was unfenced and dangerously close. Leo kept his eyes on the road ahead.

As he climbed higher he could hear the tinkling of goat bells and he knew that somewhere close by was a herd of mountain goats. The hardy goats provided an income to an area so inhospitable that survival was often not only difficult but impossible. Abandoned farms and houses bore witness to this.

When the climb levelled out, Leo stopped the car and got out. The view was incredible. In the distance the mountain range undulated and the snow-clad tops were bathed in a gentle pink haze. All other distant features were obscured or softened by the haze.

Leo marvelled at the scene, a scene lacking any hard edges. It was a scene of transient beauty and one which Leo wished he could implant into his memory and reproduce at a later date using soft, subtle watercolours.

He got back into the car and carried on driving. Following the instructions he found the turning to The Magpie's home and pulled up by a well in the garden.

The house, an original farmhouse and connected dairy, had been converted into one single long building. Across from the house Leo spotted the wooden chalet building with its fully windowed first floor, and he knew this had to be The Magpie's studio.

He smiled when he noticed that the house was painted white. Its walls, shutters and doors were painted without a trace of another colour. The studio was painted completely black.

Clutching the bottle of wine, Leo walked past the well, but couldn't resist stopping and having a look down it.

'You'll only find water in there,' a voice called out.

Leo turned and saw The Magpie standing at the door at the side of the house, he waved. Leo waved back and walked towards him, and as he did he noticed that the mask of the party had been replaced by a pair of dark glasses.

'Greetings, Leo, and welcome to my home.' The Magpie embraced him. 'Come, let us go inside.'

Leo followed The Magpie into the kitchen. The light and airy room was homely, uncluttered but not tidy.

'I am preparing a salad for us, see?' he said, pointing to a chopping board by the sink. The board was piled high with all kinds of fresh leaves. 'But from what I can remember, you do not eat,' he said with a smile.

'I wasn't hungry at the party but today I am ravenous!' Leo admitted.

'Good!' He passed a large bowl to Leo. 'Put the salad into this and I shall go and bring cheeses and fruit.'

Leo took the bowl and began to fill it with the leaves. 'I have brought a bottle of wine, I hope you will like it,' he said as he pointed to the wine on the table.

'Wonderful!' replied The Magpie. 'The French have made a fashion out of drinking too much!'

'I suppose they have,' laughed Leo as he carried the bowl over to the table. 'I'm sorry, I forgot to wash my hands,' he said with a grin.

The Magpie opened the wine. 'I doubt if our ancestors washed before handling their food,' he said.

Leo stood by the window and looked outside. 'This view is stunning.'

'It is,' agreed The Magpie. 'It is stunning and it is always different. A slight alteration of temperature can bring about almost a completely different view.'

'Does the house disappear when it snows?' Leo asked as he sat down at the table.

'The studio is on higher ground and in bad weather it is a landmark,' The Magpie explained as he poured the wine. 'Let us eat now and then I will show you what I have brought you here to see.'

Leo helped himself to salad and cheese. The Magpie passed him a large chunk of bread and explained, 'I always eat simply at home, the extravagant side of my appetite is fulfilled when I visit Sion.'

'Do you visit him often?' Leo asked.

'We need each other. We need each other like two old men who have little time in the future and much in the past!' grinned The Magpie.

'You are not old,' objected Leo.

The Magpie took a large mouthful of wine, savoured its flavour, swallowed, and then said, 'Neither are we young. Moments are precious to us both. You know, quite often we just sit together without speaking. As companions we need little more than each other's company.'

'Does he visit you here?' Leo asked as he mopped up the salad dressing on his plate with a piece of bread.

'Yes, he visits me. He loves the snow, he is like a child and delights in its strangeness,' The Magpie peered at Leo from behind his dark glasses.

'It is brilliant,' Leo answered.

'It is wondrous,' The Magpie smiled and continued to eat. When the meal was over The Magpie went to make coffee. Leo sat and stared out of the window. As he did he tried to imagine Sion finding the joy of childhood amidst the snow- covered land.

'Do you have a sledge?' Leo asked when The Magpie returned with the coffees.

'Yes, Leo, I have a sledge. Sometime you come and stay with me and you can play out,' The Magpie laughed.

After coffee and a pause for digestion, The Magpie left the room, when he returned he was carrying a set of keys. 'Come, Leo, let us not delay, then you can return home safely before darkness.'

Leo followed The Magpie outside to the double doors of his cellar. The Magpie began to unlock the doors, and as he did he explained, 'Sadly the cave is not vaulted. It is unlike so many of the caves in this area which have wonderful vaulted ceilings.'

After unlocking the doors The Magpie began to switch off the complicated alarm system inside the entrance to the cellar. Leo watched as he ran through the complex de-activation programme, remarking, 'That's some system.'

'It took me a while to understand and remember, but I'm familiar with it now,' he turned and smiled.

When the alarm was switched off, The Magpie switched on lights and took off his dark glasses. Turning to Leo he explained, 'The lighting in here is subdued. I hope you do not mind the sight of my eyes?'

Leo shook his head. On the night of the party he had seen the eyes with their shrivelled surrounding skin and they had shocked him, but now they did not disturb him. 'Do your eyes still hurt?' he asked.

'To see colour can be painful. I can see colour but the pain can outweigh the advantage. The tones of black and white are multitude and it is these I choose to see. Colour like sound is metaphysical.' The Magpie turned and opened the glass door in front of him.

'What the...' exclaimed Leo as he followed The Magpie inside.

The Magpie chortled as Leo confronted the monstrosity in front of him.

'That is perfectly horrendous!' Leo said, as he looked at the enormous life-like model of a fly. It towered over him, and the magnified details of its body, head and legs looked horrific to Leo. He walked closer to it and examined the hairs on one of its legs. He then noticed its proboscis. 'Ugh.'

'The proboscis is fairly horrendous,' agreed The Magpie, 'but examine its wings. See how truly wonderful they are.' Leo stood next to The Magpie and looked up at one of the wings. The Magpie pointed, 'See these fine lines, fine veins. What do you think they would carry within them?'

'Energy,' suggested Leo as he studied the tracery.

'What do you think of this?' The Magpie asked as he led Leo to a small vehicle parked next to the fly.

The strange golden bullet-shaped vehicle made Leo laugh and he asked, 'What on earth is this?'

'Futuristic, isn't it?' The Magpie replied, stroking a hand over the smooth bodywork.

'Does it work?' Leo asked as he peered inside through the small oval window.

'Yes, but as yet it doesn't generate enough energy to fly,' The Magpie turned to Leo and then continued, 'It has a solar pack here at the rear but the main system is not advanced enough to utilise all the energy fully. The steering interests me, Leo, have a look. No steering wheel. The seat contains sensors which can detect the slightest body movement. Movement to the left is picked up and the steering shifts to the left. Movement to the right and the steering shifts to the right.' As he spoke The Magpie moved his body to demonstrate the process.

'It will never fly, it hasn't got any wings,' Leo said dryly. The Magpie laughed and walked on. He led Leo to a small crib. Leo walked over to it and had a look inside. 'There's a baby in here,' he said pointing to the crib.

'It's a model of a real baby. The real baby was born in the 1940s. Lift him out Leo and have a look at him.'

Leo picked up the baby. 'That's weird, it feels like a real baby,' he said as he held the tiny figure in his hands.

'Turn him over and have a look at his back,' instructed The Magpie.

Leo turned the baby over. 'This is not real. This is a hoax. It isn't possible,' he said as he looked at the two perfectly formed wing-like shapes protruding from either side of the baby's spine.

'It was real, very real. The case was well documented. The wings were surgically removed soon after birth.'

As Leo lay the baby back in its crib he asked, 'Was it a genetic hiccough?'

'Perhaps. Or maybe it was a jump in evolution, who knows?' The Magpie shrugged.

'Or dares to dream,' added Leo, looking back at the baby. All four walls of the cellar were covered with paintings and prints. Shelves containing statues and books were dotted all around. Leo spotted a picture that interested him and moved closer for a better look. It was a framed section of a papyrus.

'It is an original,' explained The Magpie. He pointed to the hieroglyphics, 'Look at this, this is Horus the Hawk.'

Leo looked at the hieroglyph. 'Why is that one important to you?' he asked.

'Horus mastered celestial flight,' answered The Magpie as he moved on.

Leo caught him up. 'You are obsessed with wings!' he said.

'Flight!' The Magpie corrected him.

They both stood together in front of a towering statue of The Messenger. Its fine slender form reached its arms up to the skies as its head, tilted backwards, looked up to the heavens. His feet each wore two wings.

The Magpie moved away and led Leo to a huge painting hung on the gable wall. The painting almost covered the wall. Leo recognised it straight away.

'It is not an original,' explained The Magpie. 'It is only a copy. If I could afford the original, I very much doubt that I would be able to afford the insurance.'

'How on earth did you get it in here?' asked Leo.

'It arrived in four sections. If you look very carefully you will be able to see where it has been joined.' The Magpie pointed to the middle of the painting.

'Why did the artist paint on wood and not canvas? You would have been able to roll a canvas up,' said Leo as he studied the painting.

'He only paints on wood and I commissioned this piece. The joins are barely noticeable.'

Leo looked up at the angel. Her face, radiant with divine contemplation, gazed into the heavenly sphere. Her flowing white gown revealed her two perfect wings and on the ground by her feet lay two white lilies.

'It's a perfect copy,' Leo said in amazement.

'A perfect copy of a Pre-Raphaelite masterpiece,' The Magpie agreed. He then took Leo by the arm. 'Come, come and sit down for I wish to show you something. It is the reason I have brought you here.'

Leo sat down on the small double seat as The Magpie moved a small cabinet towards him. 'This is my collection,' he said, sitting down besides Leo. 'The reason they call me The Magpie.'

The Magpie unlocked the drawers of the cabinet. Leo moved to the edge of his seat in order to get a better look. As the first drawer was pulled out, Leo could see that the dark velvety interior was filled with gold jewellery.

'These are not copies,' he said, 'they are original pieces.' Each piece was an example of not only the work of the finest craftsmen and women but also of the movement to which they belonged. Each piece, harmonious and beautiful, radiated the energy of its time.

Leo looked at the pieces with amazement. Each one had a connection with celestial flight. One in particular caught his eye. It was a finely crafted figure of a woman. She was positioned in the centre of a brooch and with arms outstretched she held above her head a circular disc.

'This figure hasn't got any wings,' commented Leo as he pointed to the brooch.

'She doesn't need any,' chortled The Magpie.

'Why not?'

'Because she travels with and on the movement of the moon,' explained The Magpie. Picking up a pendant, he said, 'This one is interesting. It is the design of Aubrey Beardsley. What a wonderful blend of the grotesque and beauty.' He passed the pendant to Leo.

Leo held the pendant carefully and studied it as The Magpie explained, 'That figure is Mephistopheles and this one here is Faust.' He turned the pendant over and Leo read the inscription on the back, 'Evil clutches at the heart of good.'

After putting the pendant back into its drawer, The Magpie began to open the final drawer but hesitated. He turned to Leo and said in a quiet, serious tone, 'This single piece is the reason why I have brought you here and the reason why we have been drawn together.'

Leo watched as the drawer was slowly pulled open. He could see that the velvet-lined interior was empty apart from one tiny thing. Leo moved forwards as The Magpie removed the small protective dome.

The silence which followed was shattered as Leo finally exclaimed, 'My God!'

'I knew you would recognise it,' said The Magpie as he stared at the tiny gold bee.

'I am hoping this is a copy,' said Leo, pointing to the bee.

'The Merovingian gold bees are in a safe keeping apart from the ones that are...' Leo paused as the impact of what he was seeing and thinking hit him.

'Missing,' chortled The Magpie.

During the following four days, Leo felt haunted. Thoughts of the Merovingian bee would not leave his mind for long. It didn't matter what he was doing, the image of the bee would fill his mind and disturb him.

On the night of the fifth day, the haunting was broken by a dream.

In the dream Leo felt captured. He was imprisoned in a hanging cage. The cage was suspended from a crossbeam in the cellar of what seemed to be an ancient building.

As Leo looked down from the cage he could see a cloaked figure. The figure was at work below him. Leo watched as the figure prepared and began to mix an elixir.

Leo shouted to him, 'Let me go. Let me out of here.' As he shouted he rattled on the bars with such a force that the cage began to swing to and fro.

The figure turned and looked up at Leo and as it did, Leo felt he recognised the face. But the eyes, the eyes were different. The eyes staring up at him were without an iris or a pupil. They were the eyes of Merlin.

The figure stretched out his arm and held out his hand to Leo. Leo knew what the hand of Merlin wanted and he knew that parting with it was his only chance of release.

Leo closed his eyes and gently threw the Merovingian bee into the outstretched hand.

The hand caught the bee, retreated back into the cloak and as it did, the figure of Merlin chortled.

CHAPTER 9

'Please put work on the writing table on hold, and start on the bed,' Charlie said as he walked to the gate.

'I was about to begin work on the table, I've chosen the wood and studied the plans.' Giles stopped in his tracks.

'Well forget that for now and start on the bed,' Charlie said firmly.

'What's the rush for the bed?' Giles asked and as he did Steve looked at him and raised his eyebrows.

'No rush. I just want it done like that, the bed first and then the table,' Charlie explained.

Giles grinned at Steve and then said to Charlie, 'I'll start on the bed but I don't know how long it will take me. I didn't expect to be helping you lot to do this fencing or making a garden gate.'

'We'd never have got it finished if it had been left up to us two,' Charlie said as he stood next to Steve. 'We'd have struggled without your help.'

Giles stood by the gate and looked at the newly fenced patch of ground. 'It's a big vegetable garden for the two of you. That would feed a family with children,' he said, pointing to the veg garden.

Charlie turned to him and explained, 'I'm hoping the surplus will be bought by Les Lavandes and I'm hoping it will be completely organic. I'd also like to give Maurice a weekly share.'

Steve's eyes narrowed and he then grimaced at Charlie. His mind began to think of a way of covering up Charlie's slip.

'Who's Maurice?' asked Giles.

'Charlie's rabbit,' replied Steve.

Steve turned and began to walk to the log store. He felt angry. He was angry with Charlie. Angry that he had so easily made a slip, a slip which could have betrayed Maurice.

'Catch you later,' called Giles, retrieving Steve from his thoughts.

Steve watched as Charlie went into the house. He stacked the last of the logs and then set off down to the river to have a few words with Maurice.

The path which had been so overgrown was now flattened and accessible. Steve made his way down the path and into the clearing. At the far edge of the clearing he looked down to the river and could see Maurice sitting on the riverbank.

Steve scrambled down the track and as he approached Maurice he called, 'It's only me.'

Maurice didn't move but called back, 'I know.'

Steve sat down on the stones next to him and got his breath back.

'You are not fit,' Maurice said as he watched the flow of the river.

'And you wouldn't have needed your intuition to tell you that,' Steve replied.

'Anyway what are you doing here? It's not Thursday.'

'It's a social visit,' Steve said, and then began to watch the river swirl close by. A whirlpool formed in front of him.

'It doesn't feel like a social visit,' Maurice replied, and then looked at Steve.

Steve and Maurice made eye contact. Steve began to explain, 'Charlie almost let it slip that you were here and it made me realise what a situation we are all in together. It's difficult if not impossible to protect you.'

Maurice looked back at the river and said, 'I knew this would happen.' He spoke with acceptance.

'You don't seem all that bothered,' Steve felt confused as Maurice shrugged his shoulders. He continued, 'I came here to offer a suggestion. Would you consider moving into a caravan up there in the clearing? It's a dry spot but you would still be near to the river.'

'What you are really saying is make my presence known,' Maurice turned and looked at Steve.

'I suppose it is,' answered Steve. 'It's your choice though. It wouldn't be a case of hiding in that dark damp hut and eventually being discovered, it would be your own choice to make your presence known. It's too difficult to keep you hidden.'

'Everything has changed,' said Maurice calmly, 'it doesn't matter anymore who finds out I am here.'

'What has made that difference?' asked Steve.

'She has. She's coming and she hears the sound.' Maurice turned and looked at Steve, 'She hears it and I will not be alone.'

'You are not making any sense to me. Who hears this sound you keep going on about?' Steve asked.

Maurice got up and moved closer to the river, dipped his hand in the water's edge and said, 'She feels the heartbeat of the earth, she listens and hears the sound. She is the one who can make order out of chaos.'

'I don't speak that language,' said Steve. 'I only came here to ask if you would consider moving into a dry caravan, so can we speak of normal things?'

Maurice turned to him and nodded. Steve continued to explain, 'I have some money spare which I could use to buy a small caravan, with help we'd get it onto the clearing. Maybe in return you could do some work in Charlie's garden?' Steve asked, 'What kind of work did you do?'

'I was a teacher, maths and languages. The same subject really,' Maurice replied.

'Why did you pack it all in?' Steve asked.

Maurice didn't answer. He got up from the edge of the river and began to walk away. He stopped and turned to look at Steve and said, 'When she comes, tell her Maurice Vachon is here.'

Steve frowned, 'When who comes?'

'Maddy!' said Maurice as he walked away.

'Sorry Giles, you've missed him, he's over at your old place,' explained Martha.

'Damn!' said Giles, 'I was hoping he'd be able to give me a hand.'

'Can I help?' asked Martha.

'Not unless you are any good with garden machinery!' Giles laughed.

'Is it the same machine that Michael fixed for you last year?' Martha asked as she stood in the doorway.

'That's the one! It's playing up again but it doesn't matter, I can borrow Charlie's,' replied Giles.

'I don't see much of you these days,' said Martha, moving into a patch of morning sunshine. She leant back against the front wall of the house.

'I've been really busy. Busy at Charlie's, busy at home, busy in the workshop, busy in the garden. I never seem to get a minute.'

'You need to find time to relax,' said Martha as she moved to one side to make room for Giles.

'I try to find time but I fail!' said Giles.

'How are things with you and Anita?' Martha asked.

'OK at the moment but we did have another bust up recently,' Giles replied, and he leant his head back against the wall.

'So I heard,' Martha gave him a smile.

'Is nothing private around here?' Giles felt annoyed.

'Not much,' answered Martha. 'How is Anita these days? Is she better?'

'She seems to be,' Giles replied and then asked, 'When is Maddy due to arrive?'

'In about a month's time. It's giving Michael enough time to get your old place ready for her. He's insulating the loft at the moment.'

'Martha, I kept on at him to do that but he wouldn't listen to me,' Giles explained.

'Well he's had a change of heart, plus I've been on at him!' Martha turned and smiled at Giles.

Giles looked at Martha and said, 'You always get your own way!'

'Not always,' said Martha wistfully. 'Can I be honest with you about something?'

'I thought you were always honest. Go on then, speak your mind.' Giles looked into the distance as he waited for Martha's reply, and as he did a small alarm bell rang inside his head.

Martha moved away from the wall and stood facing him, she spoke softly and slowly, 'It's not the same without you around the place. I miss you. I miss you an awful lot.'

Giles looked away from Martha and said, 'I'm not a million miles away from you. You are welcome at my home anytime. Come and visit us.'

'I don't think Anita would be keen on that idea,' replied Martha.

'Maybe you are misjudging her,' Giles looked directly at Martha.

Martha touched his chest gently, 'She keeps you under wraps and don't deny that.'

Giles moved away, turned to face Martha and said, 'I am not under wraps as you put it. I am who I am and I have my own mind and my own feelings. You and Michael are both good friends and I'm happy with that, so please don't spoil it.' Martha let out a sigh and moved away. She was about to go indoors when she turned and said, 'I wish I hadn't said anything, I wish I hadn't been honest with you. I'm sorry.'

Giles walked up to her and held onto her arm. When she turned to face him, he explained, 'If I didn't have Anita and you didn't have Michael then maybe things would be different, but as it stands we both have partners to consider. We are not free...' Giles paused.

'...to have an affair.' Martha completed the sentence. 'Even one which could easily be kept private?'

Giles let go of her arm and lowered his eyes. As Martha went inside she added very quietly, 'Think about it.'

'Charlie, what on earth are you doing down there?' Steve burst out laughing.

'Yoga,' Charlie was sitting on the rug next to the woodburner in a cross-legged position.

'Here, do you want a hand?' Steve asked as he walked up to him.

'No, I don't! Can you not see that I'm almost in the lotus position?' Charlie replied.

'It did cross my mind, but your legs aren't right. That foot should be resting here,' Steve explained, and pointed to the right foot and the left thigh.

'What do you know about it anyway?' said Charlie, unravelling himself.

'I used to do a bit myself,' admitted Steve.

'Never!' exclaimed Charlie as he managed to stand upright.

'You doing yoga!'

'It wasn't through choice I can assure you, but it did turn out to be quite interesting,' Steve explained.

'Carry on,' Charlie sat down in his chair.

Steve continued, 'There were ten of us and we had to learn a method of relaxation. It was part of a programme.' He sat down and then continued, 'We were wild kids.'

'I don't believe what I am hearing!' exclaimed Charlie.

'Are you telling me that you were a delinquent and had to be reformed?'

'Something like that, and one day I'll tell you all about it but not today. But the yoga can help you to relax and find peace.'

'Did it help you?' Charlie asked.

'It did, but I didn't admit it at the time,' Steve paused and then added, 'Then I found sex.'

'You gave up yoga for sex?' Charlie grinned.

'No. I combined them.'

'Is that really possible?' asked Charlie in deep thought.

'You'll have to try it and find out for yourself!'

'What do I have to do?' Charlie asked with a huge grin.

'First of all stop looking like a pervert,' Steve began to explain. 'It can be a way of making sex spiritual. I suppose the first thing is learning to slow your breathing down.'

'While I do yoga?' Charlie asked.

Steve nodded and then continued to explain, 'Yoga can produce very deep relaxation and this can bring about a sense of heightened awareness which can be used during sex.'

'It's all linked together then?'

'Completely!'

'What about the orgasm?' Charlie grinned.

'The art of lovemaking is wasted on you!' Steve said, shaking his head. 'There's more to it than the big bang! Sensitive foreplay for one.'

'Do you not find that bit boring?' Charlie asked.

'You, Charlie, are a hopeless case. Foreplay can be an art form, that's if you are able to use your imagination.'

'What do I have to do?' Charlie asked.

Steve sat back in his chair and laughed, 'I don't believe I'm hearing this.' He put his head in his hands and then continued,

'I can't give you instructions like that, it's not like baking a cake.'

Charlie moved forwards in his seat, then said, 'Teach me yoga and I'll figure the rest out for myself.'

Steve looked up, 'Yoga isn't just moving your body into different positions, it's a spiritual thing too.'

'Be my guru and teach me,' Charlie said with a grin.

'Do you know, you are an unbelievable challenge!' Steve got up from his chair and walked over to the table. 'Practise the lotus and when you have got it together, I'll teach you the breathing.'

As Steve went into the kitchen, Charlie shouted to him,

'When's Maurice's caravan arriving?'

'Tomorrow afternoon,' Steve called back, 'Giles has offered to help us to strim the brambles down to the clearing. In return can he borrow your rotavator?'

'No problem,' replied Charlie. He sat back down on the rug and began to cross his legs.

Steve watched from the kitchen door. He shouted, 'Your trousers are too tight.'

'I thought they were,' Charlie answered, and then added quietly to himself, 'They're making my eyes water.'

The expected two hours of caravan siting extended to five, and Charlie was extremely irritable.

His initial annoyance had been stimulated by the man with the van. He delivered the caravan but refused to move it anywhere near where it was supposed to go. Charlie's annoyance was further developed by the man with a van's three large and unruly dogs who had proceeded to pee on everything which seemed to bear Charlie's scent. If this hadn't been bad enough, the wrestling match with the overgrown brambles certainly was.

Covered in scratches and mud, and longing for a cup of tea, Charlie decided to call it a day.

'We can't give up now,' piped up Steve and Giles in unison. Maurice turned and addressed the workers, 'No, the man is right. The forces are working against us. We must wait for the celestial tide to shift and then the van will easily slip into place.' Without a further word he marched off.

'Did that mean he's going home?' Leo asked.

Charlie nodded, 'Yes and so am I, I'll come back tomorrow. I stink of dog piss, I want a cup of tea and my lacerations are bleeding.'

The following day the caravan glided easily into the chosen place. Maurice spoke in detail about the importance and the recognition of the celestial tides.

As he spoke, Leo stared at him in disbelief, Charlie concentrated for a while but then his mind drifted on its own celestial tide and he wondered what was for supper.

Steve broke Charlie's thoughts, 'The key, Charlie, the key.' He held out his hand.

'I haven't got it, you have,' replied Charlie.

'I haven't got it, but not to worry.' Steve felt in his pocket and pulled out a penknife, and with one of its attachments he began to pick the lock. With ease and in record time the lock clicked open.

'Wow. That was cool! Where did you learn that trick?' asked Leo.

'Borstal,' suggested Charlie.

Steve ignored him, opened the caravan door and climbed inside. Leo followed. 'I want to check that everything is as it was when I bought it,' he explained to Leo.

Outside the caravan Maurice was explaining in detail about the influence of the planets. Giles, who was listening, asked,

'Are you saying that it's not just the moon's influence that's important?'

'All the planets have their influence. For example look at our personalities, they are influenced by the planets present at the time of our birth. They govern our birth signs,' Maurice explained.

'Most people know that,' Charlie chipped in.

'Most people know a little. In the ancient times people were more receptive, more willing to understand and to work with the planetary influence,' Maurice explained to Charlie.

'Why can't we do that now?' Giles asked.

'We have taken a different turning. We are on a different course, whether we like it or not. Planetary influence doesn't have the importance it used to have, people's minds are clogged up with the stimulus from their TVs, their computers...'

'Machines!' interrupted Charlie in disgust.

'But even you, Charlie, have machines,' Giles reminded him.

'It's a modern dilemma,' Maurice said to Charlie. He explained, 'You can still awaken and tap into the ancient wisdom, for it is locked within yourself.'

'How on earth could we do that?' Giles asked.

Maurice sat down on a fallen tree trunk and continued,

'Each of our cells contains the information, the code. We all carry that code around within us from birth to death and beyond. It is not only part of us, it is us. It is our link with the rest of the universe and when we unlock this energy we become interlinked with the great universal mind to a greater degree.'

'Maurice the Mystic is in full flow,' Leo said in a quiet voice to Steve.

Steve looked at Leo and laughed. He opened the cupboard under the sink and then closed it again quickly. It was filthy.

'When he's finished out there it looks like he'll be doing some cleaning.'

'Well at least this looks clean,' said Leo as he checked the mattress. 'In fact it looks new and the little cooker looks new too. I reckon you got a good deal.'

Steve looked around and said, 'You're right, it's a good little caravan. The dirt can be cleaned away.'

'It's a damned sight better than the hut!' exclaimed Leo.

'He'll be OK here,' Steve agreed.

'Should we leave him to move in or give him a hand?' Leo asked.

'Let's leave him to it, it's his domain now.'

'Do you reckon we can get past him without getting caught up in his mumbo jumbo?' Leo asked with a grin.

'We'll just wait for a break in his speech and then make a run for it,' Steve said as he made his way to the caravan door.

'Everything has a cycle and is tied to a cycle. It is the ebb and flow of nature,' Maurice concluded.

'We are away now, Maurice. Everything looks fine in there but one or two things need a bit of a clean,' Steve explained as he and Leo climbed out of the caravan.

'Giles has offered to lay a water pipe down here,' said Charlie, pointing to the caravan.

'It will only lie on top of the ground. I haven't time to dig it in,' Giles said.

'No but I have,' said Maurice. 'I just need to borrow a spade.'

'I'm sure I can find a spare one for you,' offered Giles.

'With running water you'll be able to clean this place up in no time,' Steve said.

As Martha closed the bedroom door, she felt young again. She felt all that she had felt when in her forties, but she felt more, she felt the experience of a woman in her sixties.

Giles noticed the change. He saw the lines of her face smooth away and he saw a brightness in her eyes that he had never seen before. The glow from her radiated outwards.

Her full mouth opened slightly as her hands softly and gently pulled Giles towards her. Giles felt the strength, the power and the desire of this transformed woman.

He was trapped in the turmoil of his own needs and his deep desires. He wrestled with himself. He wrestled until the point came where the feelings within became far greater than an aching need, they became a huge surging pain and he could wrestle no more.

Accepting his defeat like a condemned man he gave into the roaring tidal wave of desire and switched off the part of himself that lived with love.

He did not make love to Martha. Together equally in passion, unashamed and with great hunger they satisfied their desire. The intensity of their sex finally made Martha cry out. For Giles the moment of his release mingled with a stronger, more overpowering feeling. It was the feeling of complete betrayal.

As he opened his eyes he saw complete satisfaction etched on Martha's face. In his heart he knew that he was now lost.

Covered in sweat he awoke, reached out and held the sleeping body next to him. 'What is it? Are you OK?'

'A terrible dream, it was a terrible dream.'

'Let me hold you,' Anita said as she rolled over and wrapped her arms around him. She held him close until the sound of his breathing became calm. Together they both drifted back to sleep.

CHAPTER 10

The final box, small but heavy, contained a mixture of artefacts collected during trips to India, all of them a link with the past. Maddy closed the lid of the box and carried it into the spare room, and made her way downstairs.

Anita's old kitchen was a happy place to be. On the floor, by the table, Anita had left a bold handmade rug. Its deep red stripes bordered by narrow black stripes brightened the whole room. The other thing she had left was a large hand- thrown jug. Its intense glaze, primary colours of reds, yellows and greens, decorated its midnight-blue background. Maddy moved the jug onto the table and went outside into the garden.

She had arrived at the same time as the swallows, and as she walked down the garden path they chattered noisily overhead.

The path, lined with semi-wild sweet violets, had formed a carpet in places, their dark green leaves a background for the tiny, sweet-smelling flowers. Maddy breathed in the fragrant air. Spring and the promise of the new life filled her lungs and her mind.

She began to tidy the garden. Carefully and with respect, she removed the weeds from the clumps of tiny narcissi, rescued from the stranglehold of the weeds they relaxed happily.

The pear and the peach trees were in full blossom, and tiny white petals fell onto the ground like confetti. Maddy walked through the fallen blossom to the other end of the garden, and there she found an old hazel tree. It had been coppiced many moons ago leaving the branches to grow from the base of the tree. Maddy bent down and carefully chose two straight branches. She picked the branches and examined them.

Holding a branch in each hand, she stretched out her arms. The branches, like two ancient wands, felt alive. Maddy spoke, 'Wych Hazel finder of water, find it for me.'

The hazel rods pulled gently and began to guide Maddy to an area of overgrown wilderness beyond the garden. Alert to the possibility of snakes, she looked around her for any sign of movement. When everything around her continued to be still, she carried on walking. She walked following the pull of the wands.

The further she walked, the stronger the pull became. Its strength made the muscles in her arms ache, and her shoulders began to feel as heavy as lead.

As the energy and the sensations grew in intensity she knew that they were almost there. A few more steps and the wands had done their work. They had performed their magic.

The hazel rods led her to the site of an ancient well. The stone walls of the well had long since crumbled and fallen away. Maddy knelt to the side of them, moved away the clumps of weed and peered into what remained of the deep cavern. She could smell the dampness.

As she sat back she noticed a round stone shape next to the well. She cleared away the weeds partially covering it, and the chiselled-out stone revealed itself. It was some kind of man-made trough, ancient but intact.

Maddy lay down the hazel rods, placed her hands on the trough and closed her eyes. Images from the past began to flood her mind. She could see babies, children and adults alike, and she could sense divine energy. The stone had been a baptismal font.

As the images faded they were replaced by more turbulent ones. She could hear the cries of the sick and the injured and she could feel their pain. The water bathed and washed away their torments.

Maddy opened her eyes and looked down at the two hazel rods; the branches had led her to the site of a holy well. She picked up the rods and placed them side by side next to the well.

She walked slowly back to the house. As she came close to home she noticed a figure sitting on the wall. Maddy recognised who it was.

'Steve!' she called out as she ran to him. He turned and smiled.

'I've been waiting here for ages!' he said as he got down from the wall and hugged her. 'I didn't think you were ever going to appear.'

'Well I'm here now and it's wonderful to see you,' she said as she stood back and looked at him. 'And you look really well,' she added.

Steve smiled and asked, 'But how are you?'

'Almost completely healed! Almost. Come on, let's sit in the shade and have a cool drink.' She led him into the garden.

'This wonderful garden is Anita's medic garden. Sit here and I'll get us a drink.'

Steve sat surrounded by large bushes of lavender. 'It's so peaceful here,' he said as Maddy returned with the drinks.

'It's perfect for me at the moment,' she replied and then asked, 'How is life here for you?'

'It feels like the coin has just flipped over, not just for me but for Sylvie too. We seem to have been given the chance of making something of our lives, your sister and Michael have been brilliant,' Steve said as Maddy sat down next to him.

'What about Charlie? How is he?' she asked.

Steve looked at her and smiled, 'He is busy being Charlie!' As Maddy looked at him he said, 'I think I should prepare you, he may invite you to dinner.'

Maddy laughed, 'I kind of expected that!'

'Good, it won't come as a shock then!' Steve took a drink, looked at Maddy with her flowing auburn hair and her strange green eyes and could see what Charlie found attractive. She was beautiful.

'No shock,' she answered smiling.

'You may have heard that we have got a lodger, not in the house but in a caravan,' Steve said.

'No, that is news to me,' she said, taking a sip of her drink.

'He's a bit odd but I like him. There's something about him that doesn't fit into one of those little boxes.' Steve tried to explain, 'He's different.'

'You mean he's just being himself?'

'I suppose so but he can go a bit too far!' Steve laughed and then became serious, 'Maddy, I think you might know him.'

Maddy's face grew serious. She looked hard at Steve and saw in his eyes the image of the stranger. She turned away and asked, 'Who is he?'

'He told me to tell you that Maurice Vachon is here,' Steve said quietly.

Maddy sat silent and still for a long while. Eventually she said to Steve, 'That was a shock and I will explain to you why, but not now. I'm sorry, I need just a little time to think about what you have told me. We can speak about it next week, but Steve...'

When Steve turned to face her, she asked, 'Is he all right?'

'He is now,' Steve answered.

Leo was the last one to jump in. Sion and The Magpie swam to the far side of the lake, turned over onto their backs and floated.

Startled by the coldness of the water and slightly horrified at its greenness, Leo moved slowly. As he swam towards Sion and The Magpie, something slimy wrapped itself around his calf. 'Get it off, get it off!' He shouted, writhed and splashed.

Realising that the phantom snake was only a section of decomposing vegetation, he felt a fool. As Sion smiled to himself, The Magpie howled with laughter.

Leo wrenched the phantom from his leg and threw it at The Magpie. It landed with a slap on his belly, splattering bright green globules over both men.

'Sorry, I didn't mean to get you,' Leo said to Sion as he began to rinse away the green blobs.

'You meant to get me though, didn't you?' asked The Magpie. He flipped over onto his belly and then flipped back again.

Leo joined the two men and floated alongside them. Above was a canopy of branches and leaves which shielded the sun's glare but still allowed the dappled light through. 'Back home we call this skinny dipping,' said Leo, enjoying the sensation of being naked.

'You have many sayings in Britain,' remarked Sion.

'I suppose we do,' Leo answered. 'But some have fallen from use.'

'That is how language develops,' stated The Magpie.

'Tonight,' Sion turned his head to The Magpie, 'we won't play chess, there are three of us.'

'You and Leo play, for I shall take an early night,' The Magpie replied.

'Do you play chess?' Sion asked as he turned to face Leo.

'I do but I'm not very good,' Leo replied.

'That's fine because neither am I. It would be delightful to have the opportunity to win a game. The Magpie always steals the glory,' Sion explained.

'I do not!' objected The Magpie. He chortled and said,

'When I win he accuses me of cheating. He is a very bad loser and you may find that out for yourself.' The Magpie rolled over and swam from under the shady canopy into the warmth of the sun. He flipped over onto his back and closed his eyes.

Enjoying the warmth of the water, he called out, 'It's like being in the womb.'

'Describe it in thirty words,' called back Sion.

'English or French?'

'English,' replied Sion.

'Too many,' called back The Magpie.

'What is this about?' Leo asked.

'It is a game we often play. It keeps our memory faculties intact,' Sion explained, and then called to The Magpie,

'Fifteen and no less.'

'Warm, wet, safe, soothing, mysterious, alive...'

'He's struggling already,' Sion said to Leo.

'I would be and it's my native tongue,' replied Leo.

'Subconscious, deep, dark, vital, universal, transforming...'

After a considerable pause it became obvious that The Magpie had fallen asleep. Sion laughed quietly, 'It won't be long before he awakes.'

Leo lay and watched the pond skaters skim across the water, their fragile legs barely touching the surface. A large dragonfly with its rapidly moving wings investigated and then flew off.

Suddenly the peace was shattered. The Magpie's buoyancy had disappeared and his heavy body had begun to sink below the surface of the lake. His coughs and splutters as he inhaled water broke the silence.

Regaining a safe position, he then swam towards Leo and Sion. 'Why do you always allow me to fall asleep, I could drown!' he said to Sion.

Sion reached for The Magpie's arm and pulled him gently towards him. 'I would always save you,' Sion said to him.

'You already have,' The Magpie answered.

After supper and a large brandy, The Magpie made his way to bed. Leo and Sion, sitting cross-legged in front of the fire, had begun their game of chess. The large log in the open hearth provided just enough light to play chess by. After taking a mouthful of brandy Leo put his plan into action and made his move.

'That move doesn't make sense,' Sion said as he studied the board.

'But it will do,' Leo answered with a smile.

'And that is what I am afraid of.' Sion rested his chin on his hand as he tried to work out the possible moves that could lie ahead.

'Come on, Sion, I'm falling asleep here.'

'Then take a nap while I formulate my plan.'

'You haven't got one,' said Leo.

'I certainly have,' said Sion, making his move.

'That move makes less sense than mine.'

'Do not be fooled by appearances,' replied Sion.

Leo looked at the board and smiled to himself as he made his move. The move destroyed Sion's plan and removed one of his knights from play.

Sion looked up but did not speak. His concentration returned to the game with renewed vigour.

'Mind if I go to the bathroom at this point?' Leo asked as he got up from the floor.

Once outside the room he had a desire to check on Sion's progress. He silently re-opened the door, waited and watched. It wasn't long until Sion made a move.

Returning from the toilet, Leo sat back down on the rug.

'Have you moved?'

'No, not yet.'

'You old rogue! The board is different, unlike you, my memory faculty works perfectly well! You are a cheat,' accused Leo.

'I would never cheat,' stated Sion as he looked away.

'You old rogue!' continued Leo as he burst into laughter.

'Leo, do not be fooled by appearances,' Sion said with a roguish grin. 'Do you wish to continue?'

'Not with you, you old cheat!' Leo answered.

'Then go and get us another brandy,' Sion said as he passed his empty glass to Leo.

Leo got up and went over to the drinks cabinet. The cabinet, cleverly concealed behind one of the wall panels, smelt of old wood and beeswax polish. Leo poured the cognac into the glasses and closed the cabinet.

As he sat back down Sion began to explain, 'The Magpie taught me how to cheat at chess, he has perfected it!' He grinned at Leo and continued, 'He has taught me many things, most are of great, great value and I cherish them for they are priceless. He is a very wise soul whose memory can stretch back to its first awareness of itself.'

'Is that possible?' asked Leo in surprise.

'Anything and everything is possible. The Magpie has taught me to never lock the doors to the creative imagination, for it is here that all things can be possible. For The Magpie it is here that all things ARE possible.'

Leo sipped his brandy and slipped into thought. He remembered the dream where Merlin the great magician and The Magpie seemed to be one. He remembered the stare of the pupil-less eyes and the chortle as Merlin caught the bee in his hand.

Sion watched as Leo's thoughts became concrete. 'Do not fear him,' Sion said quietly, 'for fear and love are enemies.'

'I thought it was love and hate,' said Leo.

'We cannot love when we are in fear. We cannot truly experience anything when we are in fear,' as Sion spoke he relaxed back against the armchair. Staring into the fire he continued, 'Great, diverse and ultimately profound experiences lie outside the realm of fear. Within the realm of fear we are stunted and unable to grow, unable to realise fully who or what we are. One must conquer fear for it is surely the enemy.' Sion looked deep into Leo's eyes.

In his heart Leo knew that the journey would be taken. He knew that there would be no going back, only onwards towards the goal of reaching the essence of the imagination, the creative source.

'We can all move into positive change,' Sion continued to speak. 'It is there for us all to explore. It is there for you Leo.'

'Help me to find it,' Leo said quietly.

Sion put down his glass, stretched out his arms and held out his hands to Leo.

Leo took hold of Sion's hands.

'Remember the very first time you came to me. You came without fear and because of that we were able to share the same space, the same mind. Do you remember?'

Leo stared into the violet eyes and said, 'I remember.'

'Let us share that space again. Close your eyes and allow my spirit to find you.'

Leo closed his eyes. He felt the warmth of the hands he was clasping. He felt the warmth travel into him and he allowed the energy to enter him. As he felt the energy a whole new feeling began to develop inside him.

Slowly it built up and travelled along the pathway of Leo's spine. When the energy reached his heart, he could stand it no longer. The intensity of the completely new feeling was too much and he tore his hands away from Sion's.

Almost in slow motion Sion opened his eyes and placed his own hands on his own heart. 'You felt love until the point came where you felt fear. The fear destroyed the fullness of the experience, but next time Leo, you shall feel it all.'

Sion got up from the floor and stood alongside Leo. 'I must sleep now. Do not be disappointed, Leo. You allowed the experience to happen and for however long it lasted, we experienced love.'

After Sion had gone, Leo sat for a long time. His mind, bombarded by many thoughts, was restless. Eventually acceptance allowed a sense of awareness to take shape. He felt clearly in his own mind, body and soul, a feeling he had never before experienced nor imagined. He felt true love. Then came the peace.

As he walked home, the sense of peace he had found the night before began to dissolve. Inch by inch, guilt, fear and a whole host of intermediates nibbled into his mind, located the newly found peace and devoured it. Leo struggled to hold onto it, he fought to retrieve it, but failed. He had lost something very precious.

'Leo!' called Steve as he rode towards him.

Leo's thoughts were broken as he saw Steve pedalling furiously towards him. 'Where are you going in such a hurry?' Leo called. 'And are you sure that decrepit thing will get you there?' he added with a laugh.

'This bicycle is invincible,' said Steve, putting his feet down and bringing the bike to a halt alongside Leo. 'And it will more than likely see me out,' he smiled and continued,

'I'm off to the farm to place an order, we've got four tables booked at the weekend. Anyway, where have you been?' Leo looked away and then looked back at Steve, 'Can you spare me five minutes? I know you're busy but...'

Steve got off the bike. 'Let's rest our legs.' He leant the bike against a tree and sat down on the grass verge.

Leo joined him. 'I think I'm going mad, ' he said to Steve.

'Have you only just realised?' Steve said with a laugh.

'Steve, I'm being serious, I think I'm losing the plot.'

'Why?' Steve asked as he looked at Leo.

Leo began to pluck at the grass. 'I don't know where I am anymore. It feels like someone has not only moved the goalposts, they've chopped them into tiny pieces of kindling and set fire to them.'

'Is this someone Sion Devallon?' Steve asked.

'Him and others,' Leo paused for thought and then continued, 'The Magpie, even Maurice. No one seems sane around here, it's all mumbo jumbo and abracadabra. I don't know what the fuck is going on.'

'I do agree with you, there are some odd folk around here. Perhaps something has attracted them all. Why not ask Maddy?'

'Has she arrived?' Leo asked with surprise.

Steve nodded and patted Leo's leg. 'She'll have the answers for you.'

'Come to think of it, she's another one.' Leo turned to Steve.

'You are starting to sound paranoid! Have you been smoking that wacky stuff?' Steve asked as he got to his feet.

'I don't need to, the world's going mad around me,' Leo said as he stood up.

'I thought you said you were the one going mad?'

'Yes, well, I've changed my mind,' Leo said as he brushed the dirt from his trousers. He added, 'My life used to be so normal. How I'd love to sit on the settee with the dog and watch Blue Peter.'

'So would I,' agreed Steve as he pushed the bike onto the road.

'It's facing the wrong way,' said Leo, pointing to the bike.

'I know. Hop on and I'll give you a backy home. Come on, I haven't got all day.'

Leo slung his bag across his shoulders, swung his leg over the bike and sat on the seat. 'Are you sure this boneshaker's up to it?' he asked.

Steve began to pedal. 'I hope so,' he added. 'Be careful that you don't get oil on your trousers.'

Leo looked down at his trousers and noticed a glistening black smear on the inside of one leg.

CHAPTER 11

The bed was at the far end of the caravan. Maurice felt the mattress, it was clean, dry and comfortable. At the other end of the caravan were a table and two upholstered seats. The kitchen and storage area lay in the middle of the caravan.

Maurice turned on the water tap, and the pipe, still filled with bubbles of air, produced a belch and a splutter. In fits and starts the water came out of the tap and Maurice filled the camping kettle. He lit the gas ring and put the kettle on to boil.

The wall cupboard above the sink had become the foodstore, a rat-proof foodstore. Maurice took out a packet of biscuits, put them onto the table and then went outside.

The night was dark. The moon, just a sliver of silver, was barely visible, and the stars completely hid themselves.

Maurice inhaled deeply, so deeply it was as if he was trying to inhale not only the night air but the darkness too.

He felt the odour of the night. He felt the unconscious elements take shape, and he listened. He listened beyond the sound of the river, beyond the sound of nature and beyond the sound of the perpetual movement of the earth.

Beyond it all he heard the sound. That luminous sound of the high heaven, the harmony of the spheres, the music of the stars.

Time stopped, disappeared and then returned. Maurice once more became aware of the sounds around him. He heard nature return and he heard the sound of the furiously boiling kettle. Exhaling slowly and fully, he regained his composure and went back inside the caravan.

'What are you questioning, your sexuality or your spiritual nature?' Maddy asked.

'Both,' answered Leo as he looked out of his bedroom window.

'Then explore both and find exactly what it is you are looking for.' Maddy sat down on the edge of the bed and waited for Leo to speak. Leo turned away.

'It's hard to put my finger on it. I seem to be surrounded by people who have some odd ideas and those ideas are shaking my own beliefs. Not just shaking them but blowing them to pieces! And more than that I get this very strong feeling that we are all on the brink of something and that scares me,' Leo frowned and then looked at Maddy.

'Something bad?' Maddy asked.

'Something completely new,' answered Leo.

'Life is constantly changing,' Maddy said, and then explained, 'It is always renewing itself and we are all a part of that. We are evolving and moving on into the future. We are different from the people who stood here fifty years ago and we are different from the people we were only a month ago, and who knows who or what we will be like ten years from now. We have to move with change and allow it to do its work.'

'I know what you mean, but it seems to be happening suddenly to everyone around me,' Leo said.

'But not to you?'

'It is happening to me, I just can't face up to it all because I get this feeling, if I'm honest, that it may not be entirely good.'

'You have got to be brave, strong and accept what comes. We all have.' Maddy paused and then continued, 'If something bad comes along, face it and deal with it. Don't give in to your fear.'

'You are the second person who has said that to me recently.'

'Then perhaps that is the message for you, do not let fear hold you back.'

When Maddy had gone, Leo felt the need to work. The large canvas, almost completed, had caused him concern. Something was missing.

The missing piece was a vital component. Leo searched his mind. A spark stronger than anything he had experienced before illuminated the hidden symbol. Leo seized and snatched the missing piece.

He loaded his palette with colour and frantically began to transfer the image from his mind onto the canvas. Two hours later the work was completed. Leo stood back from the painting and analysed the finished work.

The background, a deep blue of the night sky, carried an undulating wave of luminous pigment, delicately painted to resemble the mists of ether.

The woven strands of ether contained and cocooned the newly added symbol. The symbol, off centre and almost hidden, merged with the dark night sky and also with the luminous ether and bound the two together. The symbol, a cross forever bound and made whole by its surrounding circle, completed the work.

Steve relaxed on the settee, drank his coffee and listened carefully to what Maddy was saying.

Maddy spoke slowly and deliberately as her mind recaptured and replayed a section from the past, the section containing her connection with Maurice.

'We met a long time ago. We were both working on the same project. It was sponsored by the American Psychical Research Group, a study of the power of sacred numbers, sacred geometry. I won't bore you with all the details!' Maddy smiled at Steve.

'It would be completely wasted on me and would go rightover my head,' Steve said honestly.

'To cut a long story short, Maurice made a breakthrough, a huge one. Suddenly the project, and Maurice in particular, became very hot news. He had discovered not only how to unlock man's mind but his soul as well. The implications at first were truly wonderful, we really thought that we had found the solution to so many problems.'

'Unlock man's mind and soul, what do you mean?' Steve asked.

'You've heard of telepathy. Well imagine someone not only able to communicate directly with your mind but also to communicate with your soul. Cutting out the usual day- to-day mind and faculties, and getting right to the soul of the person,' Maddy paused and made sure that Steve was understanding what she was saying. Steve nodded and Maddy continued, 'We in our naivety thought that we had found the key to instant enlightenment. Enlightenment for everyone in the world and ultimately peace for the planet and beyond. The dream shattered as we realised that we had discovered something which could be used for destruction and for selfish gain.'

'Used by evil,' said Steve, comprehending what Maddy was telling him.

'Exactly,' agreed Maddy, who continued, 'Suddenly we were under threat. The government and their secret forces became very interested, too interested. We found ourselves being watched, listened to and followed, and we both knew how close we were to something very dangerous. The interest in Maurice increased and the interest in me cooled off, and I was officially advised to go home to the UK. I didn't need telling twice. Maurice disappeared and has been a missing person for the past seven years. There has always been speculation, many people were convinced that he had been killed.'

'What did you think?' Steve asked.

Maddy shrugged her shoulders. 'I wasn't a hundred percent sure but I had a sense that he was hiding out somewhere and you now tell me that he is here.' Maddy shook her head.

'No wonder my news shocked you! I would have been a bit more considerate had I known. I thought he was a maths teacher who had decided he'd had enough, and that you were old pals,' Steve smiled.

'He was a teacher of maths and language. The project was a way for us both to do something different and experience another country along the way.' Maddy paused and then explained, 'When I came back home I managed to pick up the pieces of my life, I was alright, but Maurice wasn't.' Maddy turned away and collected her thoughts, 'Maurice was a wanted man and in a very dangerous situation and there was nothing I could do. Nothing at all.' Maddy looked at Steve and then asked, 'How is he? How does he seem to you?'

'That's hard for me to say because I didn't know him before he went missing. All I can say is that he seems very vulnerable, sometimes paranoid, and he doesn't always make sense, well not to me, but he might make sense to you. He is convinced that we are on the brink of the apocalypse.'

Maddy nodded, 'I see. He seems to have really trusted you, hasn't he?'

'Yes he has. He overheard you and me in the orchard on the night of the party and I think he worked out that I'd seen enough of hell and that I was a safe bet!'

'He was right,' Maddy agreed.

'What I can't get my head around is how on earth did he end up here?' Steve looked confused.

'He would have sensed that I was here or about to come here. He would have also sensed that it was a relatively safe place to be.' Maddy paused and then asked, 'Steve, how has he managed to survive?'

'He was living off what he could find in the forest and he stole the rest. But he looks ill, Maddy. He is gaunt and a very bad colour,' Steve answered.

'You have really cared about him, haven't you?'

'I just wanted him to be OK, that's all. Will you go and see him?'

'I'll go in the morning.'

When Maddy found Maurice, he was sitting on a makeshift bench at the edge of the clearing.

From his vantage point he could look down on the river, he spent some time most days studying the river.

He observed not only the movement and fullness of the water, he carefully observed, studied and recorded the planetary influence on its nature. To himself he called this the personality of the river.

A gentle delicate personality had entered, moved and governed the river. Maurice watched, in his mind he could see the strands and threads of energy linking the planets and the water. He could feel their pull and their deliverance. He felt it all within the core of the cells within his own body, the water of his being. His essence was one with the river.

Before Maddy saw Maurice, he was aware of her. The pulse of her heart had alerted him and he had heard it long before she had entered the clearing.

As she approached him he became surrounded by her energy, an energy so safe, so warm and so familiar. He did not turn around to speak but spoke mentally to her. 'We are home,' he said.

Maddy stood behind him and wrapped her arms around him. Magnetised, they were unable to move for a long time.

Spoken words were useless. Thoughts travelled between the two minds and linked by the bond forged in the past, the two minds became one. Images of past, present and future entered the one mind, filtered down, separated and filled the two individual minds.

Maddy moved away and sat down on the bench next to Maurice. As he turned his face towards her, she saw how fragile he was.

Maurice spoke, it was the quiet voice Maddy remembered.

'Maddy, I have been ill. The years spent protecting myself have taken their toll, but I have been spared, death passed me by,' Maurice looked carefully at Maddy and then continued,

'You, Maddy, I have thought of often and the thought that you had returned to your life unharmed brought comfort to me,' Maurice smiled. 'On the night of the party I heard you speaking, speaking about the wealth of the sun. I rejoiced.'

'Why was I not aware of you?' Maddy asked.

'I have learnt how to block my output, shield myself, hide myself. I have learnt that well!' Maurice touched Maddy's hand and continued, 'I have had to learn how to disappear. I blocked myself from you.'

Maddy placed her hand on Maurice's and as she did she looked down and saw that his fingers were no longer those of the mathematician, they were the fingers of an animal. Maddy sensed the life in the forest, she saw the continual effort of self-protection, preservation and survival.

Maurice broke her thoughts, 'Our work is locked in my mind but I cannot carry it forever. It is a heavy burden.'

'Then share it with me, share the burden and we can carry it together.'

'I think that we already do,' Maurice answered.

Maddy turned and looked towards the river and her thoughts ran with it, ever flowing. Finding the source they returned anew, fresh, filled with hope, strength and vitality.

'You hear the sound?' Maurice asked.

'I hear it. With you it is so loud,' Maddy replied.

'What does it say to you?'

Maddy turned and looked at Maurice. 'It says that we have a future, a new future. The planet cleansed and healed will shelter us and give us life.' Maddy paused. 'A new life.'

'Maddy, it is not far away. It is moving closer to us moment by moment. There is no going back and no stopping it, we are on the brink and must prepare ourselves. We must prepare our souls, make them ready to dive and plunge into the waters of light and the new life.' Maurice turned and looked at the river.

'We must listen to the sound, hear it, become familiar with it and allow it to push us to the edge without fear.' Turning to face Maddy he continued, 'Only then, Maddy, will we survive the shock waves.'

'I am aware that a shock wave has been released and that it hasn't yet entered our atmosphere. I am not afraid, but I have an ache in my heart for the safety of others,' Maddy explained.

Maurice reached and held both of Maddy's hands.

'Everyone is receiving the same impulse directly into their consciousness, some will fight it or go into denial. If they cannot overcome their own fears and face up to the reality then it is their own destiny to live in the illusion. We cannot change that, Maddy.' As Maddy nodded, Maurice continued,

'Their destiny is their choice, we all have free will, that is the law of the present time.'

'I understand that,' Maddy said softly.

'We all must learn to protect ourselves, for we are all vulnerable.' Maurice smiled at the radiant face looking at him. Maddy's wild auburn hair framed her tiny face, she did not look any different from the last time Maurice had seen her.

'We can speak of these things another time. I haven't offered you a cup of tea, please let me make you one.'

Maddy smiled. 'I never thought that I would drink tea with you again!' she replied.

Maurice gently pulled her up from the bench. 'The memory of the last time we shared tea has often brought me comfort.' He smiled and led Maddy into the caravan.

The two naked figures lay side by side, unaware of the night air filling the room, unaware of the distant noises of the night.

They were only aware of each other.

The first kiss, so gentle, gave more feeling by imagination than by touch. It lasted to the point of never ending, but end it did, only to begin again. It evoked longing, it evoked the awareness reserved for lovers, it evoked sensuality.

The kiss, breath, taste, skin upon skin, body fragrant, mingled and became one with the sounds of sensuality.

A hand-held face opened its eyes to reveal its soul and in the dark secret hours between the sheets, between the stars, moon and earth, Sion and Leo became lovers.

Steve sat on the doorstep and watched the storm clouds gather. He could hear Maddy and Charlie inside, Charlie was laughing as he spoke. Sylvie came outside and joined Steve on the step and as she did she put her arm around him and rested her head against him.

They did not speak, silently together they watched the skies. The heavy dark clouds, as if magnetised, moved closer to each other. One by one the tiny luminous gaps between the clouds became extinguished as darkness claimed the sky.

The eerie silence that preceded the storm grew and became almost solid.

Steve rested his head against the stone of the doorway, closed his eyes and felt a deep sadness within. Sylvie felt it too and moved closer to him.

Neither of them knew where the sadness had come from, but it was overwhelming. It was a deep ache, a longing trapped for hundreds of years. It had been trapped in the core of the earth and it had to be released.

The birth pang was so strong that its movement pulled at the guts of the earth.

Maddy and Charlie came to the door, they too felt the cry of the earth. Maddy felt the reverberation deep within her soul. How long it lasted no one knew or would know.

A shaft of light broke through the dark skies, stabbed and pierced the earth. An overhead roll of thunder followed the lightening.

Steve watched and waited. He held out his hand and closed his eyes. He felt the droplet fall. He felt it travel downwards. He felt it land in the palm of his hand. The droplet was unique, for it was the herald of the final flood.

CHAPTER 12

Charlie studied the envelope. He recognised the delicate handwriting, it was his mother's. He opened the envelope, pulled out the letter but was completely unprepared for the letter's content.

His mother informed him that his father had died and had been buried. This had taken place two weeks before the letter had been posted. At the request of his father, Charlie was not to be informed.

Charlie walked over to his chair, sat down and continued to read the letter. Having serious thoughts about the request of his father, his mother had decided to inform him.

Charlie's name had also been removed from his father's will, but this did not surprise him. His mother wished for the funds originally destined for him to be transferred to him, and she had made arrangements for this transfer to take place via her solicitor.

In the final part of her letter, she simply added that love was the greatest healer of all and that she loved Charlie dearly and please would he try to forgive his father.

The letter was a bolt out of the blue, his father's death was, to Charlie's knowledge, unexpected.

Grief came suddenly and it too was unexpected. It was triggered by Charlie's thought that his father would never see Templar House, never sleep in the four-poster bed and never sit at the writing table. The guest room would become a haunting relic.

Charlie closed his eyes tightly and held back the tears, but unable to restrain them, they flowed relentlessly down his face. The loss, the salty tears, his father's last words to him, the unused guest room, all jumbled together into a collage of grief.

He walked into the kitchen, opened a cupboard and pulled out a bottle of scotch. He poured himself a large glass and went upstairs.

He stood for a long time in the guest room, he stood and looked out of the window. It was the place where many times he had imagined his father standing and looking out across the landscape. It was the place where he imagined his father would forgive him and understand why he, Charlie, had come to this place.

He finished the scotch. The alcohol brought a sense of numbness, it eased the pain, it also brought with it a sense of guilt.

The guilt of it all felt like a worm eating into his mind. It ate into his guts. His father's body blow was still there, still trapped inside. It had survived.

Charlie slumped to the floor and resisted the urge to howl in pain. His guts felt on fire. The fire raged and burned inside of him. The fire lasted throughout the night and all of that time Charlie huddled on the floor, arms wrapped around his knees, almost foetal.

With the morning light he went downstairs, walked outside and breathed in the air. His head, still foggy with alcohol, throbbed as he began to walk towards the river.

By the side of the river, caught in the rain and the early morning mist, with tears running freely, Charlie forgave his father. As he forgave him, he spoke the words, 'Forgive me father' and as he spoke them, he forgave himself.

The black worm of the body-blow disintegrated. The emptiness within Charlie disintegrated also and was replaced by a vital element: peace.

Maurice moved the paraffin lamp closer to Maddy, sat down opposite her and watched as she read through the notebooks.

'The final section is missing,' he explained, 'I have destroyed it.'

As Maddy continued to look through the notebooks a strong memory surfaced. She looked up at Maurice and asked, 'How did you get out of that place?'

Maurice leant back against the seat. 'After you had gone back to Britain, Ray Milligan spent more and more time with me. At first he observed me from a distance and then eventually he watched me at close range.

He knew I was aware of him at all times and he realised that his secretive observations were pointless. When he realised that I could read his mind and access his thoughts, the scene became farcical. The persona of federal agent Milligan eroded and he became simply "Ray".'

'Was anyone else aware of this?' Maddy asked.

'No,' Maurice shook his head and then said, 'On a personal level we communicated telepathically and no one was aware of that.'

'And you trusted him? You trusted a federal agent?' Maddy said in disbelief.

'I had to and I did do. Every one of his thoughts could be accessed and Ray was aware of that. He couldn't hide anything from me,' Maurice smiled. 'One day he offered me a bargain, a deal. I was to reach his soul using our code. He gave me three chances, and if I was to succeed he promised that he would help me to get out of the place and out of the USA.'

Maurice stared out of the caravan window in thought and then he continued to speak, 'If I failed I wouldn't get to go anywhere.' He looked into Maddy's eyes and then continued,

'The first attempt failed. Ray managed to block me completely and I couldn't get any further than accessing what he had eaten for breakfast.'

'Toast?' asked Maddy, with a smile.

'Weetos!' replied Maurice. 'The second attempt was much easier. Once the sacred symbols were in place, the door opened and I was in there. What I hadn't bargained for was a dense impenetrable cloak put there by the FBI during training. It would not move and I couldn't get any further, so I had to retreat.'

'Ray Milligan allowed you to get that far?' Maddy was astonished.

Maurice nodded, 'It was as if I was visiting his apartment, it felt like that for the both of us. On the third attempt I walked into the apartment, explored the open rooms and found Ray in the basement. The curtain had been completely removed.' Maurice smiled as he recalled the moment. 'I walked up to him and like two old pals, we embraced. He had been waiting for me to come. He wanted, he needed to get out of there. I took hold of his hands and guided him out of the basement, up the ladder, higher and higher until the light shone on him. The shadows and darkness disappeared, the illusions faded. Ray Milligan's ego took a back seat and his spirit was free. The golden key had unlocked his soul.'

'Amazing!' exclaimed Maddy.

Maurice nodded, 'In return Ray planned for me a steady and methodical route out of America. That route brought me here.'

'Home,' smiled Maddy. 'Tell me what Ray was like afterwards.'

'Radiant!' replied Maurice. 'Completely radiant!'

'Do you know where he is now?' Maddy asked.

Maurice shook his head, 'It is not for me to know where he is but I do know that he is safe and that he is living a very different life.'

Maddy's expression grew serious. 'God bless him,' she said, and then added, 'Without him you would not be here.'

Maurice reached across the table and took hold of Maddy's hands. 'I am here and you are here and together we have much work to do.'

Maddy gently squeezed his hands and said, 'I know.' Maurice let go of her hands and sat in deep thought, 'Leo interests me.'

'Why?' asked Maddy.

'He has a vision of the new world. He hides the vision but sometimes when he is in deep far-away thought, the vision comes to the surface. Sadly, he blocks me but he is receptive to telepathy.'

'He is intuitive,' agreed Maddy. 'It's there in his work.'

'I'm afraid I once scared him,' Maurice admitted. 'He was hiding from me in some bushes and I acknowledged his presence telepathically. He picked up the message and ran home terrified!'

'You probably scared the living daylights out of him!'

'I didn't intend to, I needed to know if he was receptive and it was an opportunity to find out. I took a chance,' Maurice explained.

'Has he said anything to you about it?' Maddy asked.

'No,' Maurice shrugged. He continued, 'But he has a pure vision of the new world and one which seems completely intact.'

'In time he will trust you and then maybe he will share it with you.' Maddy stacked the notebooks into a neat pile and then said, 'The whole sequence, including the final notes, is etched in our memory, and no one could destroy that record.' Maurice rose from the table, and as he opened the caravan door he said, 'All things are possible.'

Sylvie took advantage of the bright fresh morning and began to set the tables outside. Steve came out to help.

Sylvie stopped what she was doing and turned to face him.

'They have a right to know,' she said, 'and you do not have the right to prevent that.'

'Look,' said Steve as he stopped laying the table, 'they are due home in three weeks' time and I'm sure it can wait until then. Look how beautiful the weather is today.'

'Anything could happen in the space of three weeks. The amber alert is serious, and don't deny that.' Sylvie began to sound annoyed. 'I don't want the responsibility of looking after this place during a serious flood warning.'

'Look at the river,' Steve pointed to the distant river, 'Go on, look at it, it's too far away to cause damage here.'

'It could easily burst its banks at the bridge and the water would travel straight down the road to here.' Sylvie pointed to the back of the house.

'If that happened the flood water would more than likely continue on its route down the road and completely miss this place.' Steve shook his head. 'So stop panicking.'

Sylvie felt annoyed. She let out a huge sigh and threw up her arms, 'There are times when you are so stubborn!'

Leo came out of the door and looked at both of them. 'What are you two bickering about?' he asked.

'She,' said Steve, pointing to Sylvie, 'wants to ring Martha and Michael and tell them about the flood warning.'

'That would ruin their holiday,' Leo said to Sylvie.

'It would be far worse for them if they came home to find this place full of mud and water.' Sylvie looked at Leo. 'Their beautiful home ruined.'

Leo walked up to her. 'They have waited years for this break. They bought the fisherman's cottage to provide a peaceful bolt-hole away from the problems here, and you, Sylvie, want to take those problems to them. It's not fair.' Leo paused and then added, 'I know how you feel but why not wait and see what happens. Phone them if things get worse.'

Sylvie began to walk away. She turned and said to both Steve and Leo, 'We phone if we get the red alert, but I hope for all our sakes that it doesn't come to that.' As she walked inside she called to Leo, 'Help Steve with the tables, I'm taking my break.'

'That was tricky,' Leo said to Steve.

'She called me stubborn,' said Steve.

'But you are!'

'Why is that?' asked Steve, as he carried chairs to the tables.

'Because you won't consider moving in here with Sylvie. If you did I could have Studio Cottage.' Leo sat down on one of the chairs. 'It would be ideal.'

Steve stopped what he was doing and explained, 'Both Sylvie and I are happy as we are. We have our independence and that's important to us both. If you are getting fed up here, why don't you move in with...'

The image of Sion flashed into both minds. 'Don't say it, don't even think it,' Leo said coldly.

Steve sat down. 'Come on, Leo, he has plenty of space.' Leo picked up a spoon from the table and began to twist it around. 'In his home maybe, but not in his life.'

'Doesn't he want to see you?' Steve asked.

'Yes he wants to see me but only when HE wants. My need isn't appropriate,' Leo replied. 'I'm always waiting, waiting for his call, never knowing if or when it's going to come and when it does come, nine times out of ten Martha's listening in. I've had enough of it. I'm really fed up with it all.'

'Look on the bright side,' said Steve, 'your work is starting to sell.'

'Only through him. I'm tied to him, whether I like it or not,' Leo threw down the spoon and slumped back in the chair.

'One minute I'm in heaven and the next minute I'm in hell and I can't get out of it.'

'What do you really want to do?' Steve asked.

'I don't know, but I know I want to get out of here,' Leo pointed to Les Lavandes.

'Why not move in for a while with me and Charlie?' Steve suggested. 'Have a change of scenery.'

Leo took a deep breath and let it out slowly, 'Is there room?'

'You could use Charlie's old room, he's moving into the guest room,' Steve explained.

'What about the guests?' Leo asked.

'I don't think there's going to be any,' Steve replied and then added, 'Don't ask why, it's a long story.' Leo raised an eyebrow and Steve continued, 'There's plenty of space in one of the spare rooms for you to do your painting. What do you think?'

'I'd be interested but for one thing.'

'What's that?' Steve asked.

'You haven't got a phone.'

'You, dear Leo, could help me to persuade the Luddite to get one and we could all chip in for it,' Steve smiled and added, 'I promise not to listen to your calls.'

'They'd make your hair curl!' laughed Leo.

'So, do you want me to have a word with Charlie or what?' Steve asked as he got up from the table.

'One more problem,' said Leo thoughtfully, 'this place would be empty when Martha and Michael are away and they wouldn't be too happy about that.'

'That's not a problem, we can all take turns at housesitting.'

'Would you ask him then?' Leo asked.

Steve nodded, 'I'll ask him tonight and let you know tomorrow.'

Leo got up from the table and asked, 'Is Maurice worried about the rising river level?'

'No, he says it will subside in the next forty-eight hours, it has something to do with...'

Leo interrupted, 'Planetary influence?'

'Lunar,' said Steve, 'and I think he's probably right.'

As Leo began to walk away he said quietly to himself, 'The next lunar phase will reduce the pull and maybe then we'll all feel better.'

'Gilesy, are you awake?' Anita knew he was awake, she had felt his body become alive as the anaesthetic of his sleep had worn off.

Giles uncoiled and stretched out his legs. With his eyes still closed he answered, 'Just about.'

Anita rolled onto her side and moved closer to him. Not wishing for her words to disturb the morning quiet she spoke in a semi-whisper, 'Something strange happened in the night.' Silently she recaptured the memory and then continued, 'You woke me up with your snoring and I couldn't get back to sleep. I tossed and turned for about an hour and was thinking about getting up for a cup of tea when I became aware of someone standing by the bed. When I looked carefully I saw two figures. It was my parents.'

Giles turned his head and looked at Anita. 'But they're both dead,' he said.

'I could see their spirits,' Anita explained. 'It was a likeness of them but it was not solid. Mum told me that it was time and that I was to follow them. I felt as though I had to follow them and that I didn't really have any other option, so I did follow them. They led me to the edge of something horrendous.' Anita closed her eyes and concentrated on the picture in her mind. 'As I stood there I knew instantly what it was, I don't know how I knew, I just did. I was stood on the edge of an abyss.' She paused and then said, 'I was teetering on the edge of THE abyss.' She opened her eyes and looked at Giles. 'I don't know what happened next, I don't know if my mum pushed me or if I slipped off the edge. One minute I was teetering on the edge of this huge awesome cavern and the next minute I was falling free-fall into it. I began to make frantic body movements, movements akin to either flying or swimming. I suppose they were the movements of a person desperate to survive and I was that person, I was fighting for my life.

I don't know how long this lasted, all I do know is that I was about half way across the chasm when I became completely exhausted. I could move no more and when I realised that my energy had been used up, I began to descend. I have no idea what I thought or felt, I just knew that I was sinking and that there was nothing I could do about it.' Anita stopped speaking and closed her eyes. 'God's arm and hand reached out to me from the far side of the abyss. He caught me. He stopped my fall, placed me safely on the ground and I knew that I had survived. I had been saved by the grace of God and had survived something terrible.' Anita looked at Giles and when his eyes acknowledged what she had said, she continued, 'The next moment I was back where I had started from. I was back over on the other side and I can remember thinking to myself, "Oh no, not again," but as I looked out across the abyss I saw a bridge starting to appear. It had begun to form itself from the place where God had been and this marvellous bridge of gold and light soon spanned the full distance from one edge to the other.

I was able to walk onto it and I continued walking until I got to the far side. Once I was safely on that side I looked back across the bridge and I saw you Giles,' Anita smiled.

'You were following me and behind you I could see Leo, poor Leo, his feet would not keep on the bridge for long, he kept drifting upwards! Behind Leo walked Sylvie and Steve, they walked together arm-in-arm and did not hesitate. It was as if they knew where they were going.

Behind them walked Charlie and Maddy. I remember noticing that they were both barefoot and carrying their shoes! Maddy looked so radiant. The light shining from her merged and became one with the light from the bridge, it was as if she was actually part of the bridge.' Anita closed her eyes as a feeling of tiredness and exhaustion swept over her.

'What about Michael and Martha?' Giles asked.

'I didn't see them but perhaps they followed on behind.'

'What about Maurice?'

'I nearly forgot about Maurice and he was interesting. I caught the first glimpse of him as he waited for everyone to cross the bridge and in the next split second he was on the other side! He moved like lightening and his body seemed to be made of light. He could move so fast between the two sides of the cavern.' Anita looked serious and then frowned. 'What do you think it all means?' she asked.

Giles rolled over onto his back and looked up at the ceiling. He knew what it meant and he knew Anita shared the same conclusion, but here was the opportunity to sweep it under the carpet and carry on with normal life. He rolled back onto his side and took that chance. 'It means that my snoring has disturbed you greatly, that's all.' He smiled at Anita's serious expression and with a finger he gently closed one eye and then the other, 'Go back to sleep, baby.'

The dress was ripped, its fragile silk fibres torn beyond repair. Martha examined the dress, folded it and put it into the bin. The scratched leather shoes could be repaired and these Martha put into the cupboard.

'I've had to put the dress into the bin,' she said as she walked into the tiny sitting room.

Michael didn't hear her, he was leaning with his head out of the window. The sound of the sea crashing against the shoreline was all he could hear. Martha walked up to him and repeated what she had said, 'I've had to put the dress into the bin.'

Michael turned his head, 'You can get another one, I'll pay for it.'

Martha stood next to him. She smelt the heavy salty air and breathed in deeply, 'It was pure silk and quite expensive.'

'Why wear an expensive dress for a walk along the shore?' Michael asked.

'I had assumed we would be walking on the beach and not rockclimbing,' she said as she turned her head to look at him.

'Well, you've got to admit, it was pretty exciting! It's not every day you discover a wonderful cave. Besides, the exercise did you good, you were like a sprightly young girl!' he said as he slapped her backside.

'Why is it when we go anywhere near the sea you become exceptionally randy?' she asked.

Michael began to laugh. 'I suppose I do,' he admitted.

'It must be something connected to the power of the sea, it stimulates the root of me!'

Martha rested her head upon his shoulder. 'I wish we didn't have to go back yet, we seem to have been here no time at all.'

'We don't have to go back, we can stay here for as long as we like. Sylvie and Steve are quite capable of running things while we're away. All we have to do is make a phone call.' Michael placed his arm around her and added, 'Give them a ring in the morning and let's stay on a bit longer.'

Martha looked out to sea, became lost in thought for a while and then said, 'Nobody knows how long their retirement will last. Some people are lucky and manage to get twenty years and others get barely a handful. We should make the most of each day and enjoy them while we can.' She smiled at Michael and then said, 'I'll phone Sylvie in the morning.'

'How do you fancy having dinner at that place?' Michael pointed to the small white restaurant at the end of the promenade.

'We could give it a try, but it will probably be a fishy menu,' Martha said as she moved away from the window. She sat down in one of the armchairs and looked around the tiny room. She made a mental note - 'buy emulsion, bring curtains from spare room'.

Michael interrupted her thoughts, 'I could live off fish.' He sat down in the other armchair and added, 'I could live here.' He rested his head back and closed his eyes. 'I can't imagine anything more perfect than this. To fall asleep at night to the sound of the sea and to wake in the morning to that sound, is to my mind, heaven.'

Martha examined the frayed corner of the rug and added 'new rug' to her mental list. 'I agree. We are two very lucky people and who knows, maybe one day we will move here.'

Michael's eyes opened wide, 'Would you really leave Les Lavandes and move here?'

Martha smiled, 'I think I would.'

'Then let's do it, let's do just that,' he said excitedly.

'Slow down,' said Martha calmly, 'I said maybe one day, so don't jump the gun! We hardly know the place, so let's take our time, get to know it better and then take stock.'

'I know you,' said Michael, 'we'll get back home and you will be like a little limpet clinging to the safety and security of home, and moving here will become a dream.'

'One time I would have felt like that and yes, you are right, moving here would have become a fantastic dream, but not now, the time is different, it seems more precious. I'd love us both to be able to experience this wonderful place, to experience the joy we have found here, not just for a holiday but for each and every day for as long as we are able to do so.'

'I'll hold you to that!' Michael smiled and got up from the chair. 'Come on old girl, I'm ravenous, let's go and eat and then afterwards we can walk along the beach, hand in hand, just like in the movies.'

Martha laughed at him, 'They don't make films like that anymore, that kind of thing died along with Bette Davis.'

Michael bent down and tilted Martha's face towards him.

'After the romantic evening stroll I shall bring you back here and make love to you to the sound of the sea. Or...'

'Or what?' asked Martha with a smile.

'Or,' he said, gently pulling Martha to her feet, 'we can make love now and eat later.'

Martha laughed as she broke free of his hold and moved quickly to the door. 'Come on,' she said, smiling, 'let's get changed and go and eat.'

'I was just getting going then,' said Michael, following her.

CHAPTER 13

'Isn't nature wonderful?' Maddy asked as she walked across the garden.

Charlie smiled, nodded and carried on hoeing. Maddy walked to the far edge of the vegetable garden, where she could see the dense woodland with its variety of trees and colours. Each tree, she thought to herself, breathing and connected not only by its deep roots to the earth but also by its spirit to the heavens, complete synthesis.

She looked up to the skies, the recent stormy sky had given way to fair-weather clouds, and these clouds moved slowly and silently overhead. Charlie walked up behind her. 'What are you thinking about now?' he asked.

'The diversity of it all,' she replied.

Charlie stood quietly for a moment then said, 'Someone once told me that he believed that life on this planet was purely the result of an accident.'

'And what do you think?' Maddy asked.

Charlie looked at the ground and then back at Maddy, 'I believe that only a vast and complex creative mind could have imagined the diversity of nature and I think that the same mind would have needed to have intelligence far beyond our perception.'

'No accident?' Maddy smiled and slipped an arm around Charlie's waist.

'I think it is highly doubtful. What do you think?'

'I have faith in my inner knowledge. I believe that THE ONE exists.'

'No accident?' Charlie asked with a grin.

Maddy began to walk back into the vegetable garden. Charlie followed her, and together they walked alongside the rows of peas and beans. 'These have only just survived the weather,' Charlie explained. 'They don't seem too healthy.'

Maddy bent down and examined the leaves of one of the plants. A tiny area of furry mould had begun to develop. She pointed it out to Charlie.

Charlie looked at the plant and then examined the others.

'It's mildew,' he said glumly.

'Anita will tell you how to get rid of it, so don't get disheartened, I'm sure nature will have a cure.' Maddy held out a hand to him, 'Come on.'

Charlie tried to forget about the mouldy plants and began to think about afternoon tea. 'Did you bring those crumpets?'

'I promised I would, they're in my basket on your table, quite safe!'

'Let's get back and have crumpets and tea by the fire, I've had enough of gardening.' Charlie picked up his hoe and took a last look over the veg patch.

'It's tidy, you've done a good job,' said Maddy. 'Come on and I'll make you afternoon tea.'

Maddy placed the tray in the hearth, knelt down and poured two cups of tea from the pot. She passed one to Charlie. 'You really didn't need to light the fire, it isn't cold.'

'No, but the house is awfully damp, even the piano is complaining. It's hardly ever in tune, poor PJ has to re-tune it each time he comes. He thinks I should invest in a better piano.'

'Have you decided to invest your money or not?' Maddy sat down in the chair opposite Charlie.

Charlie gazed into the fire. 'I've had some ideas about the money, but I have this nagging feeling that I should invest it and that feeling obliterates the ideas.'

'You've got to move on, Charlie, we all have. If you invested it, it could become worthless, so why not use it while you can.' Maddy took a sip of tea. 'Make positive changes.'

'It's OK you saying that,' Charlie objected, 'I don't have your intuition and you didn't have my father. I'm sure he'd put a jinx on the money if I put it to any use other than investing it. Until his dying day he vowed that I would not get a penny of his money and I can't see death changing that!'

'I thought you had forgiven him, death changes everything.'

'I have forgiven him and maybe, just maybe, I wanted to honour his memory by investing his beloved money.'

'Do something positive with it, while you are able.' Maddy looked Charlie in the eye, he turned away and stared into the fire. Maddy continued, 'Rid yourself of this guilt and move into the future, try to make it good and whole.'

'I can't be another David.' Charlie stared at her. 'I'd like to be that humanitarian person, but I could never be him.'

'Let's get this perfectly clear. I do not want you to replicate my ex-husband. I want you as you are, who you are and as you will be. Charlie, look at me.' Charlie turned to face her. Maddy continued, 'In your own way you are humanitarian. Look at this place, you have given a home to Steve and now Leo and you provide food, warmth and security for Maurice. You are growing enough veg to feed us all!' Maddy smiled, 'Charlie, you have stepped out of the mould and it's time that you saw who you really are. You don't need a role model, especially not my ex-husband. You don't need a role model because you are the true person and that is the person

I am attracted to.'

Charlie looked back into the fire, 'Do you want to hear my ideas for spending his money?'

Maddy smiled to herself, 'Speak about it.'

'I have a few ideas. The first one may sound odd, it's connected with the personal survival of us all.' Charlie paused for thought. 'It feels important to gather together a basic survival store.'

'Why are you concerned with survival?' Maddy asked.

'I realised when I was young that I was living in an unstable world,' Charlie shrugged. 'I didn't, and I still don't, want to depend on a society I can't trust.'

'Have you thought a lot about this?'

'I've thought about gathering together a basic survival store, wheat grain, dried beans, honey, salt and the like. I once read that the Shakers or the Quakers, I can't remember which, always had three years of emergency supplies with them, and it sounded a good idea.'

'How would you store it all?' Maddy asked.

'In airtight and mouse-proof containers. I'd add to the basic store things like cigarette lighters, candles, soap, toothbrushes, hot-water bottles, blankets, spare clothes, shoes and wellies. I do have a list,' he said.

'It sounds similar to the list David had for his project in India. For many people in the world, basic survival is a serious daily consideration and isn't taken for granted,' she added. 'What other ideas have you had?'

'I want to make sure that we are in the right place, otherwise all the preparation will be in vain, a complete waste of time.'

'Maurice is the man to ask about that, his perception is not only extremely sensitive, it's one hundred per cent accurate.'

'Perhaps we could go and see him together sometime, which reminds me, he hasn't called for any food this week. Is he OK?'

'He's fine but he's fasting, it's due to end tomorrow. In fact that would be the perfect time to utilise his perception because it will be very intense after his fast.'

'I suppose he's a good one to ask about survival, he's had first-hand experience hasn't he?'

'He was starting to fail and I think if Steve hadn't intervened he would have lost. We are only human.'

Charlie finished his tea and put his cup onto the tray. 'The other day I watched a mouse in the pantry, it was fascinating, so quick and so quiet, I hardly knew it was there. It had eaten a chunk from one of Steve's pastries and when it returned for a second helping I spotted it! As I watched it reminded me that we too are only animals and have a need to survive.'

'And an instinct,' said Maddy. 'What happened to the mouse?'

'Nothing. It's probably still in there happily munching away! I did mention to Steve that I thought it was an idea to store cakes and pastries in metal tins. He said that with having Leo around, a safe would be a better idea!'

Maddy laughed, 'He does have a healthy appetite. Has he settled in?'

'I think so, he seems happy enough with my old room and he's taken to doing some of his painting in the tower, he says it inspires him, but I think there's probably another reason.'

'What's that?' Maddy asked.

'From the tower he has a brilliant view of the chateau and the other day I noticed that my binoculars had appeared in there!'

Maurice and Maddy were already seated when Charlie joined them. He sat down at the small caravan table opposite them both.

After his fast Maurice looked thinner, more fragile than usual. He spoke quietly, 'I'd like to begin straight away.'

Charlie nodded in agreement and tried to make himself feel comfortable, despite a feeling of apprehension that all but prevented it.

Maurice closed his eyes and placed his hands on the table, and without opening his eyes he asked, 'Charlie, place your hands on the table and try to relax.'

Charlie put his hands on the table and sat back in his seat. Maddy caught his eye and smiled. As Maurice took hold of Charlie's hands, Charlie watched. Maurice's breathing became deep and slow. Maddy too, with her eyes closed, shared the same pattern of breathing.

Charlie turned away and began to look out of the caravan window. He focused on a large silver birch tree in the distance, but soon found himself being drawn back into the caravan.

Maurice's hands had changed temperature, their normal coolness had given way to a comforting warmth. Charlie began to relax, the constant dull ache across his shoulders dissolved and he felt himself become almost fluid.

He could hear the rhythmical pattern of Maurice's breathing and he heard it slow to the point of almost stopping. When it reached that point Maurice opened his eyes.

Charlie looked at the eyes. He felt swallowed by their deep penetrating stare. He felt magnetised and drawn into something beyond the eyes. The eyes ceased to exist.

Words flowed from Maurice's mind and travelled directly into Charlie's. The words were accompanied by a series of images. Charlie shut his eyes tightly but the images and the words continued to flow. They filled his mind. They inhabited every part of his mind and not one fragment of space was left unoccupied.

Painful memories surfaced. His father's face contorted in rage screamed at him, time and time and time again. Charlie felt the rage stab his guts, its blade piercing deep, time and time and time again.

A new face appeared, it was Rita. Seductively she opened her mouth and licked her lips, the tongue then moved slowly in and out of her mouth. As her body pressed against Charlie's, the tongue moved closer and closer, until with a final movement it thrust deep into Charlie's mouth. Secretly Charlie ejaculated. He then relived the crashing humiliation which followed. He relived the embarrassment, the shame and the guilt, and he relived the final humiliation. Rita's hysterical laughter reverberated in his mind and as she pointed to the dark wet patch that had appeared on the front of his trousers she said, 'What will Mummy say when she sees that you've come in your pants?'

Rita's face dissolved.

A chasm of loneliness, hopelessness and guilt filled Charlie's mind and he felt captive once more to the dark chains of despair. As they wrapped themselves around him a tiny pinprick of light appeared, he felt its familiarity, it had in the past saved him from complete destruction.

But here today in the tiny caravan, here with Maddy and Maurice, that spark of light momentarily disappeared. Within the space of that moment the darkness and all its allies swelled, reproduced, grew and pushed against the limits of Charlie's mind. In that one tiny fragment of time before hell completely broke loose, Charlie's mind exploded.

He felt his mind burst and as it did his consciousness travelled upwards and outwards at the speed of light.

He felt himself travelling, travelling and unable to stop or control the situation. He let go and the travelling slowed right down. His consciousness expanded in all directions and he felt that he was in the centre of it all. He felt that he knew all that was to come and all that had been. It danced around him.

The dancing act of creation let him go and as he began to fall back into time he took with him snapshots of the future, fragments of life to come.

The stillness of the real moment surrounded him and the awareness of the coolness of Maurice's hands triggered his normal consciousness. He opened his eyes and entered a familiar scene, Maddy with her wild auburn hair and smiling green eyes took his hand, Maurice sat back, stretched out his arms and yawned.

Charlie remained silent on the way home. Maddy walked alongside him, aware of his need for silence, and she too remained silent.

As they approached Charlie's front door he turned to her and spoke. His tone was cold and tinged with anger. 'You could have told me exactly what was going to happen, but you didn't, you led me like a lamb to slaughter.'

Maddy was taken aback. 'Charlie don't, please don't be angry.'

'What do you expect? I understood that we, or should I say I, was going to see Maurice for a glimpse into the future. All I wanted to know was if I was living in the right place. I didn't anticipate experiencing that!' Charlie looked back towards the caravan.

'Were you not ready for what happened?'

'I thought things like that were supposed to happen naturally, to be frank with you my experience today seemed very unnatural. I feel violated.'

Maddy moved close to him. 'Let things settle down and then form a conclusion,' adding, 'Sleep on it.'

'Sleep on it?' he said pulling away from her. 'You sleep on it!' Charlie opened the front door, went inside and closed the door behind him.

Maddy remained outside. She was still there when Steve arrived home. 'What's this?' he asked light heartedly. 'Will he not let you in?'

As Steve walked up to her Maddy began to explain, 'I think Maurice and I have just made a mistake. I think we have given Charlie too much too soon.'

'Is he OK?' Steve asked, and then repeated, 'Is Charlie OK?'

'He's OK but he's very angry.'

'Angry with you?' Steve asked in disbelief.

Maddy nodded, 'He's angry with me and with Maurice and more than that.' She looked up at Steve. 'He's furious with himself.'

'Maddy, he's been furious with himself for years,' Steve began to explain, 'It's the reason behind his bouts of drinking. He harbours a sense of failure.'

'I realise that, but this afternoon he rose above his negative beliefs.' Maddy looked at Steve. 'He experienced the divine,' Maddy went quiet and then continued, 'He's wrapped himself back in his failings again, only more so.'

'And you know why?' Steve held Maddy's arm. 'Because you didn't allow him to do it in his own way, you tampered and interfered.'

Maddy turned away and Steve continued, 'It's the root of his problem, years and years of domination and manipulation by a cruel and selfish father. All you and

Maurice have done is to re-establish that pattern. You controlled him.'

As Maddy began to walk away, tears streamed down her face. She turned and said to Steve, 'Please ask him to forgive me.'

'We've called this little meeting because Martha and I have made an important decision and it will affect both of you.'

Sylvie carried a chair over to the table and sat down next to Steve. Steve raised an eyebrow at her and then said to Michael, 'Is it good or bad news?'

Martha reached for his hand , 'It's good news, so don't look so worried.'

'If you'd let me continue you'll find out what's going on!' Michael said with impatience. 'The decision we have made hasn't been easy but we know that it is the right one for us both. It's something we have both wanted for a long time and if we don't do it now, we never will. We have decided to move into the fisherman's cottage and to spend most of our time there. We want to enjoy what's left of our retirement,' he turned and smiled at Martha and then looked at both Steve and Sylvie, 'You two are young, full of energy, and have the rest of your lives ahead of you. You both have new ideas and those ideas would refresh this place, revitalise it, make it new, and that's exactly what Martha and I want. We want to see you transform this place into something special and we know that you have the potential. You can do it. My question is, will you take the challenge? Will you both take the next step and manage this place, run it how YOU want it to be?'

Steve let out a very long sigh. He looked at Sylvie, her face had become flushed and her eyes radiant. Steve didn't need to ask for her answer, it was plainly obvious. 'You only need to look at her,' he said, pointing at Sylvie, 'to know how she feels and I guess I feel exactly the same. It would be wonderful, absolutely wonderful to run this place. We've both enjoyed it while you have been away, we've enjoyed running things and doing it our own way.'

'That's what we hoped you'd say. We plan to come back one or two weekends a month to see everyone and pick up our mail. If you had any problems we could discuss them during our visit.'

'Will you be happy?' Sylvie asked Martha.

'I'll have the best of both worlds, the cottage is a delight and we both feel we have found home there, and we'll still get to spend time here.'

'And we've got a new lease of life,' said Michael. 'It must be something to do with the sea air.'

Martha laughed, 'It's made a new man of him!'

'I thought he seemed on form,' said Steve with a smile.

'Now listen,' Michael became serious. 'We want you to develop your ideas and we'll fund them as long as they are workable. Do your own brochures and advertise in your own way.'

'Leo could help with the brochure,' Steve enthused. 'In fact he came up with a brilliant idea, he suggested exhibiting artwork in the dining room. It could help increase the numbers of folk using the restaurant.'

'Devallon and his cronies!' laughed Michael.

'And why not! It would be quite something,' exclaimed Martha.

'Down to practicalities,' said Michael. 'Will you two move in here?'

Both Sylvie and Steve remained silent. 'I take it that means no,' said Michael. 'But not to worry, just make sure that you lock up when there are no guests and when there are make sure they know where to find you. Especially you Sylvie, as you are the closest. Oh, and keep the office locked.'

'It's not that we don't want to be together,' explained Sylvie. 'We are happy as we are.'

'Then stay that way!' smiled Martha. 'We plan to go back on Monday so if there's anything you need or anything you want to know, mention it now.'

'I have a list,' Sylvie reached for the notepad on the window ledge. She tore off a sheet and handed it to Martha.

Martha studied the short list. 'But what's this last thing?' Martha pointed to the bottom of the list.

'It says flood warning,' Sylvie went on to explain, 'We need to know what to do if we get another flood warning.

This last one was awful because we didn't know whether or not to let you know.'

Michael answered, 'If ever there is another flood warning don't hesitate to phone us, we wouldn't be able to do a great deal but it would ease your minds.'

'It was awful because I had this terrible feeling that you we're going to come back to...' Sylvie paused.

'A few feet of mud!' Michael smiled at her.

'Exactly,' said Sylvie.

'Well, my dear girl, as much as you want to turn back a flood, you will be unable to do so. The best course of action is to make sure you, Steve and the guests are safe and then give us a ring. This place is only bricks and mortar.'

'Stone,' corrected Martha as she inspected her nails. 'But Michael's right, the safety of you two and any guests must come first.'

'Was the river close to bursting its banks?' Michael asked.

'Fairly,' Steve answered. 'Maurice was right though, he predicted exactly when the waters would recede.'

'Listen to him should there ever be another warning! Right, let's move onto other things,' said Michael.

Martha pointed to the fridge. 'There's a bag of fish in there, use what you want and freeze the rest. Michael chose it for you.'

'So no complaints,' said Michael with a grin.

'What kind of fish is it?' Steve asked.

Michael shrugged, 'All I know is that it was caught yesterday and the fish merchant recommended it.'

'Interesting,' said Steve.

'I tell you what,' Michael suggested, 'why not batter and fry some of it and make some of those wonderful big chips to go with it, we could have them for supper. What do you think?'

Steve got up from the table, 'I knew there'd be a catch!'

CHAPTER 14

'Not this bloody music again,' complained Leo as he stacked the bowls and plates by the sink.

'You don't like Vivaldi?' Steve asked as he began to wash the breakfast pots.

Leo searched in the drawer for a clean towel. 'In moderation. It's 8.30 in the morning and we've heard Gloria three times already.' He found the towel, and in a low voice asked Steve, 'What the hell is up with him at the moment?'

Steve stopped what he was doing, wiped his hands on the sides of his trousers and then gently closed the kitchen door.

'Be patient with him, he's going through a bad time.'

Leo pulled a face and began to dry the pots. 'I'm going through a bad time, it was much quieter at Les Lavandes.'

'Well, go back then.' Steve wiped the worktop and then grinned at Leo.

'I thought you were being serious for a minute!' Leo faced Steve, 'I thought maybe he was upset because I'd moved in here.'

'No, it's nothing to do with you, so get that idea out of your head.'

'Well what is it then? One minute he's as high as a kite and the next minute it's doom and gloom. I can't figure it out. If it's not me being here, then what is it?'

Steve rested against the sink and collected his thoughts, 'I can't tell you everything because I don't know exactly what happened. All I do know is that he's been through some kind of mystical experience.'

Leo raised his eyebrows. Steve continued to explain, 'It was an experience triggered by Maurice and Maddy and it seems it was too much too soon.' Steve looked towards the door, 'And now he's having to sort his head out.'

'Have they fucked him up?' Leo asked.

Steve shrugged his shoulders, 'I've no idea, but hopefully it'll be something he'll be able to sort out.'

'What is this crack with Maurice?' Leo asked. 'He seems to be able to do some pretty weird things.'

'What kind of things?' Steve asked.

'He can put words directly into your mind without using speech.' Leo tapped the side of his head, 'Directly in here.'

'Telepathy,' said Steve. 'Have you experienced it?'

Leo remembered the experience and then said, 'He once spoke to me like that and it freaked me out, I nearly shit myself.'

Steve grinned, 'He's supposed to be very good at it, it seems to be his thing. You must have been receptive, otherwise you wouldn't have heard him.'

'I'm not receptive anymore, I've installed 6-inch thick sheets of protection around here.' He pointed to his head.

'He'll not get through that unless I want him to.'

Steve went back to the washing up. 'Don't be too sure,' he shifted his gaze back to Leo. 'He's very powerful.'

'He's also very vulnerable,' said Leo.

That night sleep would not come. In the darkened room Leo reached for his watch, turned on its tiny light and read the time. 4.00 am. He put the watch back on the cabinet, turned onto his side and pulled the covers up around him.

Sion floated in and out of his mind, bringing with him a myriad of feelings and sensations. He wondered when he would speak with him again, laugh with him, sit and think with him, be with him.

His thoughts then turned to Charlie. For the past few days he had been so unlike his usual self. Leo remembered how he had felt on the night outside Sylvie's cottage, the night when Maurice had invaded his mind. A curious idea then came to him.

He turned over onto his back and focused on Maurice. He filled the frame of his mind with the image of the gaunt stranger.

When the picture of Maurice had become accurate and as real as possible, Leo said with his mind, 'Maurice, if you can hear me, tell me what it is that is about to happen.' Leo cleared his mind and allowed his barrier of protection to fall away. He then waited.

He didn't have to wait long. The reply, very slowly at first, but clearly, began to form in his mind. The reply said, 'I hear you.'

Leo kept his mind open.

Maurice's strong voice said, 'I can show you brief episodes, but...' his voice faded and then returned, 'In return show me your new world view.' Maurice then went silent.

Leo tried hard to find the channel he had first used to contact Maurice, but it eluded him. He went back to the start and once again filled his mind with the image of Maurice.

The image suddenly came to life. Leo answered Maurice, 'One day I will show you.'

Maurice's features began to fade and as they did, Leo saw a drop of water fall, he heard it land, he heard the splash and then he heard the others follow. The water seemed to fill his mind.

As if stepping back, he could see the rains from a distance. The landscape, a mixture of rural and urban life, tolerated the storm.

Winds blew the rain, they blew the water into an almost solid form. The solid mass magnetised to its core, solid sheets of rain. Leo could see the effects.

The trees, unable to sustain the blow after blow of the heavy rain, ruptured and burst. They sent out fragments of shattered leaf, branch, bark and trunk.

The ground almost tolerated the rains. It supported and collected it. Puddles formed pools, and still the rain fell.

Leo saw the sun turn into the moon, light into dark. He saw the change of day into night, it appeared more times than he could count. The days flicked by and then rested.

The next image showed the same landscape but now it was a landscape in despair and of despair. Its surface had been washed away. Shades of brown replaced the fertile green. Rivulets had turned into rivers, swollen and pregnant beyond human imagination. They roared. The sound seemed to be emitted from the bowels of the earth but it roared too from the heavens. The two sounds became one.

The lightening penetrated and illuminated the structure of the earth. The lightening cascaded, danced and wove itself into a web-like form. Its guidelines rooted themselves into the ground and linked heaven and earth together. Constant energy travelled between the two. Earth communicated with the heavens. The heavens bore down and released its nature on and to the earth.

The image flickered and moved on. Leo saw a huge tidal wave gather strength, form an arch and land, crashing and destroying all things in its path.

He saw the face of a frightened woman, alone she ran. He saw her transformed into a floating, almost sleeping, bloated body. The strands of her long white hair surrounded her head like the rays of a silvery sun.

He saw a younger woman hiding, cowering in the safety of her home. She too was alone. She held her breath as the unseen force of water made its impact. Leo saw the house destroyed. He saw the woman destroyed. She lay face down in the mud, alone in her muddy grave.

In the final image Leo saw a young man. Moving like an athlete he ran to escape. He did not look back but ran, ran and climbed. Unprepared and almost naked he clambered, climbed and hurled himself to a place of safety. Leo saw him wrapped in a blanket. He had survived.

The images faded and disappeared. Maurice did not speak, there was no need. It was what Leo had known. It was what he had feared. It was the imminent apocalypse.

For Leo sleep finally came and with it came one more image. The image entered Leo's dream space. It entered gently and did not form fully, but the slightly faded image made impact. Its startling content abruptly awoke Leo.

Now fully awake, he saw in his mind the silhouette of a man. The man was no longer a man. His icy cold features, almost stone-like, bore no life spark.

Waiting in his armchair, he had waited too long, food and warmth had deserted him and death had claimed him. The man was no longer a man, he was a corpse, and the corpse was Sion.

Leo knocked, rattled and banged on the caravan door. His knuckles bled. No reply came from the locked caravan.

Leo shouted and as his anger and frustration intensified, he screamed with anguish and in despair. He screamed, 'Where are you? Where are you, you bastard? You bastard, you absolute fucking bastard!'

Defeated he turned away from the caravan and came face to face with Maurice.

Leo's tear-stained face, anguished and confused, looked straight at the gaunt stranger. 'Why?' was all he could say.

'Why?' was all he wanted to know.

Maurice unlocked the caravan, pointed to the seat inside and invited Leo to sit down.

As Leo sat down, his body felt drained, as if his burst of anger had taken with it too much energy.

Maurice, sitting opposite, began to explain, 'I did not transmit the final image. I sent the others but not the last one. The last one was of your own making.'

Leo slumped back. 'My own making!' he objected.

'Let me finish,' said Maurice. 'That distressing scene was conjured by your own mind, your own imagination. It was created by your own fear. We have the power to create and manifest these things. We can draw these things to us, fear is like a magnet. You saw what you saw as a result of your own fear. Learn to conquer your fear,' he added, 'and learn to master your anger.'

As Maurice got up from the table, Leo half stood and grabbed him by the arm. 'Will he survive?' he asked.

Maurice broke free from Leo's hold and said, 'Ask him.'

'And what do I say? Excuse me Sion are you going to survive the apocalypse?'

'He knows,' answered Maurice. 'I can't tell you because it is not my place. All I am concerned with is the small group of people who will need my help.'

'And who is in this group?' asked Leo.

'Including myself there are eight of us, and you are one of them.'

Leo wiped the remains of his tears from his face. 'Me?' he asked.

Maurice continued, 'You know that you are carrying around with you the view of the new life, the new world, don't you?' Leo answered very quietly, 'I suppose so.' He looked at Maurice and added, 'God knows why.'

'It is for the future.' Then Maurice asked, 'What is this view?'

Leo shifted his gaze from Maurice and looked down at his hands. 'I think it's the New World. It has always been there in my head, always. I didn't want it there, I just wanted to be normal like everyone else. I thought becoming an artist would be a way of getting it out, letting it out without seeming some kind of freak. It doesn't work like that, it's too vast, too huge to put onto a canvas,' Leo grew silent and then continued, 'I've ridiculed people who have seemed different, I've ridiculed them because I didn't want to accept that I was different. I was afraid and there you have it again, my fear is destructive,' he looked at Maurice and then said, 'I don't really want to be an artist, my fear has put paid to what I really want to do.'

'You want to keep bees don't you?' said Maurice.

Leo nodded, 'How did you know?'

'Just as the bee is always in your paintings, it is also always around you,' he touched Leo's head. 'It is always present.'

Martha dragged the bin bags into the sitting room. 'Any more rubbish?' she asked Michael.

Michael climbed down from the stepladder and pointed to a pile of framed pictures in the corner of the room. 'Let's get rid of those,' he said.

Martha walked over to the pile and began to look through them. 'Maybe we should keep something, what about this one?' She held up the small print of a spaniel.

'I'd rather have the American Indian, that's a hunting dog.' Martha compared the two pictures and put them both back onto the pile. 'I don't really like either of them.'

'What do you think of the room now it's finished, are you happy with it?' Michael asked as he folded the ladder.

Martha looked around the newly decorated sitting room. The white walls and ceiling had transformed the room. 'I can understand why artists love this area, it's because of the light.' Then she had an idea. 'I know, let's put all this lot into a bin bag for the charity shop, go into town and buy a couple of pictures from one of the galleries.'

'That'll cost an arm and a leg,' grumbled Michael as he carried the ladders out of the room.

Martha followed him. 'Is that a yes or a no?' she asked.

'You get the stuff ready for the charity shop and I'll get changed.'

She went back into the living room, opened up one of the bin bags and began to put the pictures inside. The last picture, a small woodland scene, she placed onto one side.

Martha peered in the window of the small gallery. The window display featured local scenes and seascapes, captured in watercolour, oil, ink and pencil. Michael walked up to her and began to look in the window. 'The bigger stuff is inside,' she said. 'Do you want to go in and have a look?'

'How much are they?' Michael asked.

Martha opened the shop door and went inside. Michael followed. Together they studied one of the large oil paintings.

Two Catalan fishing boats with their brightly coloured sails dominated the painting. 'I really like this one,' Michael said, 'and what's more it's not too expensive.'

Martha walked over to a watercolour. The painting, almost abstract, was made up of delicate strokes of pastel colour. The strokes formed the image of a poppy. 'I like this one,' she said to Michael, 'but it is rather expensive.'

'It would be,' he said as he led her away from the poppy and towards a vertical black and white sketch. The sketch showed a section of the quay. It was made up of a blend of architectural and loose sketching.

'It's different,' said Martha, 'and it certainly captures the feel of the place.' She turned back to the poppy. 'But I still like the poppy best, it's soothing and peaceful.'

'Well I like the Catalan boats, they're bright and cheerful. Come and have another look,' Michael said, leading Martha by the arm. 'It would look wonderful over the fireplace.'

'No, Michael, no. Not over the fireplace, I couldn't live with it there, it's too busy, I'd never be able to relax.' After a moment's thought she conceded, 'Maybe on the back wall of the sitting room.' She then added, 'The poppy would be far better hung over the fireplace.' She walked back to the painting, 'It is so beautiful.'

Michael looked at the painting, 'I couldn't live with that over the fireplace, I'm very sorry but I couldn't. It would be all right behind my chair, I wouldn't be able to see it there, but you would.'

'What could we put over the fireplace?' she asked.

Michael walked up to the black and white sketch of the quay. 'This would be perfect,' he said.

Martha sat down in her armchair, 'Let's switch on the table lamp and turn off the main light.'

'How do you expect me to read?' Michael asked, as he put down his newspaper.

'We can move the lamp closer to you.'

'You mean I can!' said Michael as he got up from his chair. He unplugged the lamp and moved both it and the table to the side of his chair. He plugged in the lamp and switched off the main light. 'Happy now?' he asked as he sat back down with his paper.

'This is so lovely, so relaxing,' she said. A moment later she began to examine the rug. 'What do you think of this rug?' she asked.

Michael put down his paper. 'Switch yourself off will you.'

'I can't,' answered Martha. 'All those years spent rushing around have conditioned me, I can't stop.'

'Of course you can, in fact you have to. We are retired and you know as well as I that we have to make the best of our time. That doesn't mean rushing around and trying to cram everything into one moment. It means appreciating the moment, fully.' Michael leant forward and placed a hand on Martha's leg. 'So come on old girl, relax. Why don't you read a book, I'll share the lamp with you.'

Martha smiled, 'And I thought it would be you who would find retirement difficult, but you have taken to it like a duck to water.'

Michael moved the lamp closer to Martha. 'I'm enjoying every minute of it, so don't let the side down, get your book out and relax.'

'I'll try,' she took her book out of her bag.

'What is that book?' Michael asked. 'It's got a darned strange cover.'

'It's one Maddy lent to me.'

'Warlocks and witches?' Michael asked.

'No, it's about a child who is denied normal stimulus and he develops ESP.'

'Warlocks and witches!' said Michael, lifting up his newspaper.

Martha interrupted his concentration again, 'Sorry, but do you think Maddy and Charlie will make a go of it?'

'Who knows,' he answered from behind his paper.

'They haven't slept together.'

'Hell's bells!' Michael exclaimed. 'That is really none of our business.'

'We sisters share such information.'

'Well keep it to yourself, I really don't want to know.' He lifted up his newspaper and added, 'And don't go telling her intimate things about me.'

Martha laughed, 'Like you have turned into a randy old man!'

Michael put down the paper, smiled and put it back up.

'Don't open the window, we'll be cold,' complained Martha as she got ready for bed.

'There's a hot water bottle in there,' he said, pointing to the bed. 'The tide is full.' He opened the window wide.

'Just listen to the sound.'

Martha climbed into bed and searched for the hot water bottle with her feet. 'Here,' said Michael as he moved the bottle across to her.

As they lay together they listened to the sounds of the sea. The sound of the full tide as it moved backwards and forwards was broken only by the crash of the waves as they hit the rocky shoreline. The bedroom soon filled not only with the sound of the sea but also its smell and salty taste.

Michael reached for Martha's hand and spoke quietly, 'You know the one thing that I deeply regret? It's not having given you enough of my time. I didn't realise that I was neglecting you.'

'We neglected each other,' said Martha, 'and it was because of the circumstances, so let's not have any regrets.' She gently squeezed his hand. 'We are here together now and we have the rest of our lives to spend together.'

'I'm a really lucky man. I have you beside me and I can fall asleep listening to the sea.'

CHAPTER 15

The days began to fall short. Something was missing. It felt like a vital component had been misplaced, leaving the days incomplete, and more than that, finding and obtaining simplicity had become increasingly difficult, if not impossible.

Charlie's land had become a battleground. Disease wiped out more and more of the crops. The disease flourished in wet weather, it flourished and denied all attempts to wipe it out.

Charlie, with the help of Anita, Giles, Maddy and Maurice, battled. Armed with a variety of potions, herbal extracts, ancient remedies, lunar and planetary lore, healing remained absent. The plants withered and died.

He stood by the regular bonfires and watched as the diseased leaf and root turned to ash. 'The garden is doomed,' Maurice had told him. 'The soil is unbalanced,' Anita had offered. 'It is not the right garden,' Maddy had thought.

Collecting fallen trees for fuel generated much of the same disappointment. The lie of the land made moving the timber difficult and the wet weather hindered every attempt. The task became extremely time-consuming.

His machines could not help him, and eventually Charlie was forced to buy in his vegetables and his logs. With this simple act, discontentment ate its way into daily life. Self- sufficiency and self-reliance turned into dependence. His life was being transformed into a new version of his old life.

Disillusioned, he wondered if there was any solution, anything that would push things forwards instead of holding things back. A nagging doubt whispered in the far corner of his mind but he could not hear it. It was only when he was forced to take another setback that he began to listen.

The setback came out of the blue and it affected everyone far and wide. Due to the prolonged wet weather European wheat crops had suffered greatly. Overnight the cost of wheat soared, and bread became a luxury item.

The whispering, nagging doubt at the back of his mind shouted to him. It shouted with such volume that Charlie winced and closed his eyes tightly. The doubt said, 'You are living in the wrong place.'

When the doubt had grown quiet he could see clearly a part of his future. He could see a homestead.

He could see a farmhouse with a clear view of the mountains. He could see the well-stocked barn and woodsheds, a garden of healthy vegetables and herbs. He could see a field of wheat and a woodland with easy access. He could see sheep grazing and their wool being spun and knitted into clothing. And he could see his friends, healthy, industrious and happy.

The nagging doubt broke its silence and whispered once more. It said, 'This is the safe house for you all. Find it.'

Steve explained the difficulty to Sylvie, 'We have to change the menu. The one we have is working out too expensive per head, the cost of the ingredients has gone up so much that we're making a loss.'

Sylvie pulled a face, 'And we'll turn into a second-rate establishment, you can't possibly change the menu, it would be a disaster. Everyone who comes here, comes because of the menu.'

'Why are you always so stubborn? We cannot afford to keep that menu, so end of story,' he turned away and sat down at the table. Flicking through his notebook he found a clean page. 'I'll devise meals that will work out cheaper and still be popular.' He looked at Sylvie and added, 'Be willing to give it a try.'

'I haven't any option, have I?' Not waiting for a reply she left the kitchen and went upstairs.

On the landing she stopped and looked out of the window. She could see Monty's old paddock, it was empty now. She remembered her first weeks at Les Lavandes. She remembered seeing the place for the first time, with its borders of lavender and its mellow stone resting under a powder-blue sky. She remembered Monty greedily eating all the left-over pastries and still shouting for more. She remembered Leo red-faced and laughing as he ran after her when she was learning to ride the bicycle. She remembered dancing in the garden with Charlie, laying down exhausted and then watching the stars together. She could see Maddy speaking joyfully about the power of the sun. Lastly she remembered Steve. The memory of that first night together at Studio Cottage came flooding back. She recalled how gently he had made love to her, how he had opened her eyes and how she had seen his soul.

Everything then clicked into perspective, those moments were the precious moments. They were the moments when time, rush and hurry all moved aside and allowed the true nature of things to emerge. She then realised that joy and love lived at the root of the true nature of all things and that nothing else really mattered.

The following day Steve joined Leo for breakfast. Leo pointed to the CD player. 'Put a CD on, Charlie's on his way and I can't stand another of his renditions.'

Steve switched on the CD player and then sat down. He looked at Leo's breakfast. 'How many's that?' he asked, pointing to Leo's boiled egg.

'What, since birth?' Leo asked.

'No, since you got up,' Steve reached for the jar of jam.

'Two,' answered Leo as he broke off the top of his egg.

'That's your weekly ration,' Steve said seriously.

'Aw come on, we can get eggs easily and cheaply from the farm.'

'More than two eggs a week is not good for your heart, they are high in cholesterol.' Steve spread the jam onto his toast.

'I can think of worse ways to go. I reckon a heart attack is fairly quick.'

'Quick maybe but not a pleasant experience,' Steve replied.

'I knew someone once...' began Leo.

'Oh here we go again,' Steve interrupted.

'No honestly I did. I knew this guy who...'

'Morning,' said Charlie, brightly.

'Morning,' said Steve. 'There's tea in the pot.' He then looked at Leo, 'And what did he do?'

Leo cringed, 'It's really gruesome.'

'Well save it, I think I'm better off not knowing.'

Leo scraped clean the inside of his eggshell, put down the spoon and pushed his plate to one side. 'I could eat another of those,' he said and then added, 'but I'd be terrified.'

Charlie walked over to the table, put down his plate and cup and sat down. Steve was horrified as he looked at the huge pile of toast. 'Charlie, bread is a luxury.'

'Yes I know,' Charlie replied as he stirred his tea.

'What he's saying...' began Leo as he looked at Charlie's plate.

'I know exactly what he's saying,' Charlie said, then added, 'but I'm making hay while the sun shines.' He looked at Leo.

'What I'm saying is, enjoy it while you can.' Charlie smiled and then said, 'I'd enjoy it even more if you would kindly turn your music down.'

Leo got up from the table and turned down the volume. 'Do you not like this music?' he asked.

'It's too lively for this time of day,' Charlie replied. 'It would be better suited to a disco.'

'A disco!' Leo exclaimed. 'People stopped having discos years ago.'

'What do they have now?' asked Charlie as he ate his toast.

'Raves,' replied Leo as he sat back down.

'Whose music is this?' Charlie asked.

'System 7.'

Charlie looked nonplussed, and then looked at Steve, 'I want to ask a favour.'

'If it involves gardening or collecting wood, the answer is no.'

'It isn't. I need a co-pilot for this afternoon, we'll be gone for around two hours.' He paused and then added, 'I'll pay you.'

'I'll do it,' offered Leo.

'No offence,' said Charlie to him, 'but I'd rather have Steve because I may also need his advice.'

'Charge him extra,' said Leo, getting up from the table. He collected the plates. 'When I've washed up I'll be upstairs if you want me.'

'Where do you want to go?' Steve asked Charlie.

'Not far. I have the directions on a bit of paper. There'll be a couple of stops but they shouldn't take long. I won't keep you hanging around.'

'What time do you want to leave?'

'Two, we'll be back around four.'

'OK, pick me up at two, but don't be late, I know what you're like.'

Leo bobbed his head out of the kitchen, 'At 1.30 I'll put on System 7 and turn up the sound, that'll get rid of him.'

'Opera is what you need,' Charlie retorted. He then admitted, 'Opera was my first love.'

'You were one hell of a sad git,' said Leo, going back into the kitchen.

'Pull up here,' said Steve. He looked closely at the map and traced the road with his finger. 'I don't think we've gone past it.'

Charlie pulled the map towards himself and looked where Steve was pointing. 'I'll carry on a bit and if we don't come to it I'll have to turn the bus around.'

Steve folded the map and then wound down his window.

'The view from up here is amazing. You can see mountains in almost every direction.'

Charlie put the van into gear and set off slowly along the winding road. 'There's a turning ahead on the left. It looks like a track.'

'It is a track,' said Steve, 'and it looks rough.'

'I'll pull in here, there's no way we could drive down there.' Charlie parked the van as close as he could to the side of the road and then asked Steve, 'Do you fancy a little walk?'

Steve opened his door and climbed out of the van. 'It's a windy spot,' he said as he braced himself against a strong gust of wind. 'Who in their right mind would live here?'

'The people selling the farm,' Charlie answered, as he began to walk along the track.

Steve grabbed him by the arm, 'Selling the farm? I thought you were buying vegetables. That is why we are here, isn't it?' Charlie looked Steve in the eye, 'I want to have a little look at the place.'

'Why?' asked Steve.

'I'm considering buying a farm up here.'

'I don't believe you, I really don't believe you,' said Steve, shaking his head.

Charlie grew serious. 'Templar House isn't the right place. I'll explain all to you later and you'll understand, but for now let's get a move on or we'll be late.'

Steve followed behind. 'I'm angry with you, so bloody angry.'

'I thought you would be,' said Charlie without turning around.

Steve followed, silently fuming as Charlie marched on.

'This isn't it,' Charlie called out as he spotted the farmhouse.

'Turn around and go back before anyone spots us.'

Steve blocked him. 'Wait,' he said angrily, 'this is madness, what the hell is going on?'

'Get in the van and I'll explain everything, but just don't be angry.'

Charlie sat in the driver's seat and closed the door. Steve waited for the explanation. 'I know it seems madness,' began Charlie, 'but it isn't. Templar House is not the right place, it's too damp down there and it's impossible to grow anything. I'm wasting all of my time. Even getting my own firewood is impossible.' He looked at Steve. 'My dream of being self-sufficient has shattered and I need to find the right place.'

'But you didn't even look at this place.'

'It wasn't the right one. I know now what the right one looks like and that one wasn't it.' Charlie turned the ignition and started up the van. 'Please direct us to the next place.'

Steve pulled out the map grudgingly. 'I'll direct us to this place and then we go home.'

The VW turned onto the neatly-surfaced farm track. 'With a bit of luck we'll be able to drive to the door,' Charlie said sounding enthusiastic.

Steve was folding up the map when suddenly without any warning Charlie slammed on the brakes. 'My God!' he exclaimed.

'What the hell!' said Steve as the sudden stop jolted him against the dashboard. 'What was that for?'

Charlie looked ahead. They had approached the farmhouse from the rear and from where they were he could see on the left the healthy field he had glimpsed in his mind. Ahead he could see the track leading to the woodland. 'I saw that in my mind,' he explained.

'What about the house?' asked Steve, as he looked at the farmhouse.

'Most of my view of the house was from the front, but I saw that arched cellar door and those steps. I saw the barn too.'

'Are you going to get out and have a look?' Steve asked.

'Do you want to come?' Charlie asked.

Steve opened his door and climbed out. 'It's more sheltered than the last place.'

'The agent said the key is under the frog by the back door,' Charlie explained.

'This place looks lived in,' Steve remarked.

'The elderly couple who lived here have only just moved out, they were here for thirty-three years.'

'It's this barn and those goat sheds that make this courtyard so sheltered, but I bet the front of the house catches the wind.'

'We'll have a look around the house and then have a look at the front. The agent said the view is superb.' Charlie climbed the steps to the backdoor, found the key under the frog and called down to Steve, 'Are you coming?'

'Hang on a minute, there's an old wooden machine in here,' he said as he peered into the barn through a small window.

Charlie unlocked the door of the house. 'Hurry up,' he called.

Steve ran up the steps. 'You could always make an offer for that, it's an old threshing machine, even you would like that one.'

Charlie opened the door wide and went inside. Steve followed and switched on the lights. 'Electricity's on.'

'This is the vestibule!' Charlie announced as he looked around him, 'With two doors. Which do you reckon is the kitchen?'

Steve opened the door on the left and walked into a large, old-fashioned, well-equipped and well-cared for kitchen.

'I just love these,' he said walking up to the large floor-to- ceiling cupboards. He opened one of the doors and had a look inside. 'Look at the depth of these shelves.'

Charlie took a look. 'There's room for everything in there. I love the colour of the paintwork.'

'I think it's called dairy yellow,' Steve said. He walked over to the cuisiniere. He opened the oven door. 'Do you think this thing still works?'

'It must do,' said Charlie having a look. 'The old couple must have used it.'

They made their way over to the window and were both taken aback by the view. 'The agent said that the view was superb, but I never imagined that it would be so wonderful.'

'Magical mountains,' said Steve. He asked, 'How high up do you reckon we are?'

'I've no idea. We'll have a look at the map afterwards.' Charlie made his way back to the vestibule and opened the other door. The door led into the hallway. 'There's a loo in here,' he called as he peeped into the small room under the stairs.

Steve appeared from the door at the far end of the hall.

'Why didn't you use this door?' he asked.

'I wanted to know where the vestibule would lead.'

'One front door,' Steve pointed to the door and tried to open it, 'but locked.'

Charlie stood at the bottom of the stairs. 'What a beautiful staircase. Giles would love this. It looks like oak.'

'It looks like chestnut to me,' said Steve, making his way into the living room. 'Boy, it's cold in here.'

'Get that fireplace stoked up and you'd notice a difference.' Charlie walked up to the fireplace and ran a hand across the mantle piece. 'Everything has been so well looked after, it's spotless everywhere.'

Steve agreed, 'It's been a well-loved place, nothing has been neglected.' He walked back to the door. 'Shall we have a look upstairs?'

Charlie investigated the bedrooms while Steve had a look in the bathroom. 'Hey Charlie, come and have a look at this.' Charlie smiled when he saw what Steve was pointing at.

'It's a bidet,' he said.

'I know what it is. Anyway what have you found?'

'Two large-sized bedrooms and one small one, and a huge linen press, come and have a look at it.'

The linen press was another floor-to-ceiling cupboard with deep shelves. Steve opened the door and had a look inside.

'Moth balls!' Picking up a piece of newspaper from one of the shelves he read the date, '1957.'

'That will have seen some mothballs,' said Charlie, making his way downstairs.

Steve had a look in the bedrooms and then followed Charlie. He found him gazing out of the kitchen window. 'What do you think of the place?' he asked.

Charlie turned around. 'I don't just think, I feel and I know that this is the right place.'

'What about Templar House?' Steve asked.

'I wouldn't sell it.' He turned and looked back at the view.

'Maybe you and Leo would stay on there and look after it,' he explained, 'I'm

121

going to take this opportunity to say something to you but before I do you've got to promise not to ridicule me for what I say, I've had enough of that in my lifetime.' Charlie looked at Steve and waited.

'Just get on with it,' said Steve as he leant against the wall.

'I believe, like Maurice and others, that we are on the brink of a major catastrophe. I suppose I have always known that something was going to happen, even as a child the thought would come to me. But this place, this homestead, is a safe place and here we have a chance of survival.'

'Who's we?' Steve asked.

'You and Sylvie, Maddy, Giles and Anita, Leo, Maurice and me,' Steve exhaled slowly. Charlie continued, 'We all have time to get things organised so that we will not suffer too much. Of course our lives will change drastically but with forethought and care we could make them all right.'

Again Steve exhaled slowly. 'That's some thought,' he said. After a long silence, Charlie asked, 'Just for now would you and Leo stay on at Templar House if I moved here?' Steve looked out of the window, 'I can't speak for Leo but I would. I'd hate to leave the place, I really would.'

'One day you might want to.' Charlie walked over to the back door, 'Do you fancy a look around the front?'

Maddy picked up the parcel from the table, moved the jug to its usual spot and then carried the parcel upstairs.

In the far corner of the spare room she found the small blanket chest. Kneeling down beside the chest she began to unwrap the parcel. A bundle of tiny baby vests and nappies fell onto the floor. She picked them up and placed them into the chest with the rest of the baby things. She unpinned the list from inside the lid and crossed off baby vests and towelling nappies.

Maddy tried to imagine the life of the child. She wondered what things the child would want to know. She wondered what things from the present time should be carried into the future and what things from the present time would be better lost, forgotten and left behind.

She knew that the child would have no memory of the old world for it would be born in the new. Its first steps would be taken on a different earth, an earth newly cleansed, replenished and revitalised. The child would neither be polluted nor be the polluter, for its pure spirit would be completely connected to and with the new earth, but Maddy realised with sadness that the child, like everyone else, would have to learn how to survive.

CHAPTER 16

'Sorry for barging in!'

'Leo, you're soaking.'

He took off his jacket. 'Drenched but I'll dry off!'

Anita moved a chair over to the stove. 'Here, hang your coat over this. Why didn't you use your car?'

'Can't afford the juice, prices have gone completely crazy.' He wiped his hands and face on the kitchen towel. 'Can you still afford it?'

'Only just, but if it goes up again we will have to think of an alternative. Maddy suggested a group shopping trip once a month.' As she filled the kettle she asked, 'Do you want a drink?'

'What's on offer?' Leo asked.

'Mint, lemon balm or bergamot.'

'No normal?'

'I was saving what little we have. You can have honey in the herb tea.'

'Lemon balm and honey sounds fine.' He picked up the cat from the front of the fire. 'Does this thing ever go out?'

'Only in fine weather.' As Anita spooned the honey into the cups, she asked, 'How are things?'

Leo sat down at the table and put the cat on his knee.

'Charlie's moving out this weekend and he wondered if Gilesy would help him.'

'He's in his workshop right now but he'll be in for a break soon, you can ask him then.'

'What's he doing in there?'

'Finishing off Charlie's beds!'

Leo grinned. 'Charlie has gone completely mad. He arrived home on Saturday with a huge stack of new towels, a stack higher than your stove.' Leo pointed across to the range.

'The week before it was sweeping brushes, hoes, rakes, wheelbarrows, buckets and rope!'

Anita laughed as she poured the boiling water into the cups.

'He asked me where he could get extra-large kettles from!'

'We have to move all that lot at the weekend, plus those tubs of grain, and they weigh an absolute ton!'

'He's only trying to make sure that if things go pear-shaped he'll be OK.'

'It's not just for himself,' Leo began, 'it's for all of us.' Anita sat down at the table. 'Has he told you this?' she asked.

Leo shook his head, 'Not me, but he mentioned something to Steve.'

Anita took a sip of tea. 'What did he say to Steve?'

Leo lifted the cat from his knee and put it down onto the floor. 'He said the farm was not just for himself but it was for all of us.' He looked at Anita. 'A place of safety.'

Anita began to think, 'We're very near the river here.'

Leo looked seriously at her. 'We all know that there's something about to happen, we can't fool ourselves, can we?'

'We'd be fools if we did.'

Giles burst into the kitchen. 'Christ!' he exclaimed, 'What a game that was.' He walked over to the sink and began to wash his hands. 'And what's he doing here?' he asked, looking at Leo.

'He's come to visit you,' Leo replied.

'What was the outburst for?' Anita asked as she walked over to the stove.

'Two more bloody roof leaks! It's taken me most of the morning to move my stuff out of the way.' Giles sat down opposite Leo. 'What do you want?'

'I came to pay a visit and also to ask if you'll help Charlie move this weekend.'

'I suppose so. Has he managed to hire a truck?'

Leo nodded. 'He picks it up Friday evening and has to take it back Monday morning.'

Anita passed Giles a cup. 'It's mint,' she explained.

Giles looked into his cup. 'No coffee?'

'You had the last of it.'

Giles looked back at Leo. 'What's the farm access like?'

'Steve said it's a well made and well looked after track.'

'No tight bends?'

'I don't think so,' Leo answered and then said, 'Me and Steve will help load and unload.'

'How will you get over there?' Anita asked.

'Charlie will put juice in my car.' Then he said to Giles,

'The piano will be going.'

'I had a feeling it might be,' Giles said. 'I'll bring rollers with me.'

Sheepishly Leo explained, 'There are steps up to the house.'

'I'll bring some ropes,' Giles offered.

'You won't need to,' Leo laughed, 'Charlie has bought heaps of the stuff.'

'What on earth for?' Giles asked.

'Apparently it's for any and every possible eventuality.' Giles raised an eyebrow, 'Oh.'

Anita touched Leo's hand. 'Have you finished your commission?' she asked.

'Almost.'

'What's it all about?' Giles asked.

'The painting depicts the unseen threads of the universe. I've called it "The Celestial Web".'

'Unseen threads of the universe?' said Giles. 'If they are unseen how do you know they exist, and how on earth can you paint them?'

'You use your imagination,' replied Leo. Changing the subject, he said to his mother, 'Charlie wanted to know if you would help him to propagate and plant medicinal herbs.'

Anita nodded. 'Tell him I'll help. Is he still planning to buy a greenhouse or a polytunnel?'

'You'd have to ask him. At the moment all he keeps going on about is buying some sheep!'

'What on earth for?' Giles asked.

' "Wool" was the answer that I got. I think he's hoping that Maddy will take up spinning and knitting.'

'Are they a couple yet?' Giles asked. 'If you know what I mean.'

Leo looked across at his mother, shook his head and then answered Giles, 'Why don't you ask him yourself?'

'Don't forget I was the one who was put under considerable pressure to get that double bed finished for Maddy's arrival.'

'If you want to know if I've seen Maddy in it, the answer is none of your business.'

Maurice lay down on the ground next to the river. The wet earth did not concern him. He outstretched his arm and rested his hand on the moving current.

As the current brushed past his hand its circuitry left a trace. Maurice picked up the trace, he connected to it and he analysed it.

It evoked a distant memory, a memory steeped in the wisdom and the knowledge of the ancients.

The memory did not stay in the past, it moved into the future and it was there in the future that Maurice saw it clearly.

He saw materialise before him the manifestation of the golden lion. The lion sat on a golden throne and stared at him. Its head was encompassed by seven golden rays and each ray was linked to the sun.

The energy radiating from the lion was immense, vast and far reaching. It illuminated the shadow of man. The message was clear. The time was almost near for the golden age to be realised by mankind.

The lion dispersed its energy and moved back into the river. It moved back in time.

Maurice lifted his hand from the water and said a silent prayer. The prayer was simple, it came from his heart. It came from his soul. It said, 'May the mighty roar of the lion bring peace to the earth.'

The rain continued to pour. The heavy showers were broken by short interludes when the sun would try to break through, only to be forced back by another accumulation of cloud and then more rain.

Each downpour brought Charlie dismay, and in a state of great agitation he continued to pack his things. The removal day was close at hand and the weather had the power to turn the day into absolute disaster.

At 7.00 on the Saturday morning, Charlie took a look outside. The rain had stopped and although the ground looked very wet, the sky was promising. The day looked fine. The removal was on.

'What's in this bloody barrel?' asked Giles as he attempted to lift it.

Leo walked up to him with the trolley. 'Bars of soap,' he answered. 'And he's got towels to go with them.'

Giles took hold of the trolley and pushed its forks underneath the barrel. 'What's he going to do, take one hell of a bath?'

'I heard that,' said Charlie, as he came into the barn. 'One day you'll be very pleased and thankful that I've got these.' He pointed to the barrel.

'I'm sure I will,' said Giles as he began to move the trolley. He caught Leo's eye. 'Here you take this, I'll help Charlie.'

Leo took hold of the trolley and wheeled the barrel to the truck. 'There's only room for that,' said Steve from inside the truck. 'We'll have to come back for the rest of the stuff.'

'What about his beds?' asked Leo. 'They're over at mum's.'

'We'll pick them up on the way back, do they dismantle?'

Leo shrugged, 'Best ask him.' He nodded towards Giles. Giles came out of the barn with Charlie, together they were carrying an old tin bath filled with gardening tools.

Steve repeated his question, 'Do the beds dismantle?'

'Of course they do,' replied Giles.

'We've no room for that on this run,' Steve said, pointing to the tin bath.

'Leave it here,' said Charlie, putting down his end of the bath. 'We'll take it next time.'

'Will the piano be all right?' Charlie asked with concern.

'Don't worry, it won't budge,' said Giles. 'It's tied firmly in place. I just hope we can get it up the steps, and that reminds me.' Giles walked back into the barn and came out carrying four planks of wood. 'We'll probably need these, can we squeeze them in?'

Steve jumped down from the truck and together he and Giles lifted up the planks and slotted them into a free space at the top of the truck. 'That's definitely it,' said Steve. 'Let's close up and get going.'

'I'll follow in the car with Leo,' said Charlie, wiping mud from his hands. 'Can you remember the way?'

Steve thought for a moment, 'You go first, we'll follow you.'

'Whatever you do, do NOT stand behind the piano. Keep to the side of it. Do you understand?'

Leo rolled his eyes. 'Yes, Father,' he replied in monotone. Giles continued, 'And when the back roller comes free, take it and push it under the front edge, but keep to the side.'

'Are you sure this is easier than trying to get it around the front?' asked Leo.

'Much,' answered Giles.

'I didn't think it would be dangerous,' said Charlie. 'I don't think I can watch.'

'Then go inside and close the door,' said Steve, making room for Charlie to get past. He asked Giles, 'Is there enough space at the top to turn it?'

'It'll be tight,' answered Giles. 'Where do we go then?'

'Straight down the hallway then a right turn into the living room.'

'Let's get it over with,' said Leo, moving into position. Steve and Giles picked up the ropes, checked that they were firmly tied around the piano, double checked the makeshift ramp, then made their way to the top of the steps. Steve put on his gloves and straightened out the rope. 'You got a firm grip?' Giles asked.

'Yeah, ready to go,' Steve replied.

'After three,' Giles tightened his grip. 'One, two, three, go!' As both men heaved on the ropes, the piano, with a sudden jolt began to move. As it moved slowly up the ramp, Leo grabbed the first roller to come free, ran to the front side of the piano and pushed it under the edge. As Steve and Giles continued to tug the ropes, Leo ran backwards and forwards with the rollers. The piano slowly made its way to the top of the steps.

'We need to get it as far as possible over this top step and then try to turn it,' Giles said to Steve.

With his role now completed, Leo stood back and assessed the situation, 'You won't be able to turn it, there's not enough room.'

With the piano safely resting on the small balcony, Giles took stock. The handrail and upright supports would need to be removed. 'Charlie,' he called out, 'We've got a problem.'

Charlie came out of the door, looked at the piano and then at the turning space. He shrugged. Giles explained, 'I need to saw these off.' He pointed to the rails.

'There's a saw in the tin bath,' said Charlie.

'It didn't come this trip,' said Steve.

Giles took a look at the rails, 'I reckon we could boot them off.'

Charlie looked horrified, 'Boot them off? What if they get damaged?'

'I'll replace them for you. Now do we boot them or not?' Charlie nodded, 'But let me get back indoors.'

'Stand back, Leo,' said Giles.

'You get all the fun,' said Leo, moving out of the way.

With three robust kicks of his boot, Giles managed to dislodge the upright supports, and the top rail was sent flying.

'Nice one,' said Leo as he watched the rail land on the ground below and shatter into pieces.

'It'll turn now,' said Giles.

Compared with the first part of the removals, the almost completed final part went without a hitch. 'That's it,' Giles told Charlie, 'the truck's empty.'

Together they carried the beds up the steps and into the house. 'Next time, buy a house without steps,' complained Giles. 'It beats me why he wants so many beds,' he said to Steve.

'Possible eventualities,' said Leo, helping to move the beds.

Charlie reached up and pulled a key from the ledge above the front door. 'It was there all the time,' he said to Steve as he unlocked the door.

All four men walked out to the front of the house. The view made its immediate impact.

'Wow!' said Leo. 'Look at the colours.'

Giles stared at the distant mountain range. 'Is it always so clear?' he asked.

Charlie shook his head. 'No. The last time I came up here the mist and the rain obscured everything, you couldn't see the mountains at all.'

Leo pointed to the area on his right. 'I have a friend who lives over there. I bet you could see his place with a pair of bins.'

'Do you always spy on your friends through binoculars?' Charlie asked.

'Only the interesting ones,' Leo replied.

Steve wandered down through the garden. 'You've got some blackcurrant bushes here,' he said, pointing.

Charlie walked up to him. 'The last time I was here I found a huge clump of bamboo around the back of the goat sheds, it's well established and healthy.'

'You'll be OK for pea sticks,' said Giles.

'And bamboo shoots,' added Steve as they walked back into the house.

'Are you any good at making Chinese food?' Leo asked.

Steve turned to him. 'I can do a good stir fry, do you like Chinese food?'

'I love it,' Leo answered.

'I'll make you a stir fry at the weekend.'

'Speaking of food,' Giles said, 'we'd better get going, there'll be a casserole waiting for us.' He turned to Charlie and asked, 'Do you want to come? There'll be plenty.'

'Kind of you to offer, but I really want to try this out,' he pointed to the old range.

'Are you sure?'

Charlie nodded. 'I want to stay here and get to know the place.' He added, 'You lot have been brilliant and I'm so grateful.'

When Leo, Steve and Giles had got to the bottom of the steps, Charlie called down, 'There's some cash in the truck, split it between you.'

'How much?' Leo asked.

Giles elbowed him in the ribs, 'You don't ask things like that, you discreetly go and look.'

Leo set off at a run towards the truck, with Giles sprinting behind him.

Steve turned to wave to Charlie but he had already gone back inside the house.

As he closed the door behind him, Charlie stood quietly for a moment and then said, 'I've come home.'

Anita stacked the plates and dishes together. 'I'll get these out of the way and then make a drink.'

'It was a lovely meal, just what we needed,' said Steve.

'Will Sylvie be all right on her own?' Anita asked him.

'Maddy's over there. She's showing Sylvie how to thread the old sewing machine.'

'Martha's old hand machine?' Anita asked.

Steve nodded, 'Martha said that she has no more use for it and Sylvie could have it, but she's no idea how you thread it up.'

Leo put the pots into the washing-up bowl. 'She learns fast! She learnt how to ride Mum's bike in next to no time.'

'I reckon if fuel prices go up any more we'll all have to get our bikes out,' said Giles, 'and I'm not joking.'

Steve agreed, 'You're right. If we'd have used our cars less and our bikes more,' he added, 'maybe we wouldn't be in this mess.'

Anita walked over to the table. 'It was in today's paper that there's to be another price rise, not just fuel but food too.'

Steve looked up at her. 'That's bad news, I've just had to re-do our menu to make it cost effective, I can't keep doing that.'

'Doom and gloom,' called Leo from the sink.

'Well it is,' said Giles. 'It's serious.'

Anita walked over to the stove and filled the large pot with boiling water; she placed it on the tray alongside the cups.

'And it's global,' she added. She placed the tray on the table.

'Every country is being hit.'

Leo wiped his hands on the towel and walked over to his seat. 'Maybe Charlie has got the right idea,' he said as he sat down.

'Being self-sufficient?' said Giles.

'Self-reliant,' said Leo. 'Preparing for every eventuality is what he calls it.' Leo looked at Giles. 'Maybe he hasn't gone crackers.'

'That's OK if you can afford to do that, but what happens to the folk who cannot afford to "be prepared"?'

'Make do and mend,' suggested Anita.

Steve looked at her, 'My grandparents lived like that. Nothing was thrown away and nothing was wasted.'

'Were they happy?' she asked.

'As far as I know. I always remember their home as being a happy home.'

Anita poured the tea into the cups. 'People had simple pleasures.' She passed a cup to Steve.

'What are Charlie's plans?' Giles asked as he took a cup from the tray. 'I can't quite understand him.'

Steve paused for thought. 'Things are not working out at Templar House, he can't be self-sufficient there, he says it isn't the right place to be.'

'That's not all though is it?' Giles asked.

Steve became silent and looked down at the table. In that same silence Leo saw in his mind flashes of the flood. He trembled visibly. 'Are you all right?' Anita asked.

'I'm just tired mum, that's all,' Leo replied.

Steve began to answer Giles, 'Charlie's worried about us all and in his own way he's trying to safeguard our future. He might seem a fool but really he isn't.'

'I wondered if Maurice had planted some of his ideas into Charlie's head,' said Giles.

'His ideas are his own, he's had them a long time,' Steve stretched out his legs under the table. 'I'm beginning to think he's right, the way we live is starting to crumble and we are going to have to find a new way of living.'

'I think we all realise that,' said Anita.

Giles shrugged, 'Well it hasn't crumbled yet.'

'No, but it's obviously breaking down,' said Anita.

Leo leant back in his chair and rested his head against the wall. He closed his eyes. He didn't want to listen anymore.

'What are you really saying?' Giles asked her.

'I'm only trying to see things as they really are, trying to face up to it, things are breaking down,' she answered.

'I have a suggestion,' interrupted Steve, 'why don't we all try and help Charlie in a practical way. We could donate a day a week to help him. We could share the transport over there.'

'Would he want our help?' Anita asked.

'I don't think he'd manage without it and it wouldn't be fair to expect him to.'

Giles moved close to Steve and asked, 'Are they a couple yet?' He repeated his question, 'Maddy and Charlie, are they a couple, if you know what I mean?'

'I think they like each other, if you know what I mean?'

CHAPTER 17

Charlie stacked the new bedding and towels in the linen press. The new quilts and pillows would not fit into the cupboard. He carried these into the small bedroom and placed them on the shelves alongside the blankets.

The boxes of soap fitted at the bottom of the unit, and he wondered how long they would last. Survival, he thought to himself, would depend to a certain extent on cleanliness. He knew that there was enough soap to last them for thirty years, who would live much longer than that? He shook the thought from his mind and began to unpack his telescope.

As he opened the box he realised that it had been sealed since leaving Britain. He carefully unwrapped the telescope and its stand and placed them by the window. He remembered the hours of his youth spent exploring the skies, and the delight he had found when the universe became familiar to him. The stars, like friends, had revealed themselves.

He thought of Steve. Steve had been his first real and true friend and he had taken the place of the night stars. He thought about Maurice whose strange touch had awakened so many memories. His touch had also awakened faith in himself and that faith pushed aside fear and all doubts. He thought about Giles and Anita, like two opposites they made up a perfect whole, they reminded him of Castor and Pollux, and Leo was the bright and ever-constant light.

Charlie then thought about Maddy. So radiant a star, she was the embodiment of celestial light. Queen of heavens, she was the one who had brought to him the water of life.

He remembered, with a smile, lying back on the damp grass stargazing with Sylvie!

These were his true friends and they had replaced the stars he had seen through his telescope. He also knew that they shared with him a strange and unique journey.

Perched on the windowsill he looked around the room. Most of the boxes had been unpacked. The small bedroom was ideal for storage. Maybe, he thought, Giles would help to split the larger bedrooms into four smaller ones, enough space for us all.

'Slow down. How can you take everything in when you are rushing? And why do you rush?'

Leo slowed his pace. 'I didn't realise that I was rushing.'

Sion walked up to him.

'Be more aware of things.'

'What things?' Leo asked.

'Look around you.' Sion stopped walking and gestured around him. 'Appreciate what surrounds you.'

'I do,' objected Leo, 'I appreciate nature.'

'Not fully, it isn't possible to appreciate the nature around you fully when you rush through it.' Sion rested a hand on Leo's shoulder. 'We are here together in this moment.'

'That's obvious enough,' said Leo.

Sion continued, 'Everything around us shares this moment and only for this moment. Another day, another hour, even another minute, will change what you can see and be aware of. The present is precious and it deserves greater respect.'

'My mind is always racing,' explained Leo.

'Slow it down, control its speed,' Sion smiled and then continued, 'A great artist becomes one with what he sees and you can only do that when you experience complete awareness.' Sion traced a frown on Leo's forehead. 'Remove the anxiety.'

Leo turned and walked to the edge of the lake, Sion followed and stood quietly beside him. Together they watched as a group of wild ducks took refuge in a clump of rushes. One by one they began to reappear. 'They sense we are not a threat to them,' said Sion quietly.

'I wonder what they actually pick up from us?' Leo asked.

'We can only guess at the answer to that.'

'What is your guess?' Leo asked.

Sion smiled. 'It's my guess that they can sense our energy. Their survival is dependent on intuition and accurate observation, and I assume that their intuition and powers of observation are finely tuned.'

'Like mine should be!' said Leo.

Sion wrapped an arm around him. 'Yours are in the process of development, but like any process it requires commitment. Unlike the ducks here, your commitment is not fuelled by a need to survive.'

'It might be one day,' Leo answered.

'But not now. We are here in THIS moment. This moment, for us, for those ducks, for the nature around us, is the real moment.'

As Sion kissed Leo's forehead, Leo said quietly, 'I wish it could last forever.'

'We cannot crystallise this moment and we shouldn't want to. We each have a destiny to fulfil, but our love will survive.' Leo pulled away. 'What about us? What about us in the real world?'

'We each have our own destiny and we cannot manipulate what is mapped out for us. You have a view of the new world and you have been given that view for a reason.'

'But what about you?'

'I cannot share the course you take, but...' he held Leo's shoulders tightly, 'our paths will cross again, and I am certain of that.'

'Will we survive?' Leo said anxiously.

'I have answered that question.' He reached for Leo's hand.

'One day I shall teach you how to calm your anxieties!'

PJ knew Charlie well enough to be able to walk into his home unannounced.

'You're there!' he exclaimed when he found Charlie in the front garden. 'This is some place.'

Charlie took off his gardening gloves and walked up the path towards PJ, 'You like it then?'

PJ shook Charlie's hand and nodded, 'It's a wonderful place and you are a very lucky man.'

'I feel settled here already.'

'It actually looks like you have always lived here.' Charlie smiled, 'That is exactly how it feels!'

PJ followed Charlie into the kitchen. 'Should we have a coffee before the lesson?' Charlie asked.

'We have time,' said PJ, looking at his watch. 'I allowed myself twenty-five minutes to get here and I made it in fifteen.'

Charlie poured the coffee from the pot. 'No road rage?'

'I didn't meet a soul.'

Charlie passed a cup to PJ. 'It's a bit of a weak brew.'

'I can't afford it myself. Yet another little luxury has disappeared from my life.' PJ took the cup over to the table and sat down. 'So, weak or not, it will be a delight.' After taking a sip of the coffee he said, 'I'm really sorry to have cut down your lessons but I can't afford the petrol. I'll leave you with extra work to do at home, that should help make up for the loss.'

'We are all having to make adjustments, so don't worry, one lesson a month is fine. To be honest with you it suits me fine.'

'Why is that?'

Charlie explained, 'I have so much to do here. So much planning and organising as well as all the practical things. I really need to get an area fenced off for the sheep.'

PJ adjusted his glasses, 'I didn't know you had any sheep!'

'I haven't yet, they're due to arrive this afternoon and I really need to finish the fence.'

'Will you be having lamb chops?' PJ asked.

'Good God no! They will be here to provide wool...' Charlie paused, 'and they will be a bit of company too.'

'Company!' exclaimed PJ. 'What on earth happened to those two-legged creatures,' PJ went into deep thought, 'The ones with the delicious breasts and the soft backsides?'

'Our view of womankind differs slightly!'

PJ grinned, 'I get it, you shear the sheep and your woman spins and knits socks for you!'

Charlie laughed, 'Something along those lines.'

PJ looked around the kitchen. 'This room is huge, you could have wonderful dinner parties in here.'

'I couldn't afford them.'

'Of course you could,' PJ disagreed. 'Just think what glorious fun we could have. I tell you what, you spend some of that wealth and throw an opulent party and I shall entertain you all.'

'How?' asked Charlie with a grin.

'At the piano. You could wheel it in here and I would play for my supper.'

'It's an idea,' said Charlie, 'but I'm not sure my conscience would allow me to spend so much money on frivolity.'

'Frivolity!' PJ was horrified. 'Fun is as important as the air that we breathe, and laughter cures all ills.'

'OK,' said Charlie. 'You've convinced me!'

PJ finished his coffee. 'I'd like to bring Sheila with me, she'd love to meet you and she'd adore this place.' Looking out of the window he added, 'Those mountains don't look real do they?'

'That's what I thought when I first saw them. They reminded me of model railway scenery.'

PJ took another look. 'I'm envious, Charlie, you have found one huge chunk of paradise.' He then added, 'Mind you, Sheila comes close to paradise.' He closed his eyes.

'Such perfect breasts.'

Charlie interrupted, 'Shall we get on with the lesson? The piano will need tuning.'

'Lead the way,' said PJ, getting up from the table.

He followed Charlie into the living room. 'We could hold the party in here. Get a log fire going in that hearth, lay a fine spread on the table and you would have the foundation for a splendid party.'

'It's an idea,' said Charlie.

PJ opened his case and pulled out a parcel of sheet music.

'I've brought you something different to try.' Charlie sat down, 'What is it?'

'Jazz. It will give you a taster for the party. By the way, when is it?'

'NO WAY!' exclaimed Leo in horror. 'You go in and get it out.'

'Come on, you can fit in there better than us,' said Giles.

'Get stuffed! There's no way that I am getting into the back of the van with that creature.' Leo looked at it. 'It's dying to have a go at someone, look at its horns.'

'It can't get you, it's tethered to the side of the van. Just go to the back of it, undo the tether and walk it out. It'll be happy to join the others.'

'Giles, this is not a sheep, it's a ram, just have a look at this...' Leo pointed to the ram's undercarriage.

Giles pushed Leo into the back of the van. 'Just get on with it.'

The ram did not move. He allowed Leo to untie the tether and still did not move. 'Now come on, lad,' said Leo, 'Let's join your lady friends.' Leo pulled on the tether but the ram refused to move. 'He won't budge.'

Moving slowly, Giles climbed into the back of the van.

'Give it to me,' he said, taking hold of the tether. But still the ram refused to move. 'I'll pull on his tether and you pull him by his horns,' Giles suggested.

'Get lost! One false move and he'll have me skewered.'

'Well here, then,' said Giles, passing the tether back to Leo, 'You pull on this and I'll take his horns.'

Slowly Leo, Giles and the ram made their way out of the van. Charlie opened the gate, let the ram pass through and then closed it quickly. The sheep ran to the far side of the field. 'I hope they'll be alright,' said Charlie.

'We should get danger money for that job. One false move and I would have been perforated,' said Leo.

'What kind of breed are they?' Giles asked.

'Jacobs,' replied Charlie. 'The breed originated in Spain so hopefully they'll be OK here.'

'They're piebald-looking beggars,' remarked Leo. 'What do you plan to do with them?'

'Keep them for their fleeces.'

'What do you want the fleece for?' Leo asked.

'You can spin it, knit with it, stuff pillows with it, insulate your house with it, the list goes on.'

'How do you plan to shear them?' Giles asked.

'By hand,' Charlie replied. 'I've bought hand shears and shears for dagging.'

'What on earth is dagging?' Leo asked.

'The dirty bits at the rear end.'

'Good God, what do you plan to do with those?' Leo asked.

'Soak them in water,' Charlie began.

'Don't tell me anymore,' said Leo. 'It sounds disgusting.'

'Have they plenty of water to drink?' Giles asked.

Charlie nodded, 'They've a bucket full, I've put it just inside their shelter.' He pointed to the small stone hut in the corner of the field.

Giles turned to Leo. 'Come on, let's sweep out the van and then get going.'

'Before you go,' said Charlie, 'would you take a look at the bedrooms and give me a quote?'

'What's your plan?' asked Giles as he followed Charlie towards the house.

'I need more bedroom space so I want to split the large bedrooms if possible.'

'How many bedrooms do you need?' Leo asked.

Charlie wiped his shoes on a patch of grass. 'Four.'

Leo did a quick mental sum. 'No way!' he said. 'I will not.' He grabbed Charlie by the arm. 'Are you listening? I will not share a bedroom, even in the event of the worst thing you could imagine, I will not share a bedroom with Maurice.'

Giles burst out laughing, 'He might not want to share one with you.'

'Charlie, there's no way I'll share a room with him, so don't go wasting your money on making bedroom space for me.'

'It would only be a temporary emergency arrangement. So what's your problem?' Charlie asked.

'Maurice is the problem. He'd zap me in the night and I'd wake up in the morning zombiefied.'

Charlie followed Giles up the steps and said to Leo, 'Then convert one of the goat sheds for yourself.'

Leo turned and looked at the tiny row of goat sheds. 'I'll think about it,' he said.

Giles studied both of the large bedrooms. 'They won't make huge rooms, they'll be cosy. The good news is that you'd have a window in each one.'

'Will it look obvious that we've split the original rooms?' Charlie looked around him. 'I want them to look untouched.'

'We can try to make them look like that,' said Giles.

'Another thing,' said Charlie, 'can you construct a grain store in the top section of the barn?'

Giles nodded, 'We could do that.'

'When?' asked Charlie.

'To be honest, work's tailed off, people haven't got the brass like they did have. I'm trying to keep it from Anita but between you and me it's getting serious.'

'I'll employ you. I need someone to help me, I can't do it all on my own and I don't want to fail.' Charlie looked him in the eye. 'Will you help me? I'll pay you the going rate plus your fuel to get here.'

Giles smiled, 'It seems the perfect solution to both of our problems.'

'There's a lot to do, plus new skills to learn.'

'Like what?' Giles asked.

'We need to learn so much in such a short space of time.' He looked out of the window. 'Shearing sheep for one.' He looked back at Giles. 'Developing an alternative energy system. Imagine living without electricity, how would we cope? How would we wash clothes, power a drill, lighting, the list goes on. It's daunting, yet we need to find a solution. We need to find something to fall back on. I don't want to leave it until the last minute and find that it's too late and that I've...' Charlie paused for thought.

'Fucked up!' added Leo. 'You need to start collecting useful bits of junk, cogs, bike bits, metal pipes, anything that could be made into something useful.'

'That's an interesting idea,' said Charlie.

'One of your better ones,' said Giles.

'You could hire me,' Leo said to Charlie. 'I'd come in really handy.'

'Go on, convince me,' said Charlie.

'You need someone who can think of new ideas, new ways of doing things.'

'Give me an example.'

'I could help you to produce some alternative fibre so that you wouldn't be completely dependent on Dicky and his dolly birds.' Leo pointed to the field.

'Like what?'

'Hemp.'

'It's illegal,' said Giles, dismissing the idea.

'It's not. You can obtain a licence to grow it,' said Leo.

'Carry on,' said Charlie.

'I could help you and Giles install a solar water heating system to provide hot water during the summer months so that you don't have to stoke up the stove.'

'Those are good ideas,' said Charlie. 'Have you anymore?'

'I have lots,' said Leo. 'But one thing is at the top of my list. It's something that I really want to do.' He looked at Giles.

'Laugh if you like, I don't care.' He looked back at Charlie. 'I want to keep bees.'

Giles went into the other bedroom. His laughter erupted and echoed around the house. 'Just ignore that,' Leo said to Charlie.

'I am. Do you seriously want to keep bees?'

Leo nodded, 'It's something that I've wanted to do for a long time.' He added, 'You and this wacky community that you unconsciously seem to be setting up will need honey.'

Charlie agreed, 'You're right, we need to keep bees.'

'But,' said Leo, poking him in the chest, 'I'll keep the bees but don't make me share a bedroom with Maurice.'

Charlie grinned, 'You can use the small room at the front. I had started to store stuff in there, but there's room for a bed and your things. Come and have a look, it's got a wonderful view of the mountains.'

Giles was standing in the doorway wiping the tears from his eyes. Leo stopped and asked, 'Feel better for that?'

'Much,' Giles answered as he wiped his nose.

CHAPTER 18

The earth rolled closer and closer to her destiny. Each passing moon pulled at her, began to re-shape her and helped her to remodel.

Within the realm of nature all functions are linked. Every planet gave forth a finely tuned impulse to speed and ease the earth's rebirth. Each star and planet in the galaxy and beyond is linked by these strands of finely tuned energy. This is the celestial web.

The earth, once on a destructive journey towards annihilation, was now moving to a place of redemption. It was re-linking with the web and becoming, yet again, a part of the divine plan.

It was returning to its rightful place within the safety and the salvation of creation and it was about to experience its creator.

It was a wet and miserable Sunday when Maddy moved in with Charlie.

Together they had loaded up the van with Maddy's belongings, locked up the house and secured the shutters. While Charlie sat in the van, Maddy visited the holy well for the final time. The well, now filled to the brim with water, spoke to her of the future and gave to her a wealth of hope.

'You're drenched,' said Charlie, as he put the van into gear.

'Soaked.' He looked at her from the corner of his eye.

Maddy smiled and wiped the raindrops from her face. 'But I'm fine.'

The van made its way along the wet country lanes. Fallen branches had been removed from the road and placed on one side. 'I wonder who did that?' asked Charlie.

'Someone with a definite need to get through,' replied Maddy.

Charlie laughed, 'It was me! When I came to pick you up this morning this stretch of road was blocked. It was either get out of the van and move the stuff or turn around and go home.'

'Was it a difficult decision?' Maddy asked.

'Terrible,' answered Charlie. 'I hope Maurice doesn't leave it till the very last minute or I'll never manage to get through to pick him up.'

'He travels light, and if the worse came to the worse, he'd get to you! But he won't leave the river until he has to.'

Charlie looked at the road ahead, the lower sections were now submerged beneath the rising river. 'It wasn't like this earlier,' he said as he slowed right down. 'We'll be alright further on, the road rises steadily.'

Maddy looked out of the passenger window. Spray from the front wheels splattered the glass with a mixture of mud and water. 'Slow down again,' she said. 'You're going too fast.'

'We're almost out of it,' he said with a smile, 'and the road ahead looks pretty clear.'

Leo helped Charlie and Maddy to unload the van. 'Where is it all going to go?' he asked.

'Put it in my room for now,' Charlie answered.

One by one the boxes were carried into Charlie's room and stacked in a corner. 'What do we do with this?' Leo pointed to a small chest.

'Just as a temporary measure could it go in your room?' Charlie asked.

Leo picked up the chest. 'It had better be temporary,' he said, adding, 'But I'll never know why it isn't going into Maurice's empty room.'

'Because he wants it to remain empty,' Charlie closed the van doors.

'Why?' Leo asked, adding, 'Oh don't tell me, it'll be something to do with bad vibes.'

Charlie followed Leo up the steps. 'Energy contamination is how he puts it.'

Charlie found Maddy unpacking a small box at the table.

'What's all this?' he asked.

'Lunch,' replied Maddy, 'I thought it would save us having to make something.'

'Looks wonderful to me,' examining a cheese tart he added, 'this must have cost a fortune.'

'It had been in the freezer for ages,' after kissing Charlie on the cheek she added, 'it was waiting for today.'

'So was I,' said Charlie, kissing her on the lips.

'Oh God! You two aren't going to be like this all the time are you?' Leo walked up to the table. 'What's that?' he asked, pointing to the flan.

'Lunch,' answered Maddy. 'Cheese tart, salad and fruit. Do you want some?'

Leo grinned and began to set the table. Charlie opened the large cupboard. 'I've been saving something for today.' He pulled out a bottle of wine.

'I didn't know that was in there,' said Leo.

'It was hidden,' explained Charlie.

As Leo continued to set the table, he asked, 'Did you bring the chess set?'

Maddy stopped what she was doing and thought for a moment. 'The board is down the side of one of the boxes and the pieces are in the same box. Do you fancy

142

a game?'

'He,' said Leo, pointing to Charlie, 'reckons that he was a gifted child who could play chess at four years old, and I would like to check that out.'

'Five years old,' corrected Charlie, as he opened the wine, 'and I will prove that to you!'

Maddy lit the small nightlight, placed it on the bedside chest and got into bed. Charlie closed the shutters and the window.

'It's hard to believe it's only September, it feels more like November. I hope it dries up and then we can get the wheat planted.'

Maddy patted Charlie's side of the bed. 'Come to bed and stop worrying.'

Charlie took off his slippers. 'I can't help it, I feel that I'm responsible for getting things organised.'

As he climbed into bed Maddy said, 'Well you are not, we are all responsible, all of us.'

'I could buy some more wheat, it's still possible to get hold of it.'

Maddy placed her hand over his mouth. 'Shhhh.' Slowly she lifted her hand and replaced it with her mouth. Charlie closed his eyes. Maddy traced his lips with her tongue and very slowly and gently she explored his mouth.

Charlie turned onto his side and stroked the wild auburn hair. He held a lock of it in his hand and kissed it. The smell of it reminded him of a warm lazy day spent making love by the river.

Maddy gently touched one of his eyelids and then the other. Her finger traced the line of his nose, the curve of his chin and the outline of his neck. Her hand reached his chest and then rested.

Charlie opened his eyes and whispered, 'Don't stop.' Maddy closed her eyes and with her mind, her hands and then her body, she made love to Charlie.

He remained quiet. He remained still, until the moment came when Maddy, vibrant and alive, showered him with the intensity of feeling. Their lovemaking moved between them, it wound around them and it bound them together.

'If you want to stay here and commit suicide, then that's up to you.' Steve grabbed her shoulders and looked her in the eye.

'But don't expect me to stay with you.'

Sylvie turned away from him. 'I can't leave this place. It's everything I've ever wanted and more besides.' She shook free of his hold. 'I think you are just being selfish. Always thinking of yourself.'

Steve held his hands up to the heavens. 'God give me strength.' He then looked at Sylvie. 'I'm thinking of you, I'm thinking of me. I'm thinking of us. OUR survival, can you understand that?'

'To be perfectly honest, NO!' She walked across the kitchen. 'I don't see things like you do and I do not want to go running off to Charlie's.'

'Listen!' Steve began to explain, 'The water level is rising, and you are aware of that, you're not stupid.'

'And it can go down again, just like the last time and the time before. If I remember rightly, you were the one who wanted to stay here then!'

'This isn't the same, Sylvie. The water level isn't receding. The land around us is turning into bog, it's saturated and the river is still rising.'

'If it's so serious, how come we are not on red alert?'

'I don't know, maybe they don't want folk to panic, who knows what the reason is.' Steve paced across the kitchen.

'Look, you like it at Charlie's, you have said that every time we have been up there. Anita and Maddy have offered to teach you things, things you'd enjoy.'

'Knitting!' Sylvie said drily. 'I could have stayed at home to learn that one.'

'Take the old sewing machine, you enjoy sewing.'

'Yes, and I could have done that at home.'

Steve began to lose patience. 'Then stay here in this guest house without guests, in this restaurant without food,' he walked over to the door and opened it, 'and without a chef.' He slammed the door behind him and added, 'And without a partner.'

The dream shattered. Sylvie looked around the kitchen, it seemed empty. The hopelessness kicked in. Hot tears flowed for what seemed like hours. Her head ached but her mind would not give up. It cried within her head. Images of what could have been and what should have been began to collapse.

Sylvie flung herself down on the table, she stretched her arms across the polished wood and like a child she began to sob.

Then resting her wet cheek on the table she gave way to the hopelessness and the sadness.

She didn't hear Steve come back into the room but she felt him touch the side of her face. He spoke almost silently to her,

'Come on, baby, let's go, there's nothing here for us anymore.'

Charlie stood back and admired the new cooker. The black cast-iron range was beautiful. He knelt down in front of the glass door of the firebox and said, 'We can watch the logs burn.'

Maddy studied the temperature gauge on the oven door.

'We shouldn't burn things with this,' she said tapping a finger on the gauge.

'I just love this,' said Leo, tracing his finger across the words cast into one of the small lower doors.

'Now you know why I wanted you out of the way!' said Charlie.

Leo moved a chair closer to the range. 'Sorry, I need to dry this sock,' he explained as he pushed his foot against the firebox.

'You need new wellies,' said Charlie. 'Anyway how did you two get on?'

Maddy brought a chair up to the range. 'It's fairly horrendous over there, but we made it.'

'Only just,' added Leo, rubbing his foot.

'We finished clearing the house,' Maddy explained. 'It's completely empty now. We also took a quick look at the garden, it's completely saturated.'

'It's turned into a bog,' said Leo.

Charlie looked at Leo and then back at the firebox. 'A wasted effort.'

'Not necessarily,' objected Maddy. 'You learnt precious things there.'

Charlie looked at her. 'I suppose so.' He asked, 'Did you see Maurice?'

Leo answered, 'I went down as far as I could but it was impossible to get to the clearing, there are tiny streams everywhere. The whole area looks so different, you wouldn't recognise it. I tried shouting for Maurice but he didn't respond.'

'He probably chose not to, he likes to take his own course, that's who he is,' explained Maddy. She added, 'On the way back we called in to see Giles and Anita, they're packing up but Giles is not too happy about it.'

'Oh, not another one,' said Charlie.

'He's only just got his workshop sorted out,' said Leo in defence.

'He can have one here,' said Charlie. 'I've told him he can use some of the barn. We can help him to set it up.'

'Mum's OK though, she'd begun to pack things over a week ago. The plants will take some shifting and they'll need to be replanted, she was anxious about that.'

'We can all help with that,' said Charlie. 'When are they hiring the truck?'

'Giles said he'd have a word with you about that.' Leo took off his sock and warmed his foot against the range.

'Put wellies on my list,' said Charlie. 'We all need new ones.'

'When do you pick the Landrover up?' Leo asked.

'Tomorrow,' Charlie answered, 'and I want to pick up some sacks of wheat on the way home, do you fancy the trip?'

'I could map read,' said Leo.

'That reminds me,' said Charlie, 'will you add maps to my list, it seems important to get maps while we still can.'

'But the area is changing,' said Leo, 'so what's the point?'

'We may need to know what the area was like originally, the old maps could be transformed into new ones.'

'Why are you getting rid of the v-dub?' Leo asked.

'It's hardly used and I thought we might need something with four-wheel drive.'

'Is the Landy in good nick?'

'Seems to be. The seats are rather uncomfortable, they've seen better days, but apart from that it seems fine. I just hope it will cope with the weight of the wheat.'

'We'll find out, won't we?'

'Is the wheat for planting or storing?' Maddy asked.

'Both,' answered Charlie, 'and we need to get some planted soon.'

'We can all help,' said Maddy. 'What we do need are regular meetings so that we can discuss things like this and make suggestions, iron out any problems.'

'That's a good idea,' agreed Charlie.

'How are you going to harvest the wheat?' Leo asked.

'With a scythe.'

'On your own?' Leo said in disbelief.

Charlie shrugged but didn't answer. Leo waited and then began to suggest, 'We need to get a number of scythes so that we can work together as a team. That's how they used to do it.'

'How did you know that?'

'I once had to study an oil painting which showed the lads and the lasses harvesting the wheat. Some were hard at it with their scythes and others were hard at it...' Leo paused for thought.

'Enjoying themselves!' said Charlie.

'Where's Sylvie?' asked Maddy.

'She hasn't come down yet.'

'Is she in bed?' Leo asked.

'I think so, Steve's up there with her, but apart from him she doesn't want to see anyone.' Charlie opened the firebox and threw in another log.

'She's very upset,' said Maddy, 'but she'll get over it. It will just take its time, and we'll all have to be patient with her.'

Leo changed the subject. 'How did the heating guys get this cooker up here?'

'They made it seem so easy. It was hoisted up here like clockwork.'

'What did they do with old one?' Leo asked.

'It's in one of the goat sheds, why?'

'It's got some good bits on it,' replied Leo.

Charlie turned to Maddy and asked, 'Do you like this cooker?'

'I think we all will,' she replied.

When Steve, Charlie and Leo had gone to collect the Landrover, the house grew quiet.

Maddy sat in the stillness and began to sew. Her tiny stitches repaired the piece of fine cloth. When she had finished sewing she stretched out the fabric across her lap and examined her work. The frayed edges were now barely visible, they had been made strong again.

'Can we speak?'

Maddy jumped, and turned to the direction of the voice. Sylvie stood in the doorway like a lost child. Her face, usually bright and rosy, was now pale and dim.

Maddy smiled and stretched out her hand, 'Come and sit with me.'

Sylvie walked over to the range but did not sit. 'What are you doing that for?' she asked, pointing to the sewing.

'It needed repairing.'

Sylvie walked over to the window. 'Why bother?' She turned to Maddy. 'You're wasting your time. You're all wasting your time.' After a silence she continued to speak, 'What do you think is going to happen? Do you think that you are special and that he,' Sylvie pointed to the heavens, 'will save you?' She shook her head. 'Get real! You are no different to the millions of people out there who will end their days taking their last breath in a sea of mud.'

'What do you suggest?' Maddy asked as she rolled up the fabric. When Sylvie didn't answer she continued, 'It's fight or flight.'

'Flight! Where to? The moon?'

'If that is the only place to escape then we might as well stay here and fight for our survival,' Maddy pushed fabric back into its bag, 'and that is exactly what I am going to do. I'm going to give survival one hundred per cent of my energy.' She stood up and put the bag of fabric onto the table.

'I'm going to prepare lunch. Will you be eating with us? Or do you have other plans?'

'You can really be a bitch! You think that you are so perfect, so holier than thou. It makes me feel sick. I'm up to here,' Sylvie drew her hand across her throat, 'with hearing you preach!' She sniggered and added, 'Tell me, wise one, what is mother nature saying to you now?'

Maddy walked up to her. 'She speaks of the past, of the present and of the future, they are all linked together. We are a part of that chain, we are responsible for what is happening now. We are part of the problem, each and every one of us.' Slowing her speech down, she continued, 'But we can be a part of the healing. It's a choice, and a choice we can all make. It starts here.' She touched the side of Sylvie's head. 'This is where the healing begins. It begins in the head and starts with simple words, "I will succeed" are three of them.'

As Maddy turned to walk away, Sylvie grabbed her by the arm. 'You once told me to live my dream, and I listened to you and I tried to do that. Now look at me. This is not my dream, it's my nightmare!'

'Then turn the nightmare into the dream.'

The pile of cards were face down on the table. Maddy picked them up and passed them to Sylvie. 'Hold them, shuffle them, do whatever feels right and then pass them back to me.'

Sylvie shuffled the cards and when satisfied that each card had been shuffled, she passed them back to Maddy, who turned over the top three cards and placed them on the table.

'All wands,' she said. 'The light bearers,' she explained, 'This card is symbolic of harmony. It represents the peace and satisfaction that harmony can bring. It can also represent the fruits of labour, the rewards of effort.' Pointing to the next card she said, 'This shows a very determined person, she is a person who means business.' Maddy pointed to the third card. 'This card depicts moving on, advancement, going forwards.'

Before Maddy could continue, Sylvie said, 'I understand what they are saying. I'm stuck in the past, aren't I?'

'You're not stuck, you are afraid of moving on. Pick a final card.'

Sylvie picked up the pack, shuffled it and then handed it to Maddy, who turned over the top card. 'The Empress,' she said. 'This is a strong woman who is concerned with the basic things of life. She is opportunistic and successful. She is the symbol of accomplishment and evolution. She is the sister, the wife and the mother. This is you, Sylvie, you in the past, the present and the future. It is who you are, who you have been and who you will be.' Maddy touched the card. 'You can live in harmony with others and with what lies around you. You can work with determination to make things succeed and you can move on. Just like the Empress you can walk into the unknown future with grace and dignity.'

'I thought it was the end,' said Sylvie.

'It's change. The end of the old and the beginning of the new.'

CHAPTER 19

The meeting had begun. Charlie gathered together the papers and then read aloud the various entries. 'Beekeeping equipment, spinning and weaving equipment, water filtration system, distillation unit for making essential oils, solar water-heating unit, solar lanterns, wind-up radio, scythes, axes, saws, hammers, spades and forks.' He looked up. 'Is that it?'

'I would have thought that was enough to be going on with,' said Giles.

'It's important that we don't forget anything,' said Maddy.

'There's bound to be something that we'll forget,' Leo contributed. 'Paper-making equipment and pens, we haven't mentioned these.'

Charlie passed him a sheet of paper. 'Jot them down.' He looked around the table. 'Has anyone else anything to add?'

'The plants we spoke about earlier, and the trees, but I'm not sure how they will cope with the wet ground.'

'Give them a chance,' said Maurice.

Charlie passed Anita a sheet of paper, and turned to Steve and asked, 'What about kitchen stuff?'

'A large soup pan and spare cups, dishes and plates.'

Leo leant forwards and said, 'Pottery won't last forever no matter how much we buy in. We need to be able to make our own.' He looked at Charlie. 'We need to build a kiln.'

'And how long will that take?' asked Giles. 'Haven't we got enough to do?'

Leo continued, 'All early civilisations produced their own pottery.'

'Some relied on wood,' said Giles.

'Leo, do you know how to make a kiln?' Charlie asked.

'I can find out.'

'It's important that we do not lose valuable information,' said Maurice.

Charlie looked around the table. 'Is that it now?'

Sylvie spoke quietly, 'You need a hand mill for the wheat.'

Charlie smiled at her. 'WE need a hand mill.' He added it to his list.

'No one has mentioned hobbies and pastimes,' said Leo.

Giles burst out laughing, 'What planet are you on? We have enough to do trying to learn how to survive without taking up a hobby!'

'All work and no play,' said Leo.

'What hobbies do you suggest?' Maddy asked.

'I don't know?' Leo answered. 'What's everyone into?'

'I'd like to get more musical instruments,' said Charlie.

'I've got my eye on a very nice violin and also a cello.'

'I enjoy doing jigsaws,' said Anita, 'the large tricky ones.'

'Jot that down,' said Charlie. 'Anything else?'

'Perhaps a good telescope,' suggested Maurice.

'I already have one,' said Charlie. 'You can use it if you wish.'

Steve pointed to the sheets of paper. 'You will have to try and order some of that stuff.'

Charlie nodded. 'Leo's helping me to track down suppliers.'

'Can you still obtain everything?' Maurice asked.

'For a price,' Steve said. Turning to Charlie he asked, 'Do we have enough money in the kitty?'

'There should be enough.' said Charlie. 'I'll work it out later.' Placing all the sheets together in a pile he then sat back and asked, 'Who wants to start?' He looked at Anita. 'You have concerns?'

Anita, not looking at anyone in particular, began to speak to them all, 'I know it seemed like an awful lot of herbs to plant, but they are vital. The lavender, rosemary, thyme, peppermint and the echinaceas are vital for our survival, they are a part of the "wild magic", the herbal medicine.' She paused and then continued, 'Imagine a world without doctors and without hospitals, what would we do when a minor infection develops into something more serious? At the moment we seek a cure but the real answer lies in prevention. If we are going to survive we must change our attitude and prevent illness.

The herbs we all helped to plant will not only help in treating illness, they will also help prevent it.'

Maddy leaned forwards, 'Hygiene is also at the root of preventing disease. It is crucial that we keep ourselves, our clothes, towels and bedding scrupulously clean. We can also fumigate the rooms and ourselves with herbs. We can make sure our washing is done daily and that everything is washed at a high temperature.' Maddy looked around the table.

'Hygiene is something we all need to consider seriously and constantly put into action.'

Anita closed the subject, 'We may only get one chance to get this right.'

Charlie asked, 'What happens when the big plug gets pulled out? Has anyone invented the alternative washing machine?'

'Not amongst us lot,' said Leo, 'But I did read about someone who powered the belt drive using a bicycle.'

Giles put his head in his hands, 'Idiots have landed! Who in their right mind is going to sit on a bicycle everyday and drive the washing machine?'

'Well, you come up with a better idea!' retorted Leo.

'We could go back to using a dolly tub,' said Anita, 'But I have no idea where you would get one from.'

'Can we all come up with suggestions for the next meeting?' said Charlie. He then said to Maurice, 'You wanted to say something.'

Maurice collected his thoughts and then began to speak, 'There is a link between each of us and the heavens. From the heavens comes the heavenly impulse. That impulse is a flowing creative energy which will imbue us with strength. It will strengthen the core of our cells and from that core the strength will radiate outwards and enhance our immune system. Our old immune system has grown weak, it has been constantly bombarded by the negative energies around us and within us. It is collapsing in on itself, it is imploding. We are destroying ourselves.' Maurice looked at Maddy. 'Cleanliness of the body is important, but also important is cleanliness of the mind.' He looked around the table. 'And cleanliness of the spirit is more than vital.' After a pause he concluded, 'Only when we are truly clean in mind, body and spirit will God come to us.'

'I suggest we start with Dicky, he'll lose his rag if we start with one of his women.'

'He'll lose his rag if we start with him,' said Giles. 'He's had it in for me since I pulled him out of the van by his horns.'

'I'm not surprised,' said Steve.

'Treat the animal with respect and he will be OK with you,' advised Maurice.

'Charlie,' Leo called. 'Dicky's going first, can we round him up now?'

Dicky was coaxed, led and manhandled into the corner of the field, where, much to his objection, he was propped in a sitting position against Steve.

'We aren't doing a full shear,' explained Charlie, 'it's the wrong time of the year. We'll just tidy them up a bit.' Then remembering everything he had read in the sheep manual, he began to shear.

Leo collected the fleece and placed it onto an old sheet. The daggings were done last, and much to Leo's horror he placed them in a hessian sack.

The ram regained his normal posture and his freedom. He ran quickly towards the females.

Charlie inspected his hand. Two large blisters had appeared.

'That's enough for today, look at the state of my hand.'

'I'll have a go,' Leo volunteered, 'but someone else will have to do the daggings.'

Leo, Steve and Giles took it in turns to 'tidy' the three females. The piles of fleece were rolled and bundled into clean hessian sacks. Charlie collected the daggings and placed them into what Leo had christened 'The Bag-O-Shite'.

Leo inspected his blisters, two of them had burst. 'Look at these!'

Charlie looked at the weeping flesh. 'Ask your mum to put something on them.'

Giles and Steve picked up the sacks and made their way to the gate. Leo walked alongside Charlie. 'Don't swing that around,' said Leo, pointing to The Bag-O-Shite. 'You'll spread germs.'

'This will make mighty fine fertiliser.' Charlie proudly held up the sack.

'You really are one hell of a sad git.'

The spinning wheel arrived a week later. With excitement Maddy opened the parcel. Then she opened up one of the hessian sacks and pulled out a large handful of fleece. She spread the fibres with her fingers. 'Look at the mixture of colours,' she said to Anita.

Anita fingered the fleece. 'I'm not sure what colour we'll end up with once it has been carded.'

'Can you feel the oil?' asked Maddy.

'Lanolin,' Anita said.

Maddy passed the carders to her. 'Go on, you have a go first.'

Anita made herself comfortable and following the instructions before her, she began to card the fleece. She pulled the carded fleece from the carder and made it into a small roll. She passed it to Maddy. 'What do you think?' she asked.

'The fibres are quite short, which could make it difficult to spin,' said Maddy. 'Charlie didn't do a full shear, so the length of this,' she examined the fleece, 'is about half of what it should be.'

'We'll have to learn the hard way,' said Anita.

Maddy took the small roll of fleece and sat in front of the wheel. Slowly she began to treadle the two foot pedals. 'Now for the hard bit.' Gently she fed the fleece into the opening.

The wool twisted, stopped, started and twisted again. Maddy stopped moving the pedals. 'The wheel has been christened!' The first strand of wool was far from perfect, thin in parts and thick in others. All the same it was beautiful. Maddy held it between her fingers and then passed it to Anita. 'We can only get better,' she said.

'I don't think the men will be getting socks for Christmas,' Anita said. 'We've not only to learn how to spin but then we've to learn how to knit them!' She got up from the chair. 'I nearly forgot to show you.' She opened the lid of the craft chest, pulled out a small wooden shape and passed it to Maddy. 'I found it this morning.'

'A wooden mushroom,' said Maddy. 'It's for darning socks.'

'Do you know how to darn socks?' Anita asked.

Maddy shook her head. 'I've no idea but we'll learn.'

Sylvie walked into the room carrying a tray of weak tea and toast. 'Have you tried it?' she asked as she put the tray onto the table.

'Maddy's had a go, do you want to be next?'

Sylvie shook her head. 'When you get proficient you can teach me.' She picked up the wooden mushroom. 'What's this for?'

'Darning socks,' answered Anita.

'It's like being in the war.' Sylvie put down the mushroom and picked up a piece of toast. 'Who's on bread making?' she asked.

Maddy picked up a cup. 'Leo, I think.'

'Good. There's hardly any left.'

'You haven't used it all?' asked Maddy.

Sylvie nodded and carried on eating her toast. 'We could make a batch of scones to go with the soup but the flour is down to the bottom of the tub.'

'You could mill some,' suggested Anita.

'It's not my turn,' said Sylvie. She then looked at Maddy.

'It's yours.'

'What time is the electricity due to go off?' Maddy asked.

'5.30.' said Anita. 'That gives us an hour to finish our tea and toast, mill the flour, make the scones and the soup. Then it's lights out.'

'I'm fed up,' announced Sylvie, 'really fed up.' Maddy began to laugh. 'It's not funny!' objected Sylvie. 'I am, I'm really fed up.'

'Well, why are you smiling?' Maddy asked.

Sylvie looked at Anita and Maddy. 'It's you two, you're sat here like two old spinsters and it's taken you all afternoon to spin hardly enough wool to wrap around a big toe, let alone knit a sock!' She took a sip of tea. 'And this tea is awful!'

When Sylvie went back into the kitchen she found Maurice at the table. 'Sorry Maurice,' she said. 'Will I disturb you if I use the hand mill?'

Maurice looked up from his notebook. 'Not at all.'

Sylvie took the lid off the grain tub, filled the scoop with wheat and emptied it into the small grain hopper. She placed the bowl under the mill and began to turn the handle. Flour slowly began to fill the bowl.

'Do you ever get fed up?' she asked Maurice.

Maurice looked over to her. 'I try to remain positive.'

'How can you when everything around you is falling to bits?'

'It's the key to survival,' Maurice answered. 'And it once saved my life.'

Sylvie stopped turning the handle and explained, 'I feel like I'm imprisoned here and that my old life has been taken away from me.'

'You're still alive,' said Maurice. 'You are having your needs met, you are healthy and strong. Those are very positive things. Perhaps it's just a matter of changing the way you see things.'

'That's not easy when day in, day out, it rains!'

'Not constantly,' said Maurice.

'Enough to get you down, and now we have these daily power cuts. It's grim.'

'You are better off than a lot of people,' said Maurice.

'Including my own family,' Sylvie stopped what she was doing.

'Is that the real reason for your upset?' Maurice asked.

Sylvie spoke quietly. 'Who up there decides who will live and who will die? Who decides what is going to happen and how can they decide?' She placed her hand on her forehead.

'My mind is filled to the brim with questions, questions but no answers.'

'If you let your mind be still you would hear the answers.'

Sylvie walked up to him. 'If I heard the answers and I didn't like them, I couldn't change things, could I? So what's the point?'

'Are you speaking about your family?'

'I want them to be all right, that's all.'

'Then ask for a blessing. Ask with the highest part of your mind and have faith. Whatever happens will be in accordance with the divine plan. It's outside your control.' He gently stroked her cheek. 'So let go.'

Charlie poked his wet and dripping head around the door, 'Have you seen Anita?'

'She's in the other room,' Sylvie answered.

Charlie took off his boots and went into the living room.

'This is why the wheat hasn't come up,' he said, thrusting his hand towards her, 'take a look at these.'

Anita inspected the grains. She picked one up and squeezed it gently. The grain turned to mush. 'It's rotten.'

Maddy walked over. 'Will it all be like this?' she asked.

'Most of it,' said Charlie, putting the grain into his pocket.

'And what has sprouted wouldn't feed us lot, that's for sure.'

'We aren't dependent on this though, are we? We've enough in store to last us for three years.'

'You don't understand,' said Charlie, looking at her. 'We need to replace the wheat we use and always keep a store.

Besides, it was a lot of hard work preparing the land.'

'It'll be easier next time,' said Anita, 'so don't get discouraged. Come and have a look at the wool industry, that will cheer you up.'

Charlie walked over to the wheel. 'The bobbins are empty.'

'Don't look at that, look at this,' said Maddy, showing him the sample of wool.

Charlie smiled. 'Our own wool,' he said.

Maddy twisted the wool in her fingers. 'You can feel the oils.'

'At least something has turned out good,' said Charlie.

'The land here is good,' Anita said. 'It has wonderful drainage and good soil. Too much rainfall has damaged the wheat.'

'I suppose it was to be expected,' said Charlie.

'You gave it a chance,' said Maddy as she slipped an arm around his waist. 'Next year we will have a bumper harvest.'

'Is that a hunch?' Charlie asked. Maddy smiled. 'Maybe.'

After a late supper, Leo set up the chessboard. He moved the candle between himself and Charlie.

'You'll never beat me,' said Charlie.

'I'm determined to,' Leo said. He pointed to the board.

'Your turn to go first.'

Maurice got up from the table. 'Mind if I use the telescope?'

'It's set up in Leo's room,' Charlie explained.

'Just go in,' said Leo.

Charlie made his move. Leo remembered how Charlie had opened previous games and he remembered Charlie's next move. By moving his pawn he blocked this possible move.

Charlie laughed. 'I'm not going to use that old sequence! I'm not that predictable.' Without delay he made his next move.

Leo thought for a short while and then made his move. Charlie rubbed his chin. 'An interesting move,' he said as he made his own move. 'But not clever.'

Leo found himself blocked. 'I didn't think that you would have done that.'

'You have tunnel vision when you play chess and you leave yourself wide open.'

Giles walked up and took a look at the board. 'He's got you by the short and curlies.'

'Shove off,' retorted Leo. 'I'm trying to concentrate.'

Giles cranked the handle of the lantern and when it was fully charged he took it into the living room and put it onto the table.

'That's better,' said Anita, 'now I can see what I'm doing, and I'm determined to master this.' She rolled up another section of carded fleece.

'She's trying to get the better of me,' said Maddy. 'Go on, show him my achievement.'

Anita passed him the small skein of spun wool. 'It's a peculiar colour,' he said.

'Pass it back to her,' said Maddy. 'When that wool has been transformed into a pair of lovely warm socks, I doubt you'll care what colour they are.'

'Where's Steve?' asked Giles.

'Upstairs with Sylvie, why?' asked Anita.

'I need his help in the morning, I can't work on the solar system on my own.'

'They've only just gone upstairs.'

'I'll give him a knock,' said Giles, 'and then I'm off to bed. I'm knackered.'

'Hey, Giles,' said Maddy. 'Before you go, help untangle this.' She passed him a badly tangled skein of wool.

'There isn't enough light in here, wait until the morning and you'll manage to untangle it.'

He was making his way upstairs when he heard Leo loudly exclaim, 'Fucking Hell, Charlie!' Giles smiled to himself.

The following morning Maurice watched Sylvie from the kitchen window. She split the logs without pausing. Time after time she raised the axe and brought it down on the logs. The split logs she threw into the logstore.

Never stopping for rest or a break, she carried on. Undefeated, with deliberate and powerful strokes, she split the logs. During all of this time, the rain constantly fell.

Slipping on his waterproof and his wellies, Maurice made his way outside. Sylvie heard him approach and wiped the rain from her face as she asked, 'What do you want, Maurice?'

'Can I have a word with you?' He pointed to the goat shed.

'We can shelter from the rain.'

Sylvie put down the axe and followed Maurice into the shed. They both stood in the doorway and looked out. 'Don't be too hard on yourself,' he said. 'There is no need.'

Sylvie took off her gloves and tucked them under her arm.

'That's up to me,' she answered. 'I am me and you are you.' Maurice was about to speak when Sylvie carried on. 'I feel such anger inside of me. I can't be like you and say prayers for people. I have to deal with it in my own way.' She turned to look at him. 'I am not divine.' She put on her gloves, then pulling up her hood she walked outside. For a moment she stopped and looked back at him. 'I am a human being.'

Charlie and Leo set off in the Landrover to collect the parcels.

'Is that what she said?' Leo asked. 'No more deliveries ever again?'

Charlie changed gear. 'Finito! If we want our mail then we will have to collect it ourselves, and this is happening everywhere in Europe.'

'I wonder what will happen to all the postmen?' Leo asked.

'I reckon that they will become a thing of the past, but at least mail is still getting to the post office.'

'For now,' said Leo, 'but I wouldn't bet on that lasting.'

'Looks like a sea of mud ahead,' said Charlie.

'It looks worse than that, there's been a landslide,' said Leo. The road ahead was completely blocked. Huge piles of mud, fallen trees and boulders formed a barricade. Charlie brought the Landrover to a stop. 'I don't want to get any closer, it could still be unstable up there.'

'What do we do?' asked Leo.

'Go back,' answered Charlie.

Leo pulled a face. 'We can't do that, it's the beekeeping stuff. No bees, no honey, no wax.'

'Well, what do you suggest?' Charlie asked.

Leo pointed ahead, 'The post office is less than a mile away, if we could climb over this lot then we could walk it.'

'It's pouring down,' complained Charlie.

Leo poked at Charlie's jacket. 'It's waterproof and so are your boots.'

Leo scrambled over the fallen trees, the boulders and the piles of mud with Charlie following behind. 'This is dangerous, another lot could come down on us.'

'Keep going,' said Leo, 'we're nearly over it.'

With boots, trousers and jacket full of mud, Leo stood and waited for Charlie. As he climbed over the last fallen tree, Charlie broke wind.

With a grin Leo said to him, 'You should never force a fart.'

Charlie walked up to him, 'No?'

'No,' said Leo. 'You could follow through.'

Amidst the rain and the mud, Charlie began to laugh. He laughed so much that Leo wondered if he was ever going to stop. 'It wasn't that funny,' said Leo.

'It was,' said Charlie, getting his breath back. 'Here we are, you and I, it's pouring down, we are soaked to the skin, filthy with mud, we have a mile to walk to the post office, society is breaking down, there's worse to come and you instruct me on how to fart!'

Leo stared at him. 'It's surreal, isn't it?'

CHAPTER 20

As each day passed it left a mark. That mark etched deeply into the land, sky and sea, and into the consciousness of man.

Nothing and no one escaped the power of nature. Nature was regaining control. As she released her power, turmoil, tragedy and trepidation became the norm. Her reclamation and rejuvenation turned every day into an unexpected array and chain of events. Climate change had now become incomprehensible, it was outside human understanding.

The rolling ball of ultimate change was heading quickly towards its own fruition and there was nothing, nothing at all that man could do to prevent the final destiny.

Bubbling unconscious images, archetypes of ancient times, emerged, and like the unseen map of the cosmos, they drew on their roots and left clues in the minds of man.

A thread of the new 'world' wove itself around all primitive thoughts and moved those thoughts forward. Subconsciously man was on a journey and the journey was taking him far beyond the confines of his mortality.

With the earth under his feet and the skies above his head, man was changing. He was becoming a complete part of nature. Creation was restoring order.

Charlie closed his notebook and in the darkness he sat deep in thought. Far from being empty, the darkness brought inspiration, creativity and clarity.

Giles sat by the window and stared out into the night. The light of the moon was barely visible. It was hard to imagine that this now quiet and peaceful sky had only minutes earlier bombarded the senses, ripping wide open the senses of sight and hearing.

'Maybe that was the last?' said Charlie.

Giles turned from the window. 'Who knows when it will end.'

'I think we'll know when it's all over and completely finished,' said Charlie quietly.

'It isn't yet though is it?' asked Leo, leaning back in his chair and resting his feet on top of the range. 'You can tell that there's more to come, you can feel it.'

'I should go and check on the sheep,' said Charlie, getting up from the table.

'Sit back down,' said Giles. 'They're OK in the barn. You'll only disturb them if you go in there.'

Charlie sat back down. 'I suppose you're right.'

'What were you writing about?' Leo asked.

'I don't know if it makes any sense,' said Charlie. 'When the storm was tailing off it felt like something was placing words into my head.'

'That happens to me sometimes,' Leo explained. 'But I don't get words, I get images. I try to memorise them so that I can transfer them onto canvas, but more often than not they disappear. In a strange way they always seem familiar.'

'The words felt like that. It's as if they have always been a part of me, yet I can't remember ever hearing them spoken or seeing them written.'

Giles looked at Charlie. 'Read some to me.'

In the dim light from the range Charlie squinted at his notebook. 'Never shall the eternal man destroy his own path.' Giles turned and looked back out of the window. Alone with his thoughts he felt safe, they didn't seem strange or prophetic, they were normal, and that sense of normality brought comfort.

Leo spoke quietly to Charlie. He spoke to him about the realms of his own imagination. 'It's what drives an artist, it's something outside rational thought. It's the creative intellect or function,' he paused for thought. 'It's one more way for the universal creative mind to manifest itself.'

'A pathway,' said Charlie. He asked, 'Do you miss your artist friends?'

'I miss being with them, but our paths will cross again.'

'Do you miss Sion?'

'It may sound strange, I wouldn't say that I think about him, it's more like he dwells inside of me and he seems to be with me or a part of me for most of the time.'

'Love has no boundaries,' said Charlie.

The turbulent weather and the continual rain changed the days. It stripped away normality.

The structure of society was crumbling and disintegrating. Its foundations, so totally and completely dependent on technology, were ceasing to be. The great wheels of the man- made machine were grinding to a halt.

But amidst the chaos and beyond the power of man, something vital and real was taking place. Something was awakening.

Quaking within the movement of the shifting earth mass, new life was transforming the surviving elements within its wake.

The deep, ever-silent and ever-present core of the earth had ruptured and had brought to the surface particles of the potential new life. Those particles reached out towards the skies, they reached out to and joined with the stabbing shafts of light. From the heavens the lightening connected and joined with those particles. Seeds of new life formed and began their journey to heal and revitalise the earth.

The earth was being made whole.

Alone, Leo stood by the window and closed his eyes. The time had come. No longer was the scene playing in his mind, it was happening as he knew it would.

Rolling around the planet, the waters of life and death were fulfilling the prophecy. They were living their role as both the givers and the takers of life.

Every cell in his body felt the charge of energy as it crashed, rose and moved above and below. No part of anything was left untouched, everything, by the nature of its subtle energy, was being integrated.

The skies had ripped open and deep within their secret place, a sacred sound called. Leo heard it. It was the golden sound he had longed for. The sound flowed in that precise moment and reconnected the earth, man and the heavens.

Leo felt the joy as his spirit became free. Loosened and unbound, his spirit was lifted by the divine call. It was lifted, nourished and nurtured.

The one single pain carried by all men was finally being healed. The fall of man was almost over.

The new celestial phase was moving man beyond the fall, it was moving him into his rightful position. Dwelling with his feet treading carefully on and with the earth and with his head always touching and being part of the heavens, man was about to become heir to the original plan.

Leo opened his eyes. The darkness of the day or night was being fractured by the constantly shifting energy. It was being illuminated by the light.

Leo glimpsed and then acknowledged the changing light. It had formed, almost crystallised itself and the land, bathed in this light, was awash with living colour.

Leaving Maddy alone with her thoughts, Charlie quietly closed the bedroom door.

Maddy lay back on the bed and allowed her grief to surface. Tangled emotions emerged and dragged with them images from her childhood. She could hear Martha's laughter and she could see her smiling eyes. The images captured and stored since childhood replayed one by one.

The memories moved on in time and finally pulled from the archives the most recent of memories. Martha, beyond childhood, beyond middle age, turned her head towards Maddy and as her car drove away, for the very last time she said goodbye to her sister.

Martha and Michael had braved the elements together and together they had witnessed the overwhelming power of the great tide. That single tide had curled around them and had carried them far beyond the reaches of any man. Together, clasped in each other's arms, they had died.

The cameo of them both linked as one within the huge swollen belly of the ocean pronounced itself. This most recent image of her sister replaced all previous ones.

Steve helped Sylvie to give the sheep fresh water. On the advice of Maurice, the sheep had been moved from the barn and had been rehoused in the cellar. This had spared anyone from having to go outside.

Steps from within the house led down into the cellar. Steve held up the lantern as Sylvie made her way down the steps. The sheep greeted them with eager anticipation.

'You've got enough hay,' Sylvie said as she stroked the head of one of the sheep.

Steve refilled the bucket of water. 'We'll have to clean this lot out,' he said, pointing to the soiled bedding. 'It stinks.'

He opened the gate to the pen, went inside and began to rake the bedding into a pile. When the sheep realised that he wasn't going to give them anything they left him alone and focused their attention on Sylvie.

From her pocket she pulled out a piece of stale bread. Steve shook his head. 'You could have eaten that, dipped in your soup it would have been fine.'

Sylvie smiled and broke the bread into pieces. One by one she fed the sheep a small piece. 'Leo and I used to feed Monty like this. Every morning that donkey would get the left-over pastries, it was better fed than any of us!'

Steve laughed and shovelled the heap of bedding close to the door. 'I wonder what has happened to Monty?'

Sylvie didn't answer. She stroked the head of one of the sheep. 'You are safe in here. Safe, warm and well fed.' The sheep nuzzled inside her pocket and searched for crumbs.

'Don't let me forget to take some logs back up with me,' Steve pointed to the log pile.

'Do you think they'll last?' she asked.

Steve looked at the pile, 'Let's hope so.'

Giles sat quiet and still as Anita wound the wool around his hands. When she had finished she helped him to slip the hank of wool from his hands, then tied it carefully. 'That's the last of the fleece, we've definitely spun the lot!'

Giles moved over and made room for her on the settee.

'What will you do now?' he asked.

Anita sat down. Looking at the light from the lantern she said, 'That's not bright enough to read by so I guess it will be early nights.'

Giles wrapped an arm around her. 'We could have early nights together.'

'We have got single beds!' she reminded him.

'I made them so that they will link together,' Giles laughed.

Anita turned and looked at him. 'Did you really?'

'Give me ten minutes and I'll show you,' he said, getting up from the settee. Before going out of the door he repeated, 'Ten minutes.'

The two single beds clicked together smoothly, as Giles knew they would. He replaced the pillows and the quilts, got undressed and climbed into bed.

The now familiar sound of the raging storm, the rattling shutters and the roar of the wind did not disturb him anymore. His hearing, now almost selective, chose not to hear the sound of the chaos outside, instead he concentrated on the tapping of his fingers. He tried to remember the tune and the lyrics to the song 'Paperback Writer'.

Halfway through the second chorus Anita opened the door. The dim light from the lantern illuminated the now joined single beds. 'Come on, my lovely,' he said with a grin.

Anita threw back the covers and inspected the beds. 'You are really devious!'

Grabbing her arm he pulled her down onto the bed and began to kiss her neck. 'Get in.'

'Just wait will you? I'm fully dressed.'

'Not for much longer!' he said with a laugh, as he hurriedly began to remove her clothes.

Within the privacy of his room, Maurice did not eat or sleep. Lying completely still, and almost without breath, he entered the slipstream.

Conscious of consciousness and of unconsciousness he moved between the two, and by the act of mediation he helped to connect the two realms fully.

Energy flowed down through him and found its root deep in his subconscious and then deep into the earth.

Energy travelled upwards, coursed throughout him and found its release through his connection with the eternal.

Throughout the tumultuous days and nights Maurice continued to help forge the link between the heavens and the earth. He knew that it was by this bridge alone that the future man would find his true salvation.

Transfixed, Charlie watched the radiant skies from the kitchen window. The spectrum of colours flowed and formed an array of constantly moving rainbow light.

'It's beautiful,' said Leo.

Speechless and unable to form an objective observation, Charlie, like a child, continued to stare wide-eyed into the night.

That very night, so precious and magnificent, announced through the full spectrum of its radiant and majestic beauty that the time had finally come.

Leo closed his eyes, and without doubt or disfigurement of truth he spoke for that precise moment, and in that very holy sacred point in space, time spoke through him.

The sacred quiet time spoke the words, 'It is over.'

CHAPTER 21

From the kitchen door he could see Maddy, alongside her stood Giles, and together they were sowing seed. Everyone else had gone foraging.

Maurice closed the door and went back inside. His papers lay scattered on the table, he gathered them together and sorted them into groups. He re-read the top page.

The top page concerned the new law. Maurice read the words aloud, 'There will be no suffering for any living thing. There will be equality for all living things. All will live in harmony with the surrounding nature. Man shall seek to maintain honesty. He shall maintain purity of mind, body and spirit. Man will fully acknowledge the living god. Man will assist the process of creation.'

He sat back in his chair as he remembered the precise moment when the course of his life had shifted. That new direction was marked in his mind by the words he had heard at the time, 'You have received the call.'

That calling had led him into the future. It had led him to help create a new and fully abundant, integrated world.

As the image of the future formed in his mind, he felt the chains of the old world slowly begin to dissolve.

He felt the freedom of nature and he felt the richness of its core now firmly rooted into the earth.

He was aware of the stability and the safe movement of the earth under him and around him, and he felt the heavens, so close, so familiar and undeniably alive. The light of that living energy, constantly flowing and renewing itself, created the link. Man was finally regaining his position within the passage of the creative living dynamo. He was being made whole.

In its wake the floodwater had uprooted and misplaced many things. Some of these things could be repaired or re-used. It seemed important not to waste anything.

Steve and Leo scrambled part way down the steep slope towards the shed. 'We'll never get it up here,' said Leo, looking down at the partly demolished shed.

'It's the roof that could be useful,' said Steve, scrambling towards the shed. 'Come on.'

Partly walking and partly sliding, Leo followed Steve onto the ledge where the shed had found refuge.

Now resting on its side with its roof almost hanging free, the shed had, along with other things, ground to a halt. As Steve inspected the roof, Leo searched amongst the debris for anything else of use.

Tugging hard at the roof Steve called out, 'If we both give it a tug it'll come off completely.'

Leo went over and took hold of one of the corners. Together they tugged and pulled until the roof broke free. Placing it on the ground, Leo asked, 'How the hell do we get it up there?'

'We fasten this rope to it,' answered Steve as he began to unravel the rope from his rucksack, 'and then we drag it up.' Leo walked over to a child's football, which like the shed had found a resting place on the ledge. He stood still and began to think about the child.

Steve watched him for a moment and then called, 'Don't think about it.'

'You can't not think about it,' answered Leo.

'Come and help me,' said Steve.

Together they spent the rest of the afternoon dragging the shed roof up onto the higher ground, once there they were able to pick it up and carry it between them back along the track towards home.

Bleary-eyed, dazed and semi-confused, he began to walk again. As he shifted the position of the bag from his left to his right shoulder, the pain across his back lessened, but still he could not stand completely upright. His knees felt locked in the position they had been forced to endure for so long.

He couldn't remember those days, they had either been erased by shock or the memory had been simply lost.

What was now a vital thought, a thought greater than anything else, was to find a place of safety.

Roads before him did not resemble roads, fields too had been transformed. Together they had become a jumbled mass of earth, rubble and stone.

In a state of almost sleepwalking, he walked on. He walked on oblivious to the carnage, oblivious to the sight and smell of decay and he walked on oblivious to the remnants of his lost life.

'Do you want any help?' asked Giles. 'I've finished mine.'

Maddy smiled. 'No, I'm quite happy.' She opened out her hand. 'I've only got these few left.'

Giles left Maddy to finish planting her seeds and he walked over to the edge of the field. From the gap in the trees it was possible to see down into the valley and across to the other side. Although the floodwater had greatly receded, many houses in the lower valley were still submerged.

He could see a number of cars dotted along the edge of the water. At first it seemed as though they had been parked in a random fashion. He then noticed that many of them were either on their sides or with their bellies up.

Across on the other side of the valley a huge mass of sludge had formed. From a distance it looked like a large brown lake with its surface glistening in the afternoon sun.

Maddy walked up to him, 'No sign of anyone?'

Giles shook his head. 'You'd think we'd spot some sign of life but there's nothing.'

'When it's safe we can search further afield,' Maddy said.

'When do you reckon that will be?'

Maddy looked up at him. 'When the earth has settled,' she said, adding, 'It would be foolish to go too far before then.'

Giles pointed to the glistening brown lake. 'What do you reckon is in that sludge?'

Maddy shrugged, 'Mud, sewage, diesel,' she paused, then added, 'And maybe a cocktail of chemicals.'

'That's what I thought,' said Giles.

'But they are breaking down quickly,' she explained. 'Their molecular structure is changing rapidly, it's altering, and soon toxic waste will have been completely neutralised. It will become harmless.'

Giles shook his head. 'I believe what you are saying but at the same time I find it hard to believe.'

Maddy sat on the ground. 'We are moving from one phase into another and have one foot in the old world and one in the new. That's why some things seem confusing right now.'

'It's a period of transition,' said Giles as he sat down beside her. 'Isn't it?'

Maddy nodded. 'Transformation,' she added, 'And just as the earth is changing, so are we.'

The night sky closed her curtains and hid the moon and the stars from the earth. As darkness masked the disorder it brought with it the sweet familiar realm of unconsciousness.

Sleep came to the walker, who, huddled alone in the back of an abandoned car, found comfort in the semi-sentient world.

His dreaming mind cart-wheeled through the scenes and images that his waking mind could not bear witness to.

As the dream formed it dragged with it cries of death and it dragged with it the thunderous roar of nature as she twisted and turned. The sounds merged as one and culminated in the cry of release. The mother was being reborn.

The crumbling walls around him fell as they had fallen and the weight of a million years rested on him. He felt the earth's shift, he felt it twist and turn and then in the strange quietness, he felt his own life.

He moved through the dream. He moved on as a broken man, ragged and raw. He moved through and across the disassembled fragments of the civilised world. Those separate pieces did not make sense, having neither function or normal appearance, they created disorder. The map had been destroyed.

Searching, he scurried rat-like over and through the disarray and far beyond the stench of final decay. He breathed the air. He clutched with the mighty power of his lungs at the precious jewel and it gave him life.

The dream somersaulted and tipped him backwards and forwards through time. His lover, naked and in the throes of ecstasy, drifted beyond reach, drifted beyond life.

Time clicked onwards like the rapid fire of a gun and the dreamer was projected like a missile into the heart of the future. It was here that logic gave way to insight and brought the tumbling down of reason.

The illuminated scroll unravelled and the dreamer placed a hand on its upper edge and pulled it down into his mind.

Waking, he slowly stretched out his legs as far as they could stretch, and turned to face the daylight. Still tired and weary, he moved slowly. Searching within the bag he found two small chunks of bread, carefully he replaced one of them, the other he broke into tiny pieces. Each of these pieces he deliberately chewed for a long time, releasing from them as much nourishment as he could. Swallowing the bread made him aware of the dry rasping roughness of his throat and the great need for water.

Leaving the temporary shelter of the abandoned car he hoisted the bag onto his shoulders and went in search of clean water.

Steve lit the fire under the metal tub while Sylvie fetched the bundle of dirty clothes. Using a makeshift posser she pushed the washing into the tub. 'It's full to the brim,' she said.

Steve looked into the tub. 'It'll be OK. I'll keep my eye on it if you want to go and do something else,' he offered.

'I wouldn't mind,' she said. 'I hate this job.'

Steve smiled. 'I know, you make it quite obvious.'

'Do I?' she said, as she began to walk away.

'You know you do! Off you go but don't be too long.' Sylvie smiled at him. 'Can't someone else rinse and peg out?'

'It's your turn,' said Steve.

'How long will it take to get the washing machine going?' Steve shrugged. 'Giles didn't think it would be much longer, but he's got a couple of problems to solve.'

In the kitchen Sylvie found Leo at the table, with eyes red and watery. 'Give us a hand with these onions, will you?' he asked.

Sylvie took over. She sliced and diced quickly and efficiently and in next to no time the onions had been reduced to a pile of fine pieces.

Leo watched with disbelief. 'You don't mess about do you? And how come your eyes aren't watering?'

'Because I haven't rubbed them,' she answered as she placed the onions into the soup pan. 'What else is going in here?'

Leo rubbed his eyes. 'Turnips.'

'Oh, not again,' said Sylvie, 'is there nothing else?'

Leo shook his head, 'They need using up, they're going rubbery.'

'And they taste like it too,' she said as she put the box onto the table. 'Catch!' she said as she threw one at Leo.

The turnip, narrowly missing his head, smashed against the wall behind. Leo looked at the splattered turnip. 'They're not that rubbery,' he said.

Sylvie laughed and then asked, 'Do you fancy a game of rounders later?'

'If I get time,' Leo replied. 'I want to spend some time with the bees.'

'What do you do with them?' Sylvie asked.

'Watch them,' Leo replied, 'get to know them. I like to study their flight paths.'

'Do you not get bored?'

Leo looked at her in amazement, 'They are the most fascinating creatures on this planet!'

'I'd be bored stupid,' said Sylvie as she peeled the turnips.

'Well, that's you, isn't it?' said Leo, 'and we are all different.'

'Some are off the scale,' said Sylvie.

Leo stopped dicing the turnips. 'If I didn't know you well I could take offence at that.'

'That's why I said it!' said Sylvie.

Leo carried the pan over to the sink and began to fill it with water. Sylvie walked up to him, gave him a hug and said, 'I love you the way you are. Now go on tell me about your bees.' Leo took the pan over to the range and placed it on the hotplate. 'They have a hive mind,' he said.

Sylvie leant back against the sink. 'Do they not have their own minds?' she asked.

Leo nodded. 'They do, but they actively belong to a higher order. That order bubbles through into their individual minds. It's all important for their survival, and they survive as a group or a unit.'

'Like us,' said Sylvie.

'It is,' agreed Leo. 'It's their flight paths that really amaze me. They shift and alter course like the planets. They are actually influenced by the planets.'

'How do you know that?' asked Sylvie in disbelief.

'They've been studied. Their flight paths are linked to planetary influence. In short, the bees are linked to the cosmic order as well as being linked to the order of the hive and they are obviously linked to the earth as well!' Leo smiled. 'Come and watch them with me sometime, you'd really get into it,' he added. 'It's amazing what you can pick up from them.'

'What kind of things?' Sylvie asked.

Leo tried to explain, 'If you are willing to try to listen to them you can hear what they have to say.'

'I can't understand that,' said Sylvie. 'All I can hear is their buzz.'

'There's more than that,' said Leo. 'Come with me sometime and I'll show you.' Looking out of the window he then said, 'Steve's flapping his arms around down there, I think he's having problems.'

Sylvie made her way to the door. Before leaving she asked, 'Aren't you supposed to be helping Giles?'

'That's another story,' said Leo. 'We've had a disagreement. He wants to do it his way so I've left him to it.'

'Go and help him,' said Sylvie, 'and get that washing machine working. I can't stand having to poss the festering dirty washing in that smelly steaming tub for much longer. It's disgusting!'

Leo watched Steve. 'It looks like he's not too happy about it either!'

On her way down the steps Sylvie stopped, turned and looked at Leo through the window. Very slowly she blew him a kiss.

When she had gone Leo set the table, put on his work boots and went outside. He found Giles in one of the goat sheds.

'How's it going?' he asked.

'It isn't,' said Giles. 'The bicycle idea has failed.' Wiping his hands on his trousers he added, 'Completely failed.'

'Are you giving up with it?' Leo asked.

'No I'm not giving up, the idea needs modifying, that's all.'

'Do you want any help?' Leo asked.

'No, but I reckon Charlie could do with your help. He's around the corner trying to make another logstore. He's using the old shed roof and from the sound of it I reckon he's failing.'

Leo laughed. 'He's useless with a hammer.'

'I agree, so perhaps he would appreciate your help.'

Leo found Charlie red faced, puffing and blowing. 'Are you all right?' he asked.

'Do I look it?' said Charlie.

'To be honest you don't. You look like you're about to burst a blood vessel!'

Charlie passed the hammer to Leo. 'Here, you use this while I hold this in place.' Charlie picked up the corner of the roof and placed it onto the post.

Leo hammered the corner of the roof into place then together he and Charlie worked on the other corners. When it was finished Charlie stood back. 'That will make a great logstore.'

'How many more logs do we need?' Leo asked.

'Another two years supply needs to be split and stacked so that it can dry out.'

'I thought we had next year's logs?'

'We have but the logs for the following year need to be drying out. They aren't efficient if they're damp. Then come autumn we will have to cut trees for the year following. We need to be organised,' said Charlie, adding, 'which reminds me, Maurice is planning a meeting for tomorrow.'

Leo helped Charlie to collect his tools together and asked, 'What's the meeting about?'

Charlie grinned. 'I don't know but I've got an idea that it won't be anything of a practical nature.' Picking up his tool box, he asked, 'How's Giles getting on?'

'Awful,' answered Leo. 'I did offer to help but he sent me off to help you.'

'It's a good job you did. I'm wiped out!'

Leo took hold of the tool box. 'Come on Buster Blood Vessel, you've done enough for today.'

Maurice's meeting took place around the kitchen table. Without delay he launched into his speech, 'I speak to you all as members of my family. We are each in our own way aware of changes taking place. I don't mean the obvious changes, I mean the unseen.

Those changes are affecting us all, every single one of us. Even as I speak and as we sit around this table the changes continue and will continue until the point comes when we are all fully linked to the divine creative force.

We are a link between the heavens and our planet, the new energies flow between the two. They flow between the heavenly father and the earthly mother, we stand between the two, and we are linked to them both.

As we continue to absorb the new energies we will become more aware of our place. We will become more aware of the sacred celestial tide and its effects on us will bring us into a state of balance. To live in such a state of harmonious balance will bring balance not only into our person but it will affect everything we do and everything we do will have an effect on the whole of the future.' He paused, collected his thoughts and then continued, 'The planet is preparing itself for its holistic future and we are a part of that future.

Not only are we augmenting spiritually but we are also changing physically. Some of us are aware of the subtle changes taking place, others are not, but that doesn't matter, for even if you are not aware, the changes will continue to take place.

The molecular structure of our physical self is augmenting, it is altering its vibratory rate. We are becoming stronger as our immune systems yield a greater defence. Damage within our systems is being repaired.' Maurice looked around the table. 'I know that's a lot to take on board right now.'

After pausing he then continued, 'If you reject the thought of this change it will not alter the effect. The new energy is within us and it is reforming us.'

He handed out the identical sheets of paper, one for each person. The heading on each sheet read, 'The New Law'.

He explained, 'There are laws within the whole of nature, within the whole of existence, and new laws go hand-in-hand with new energies.

The laws that I have listed are only a vague guide, for the true laws are within each and every one of us. Follow your own true laws, not the laws I have set out. Follow the ones you have been given. These laws are within your own heart and soul.' Maurice got up from his chair. 'Thanks for listening.'

A moment later he had gone back to his room and had left his extended family in complete silence.

Leo broke the silence. 'Phew!' he said.

Anita got up from the table and moved the kettle onto the hotplate. 'I think we could all do with a drink.'

Giles spoke quietly, 'He can make sense of things which seem so senseless.'

Sylvie looked at the list of new laws then placed it on the table. 'We are all here for a reason,' she said. 'We haven't survived for nothing.' She pointed to the paper. 'I think those things are a good enough reason for being here, and to be honest, it's what I feel inside.'

Charlie spoke next, 'For me it feels a great and wonderful honour to be in this place and time. I don't know what I feel inside but...' he paused for a moment, 'it borders on pure joy.' As the evening wore on, an atmosphere of happiness, contentment, joy and peace flowed between them all.

The usual daily chatter and banter resumed, except for one moment when Charlie stopped speaking and stared at the wall. 'What on earth is that?' he asked.

'It's some turnip,' said Leo.

CHAPTER 22

In his search for clean water, the walker began to climb. Leaving behind him the open wound of the earth, the deep fissure that had ripped open the floor of the valley, he slowly began to climb.

He climbed out of the rancid stench that had collected and filled the valley basin. He climbed beyond the reach of scavenging animals who in their search for food had threatened him. He climbed away from what had always been his safe home and he climbed away from his old self.

Unstable crumbling rock slowed down his progress almost to a stop, but the need for water pushed and moved him onwards and upwards.

His hands, unused to the coarseness of the rough ground, bled. His knees, still semi-locked in the position of their seemingly endless endurance, grew hot with pain. His mind, bombarded with unceasing images and sounds, gripped hard the one thought, water.

The flood, with majestic power, had taken from his reach the many things that he had taken for granted, water was one of them.

As he scrambled slowly higher, loose rocks and debris fell into the open wound of the earth. The walker stared down into the seemingly bottomless pit as it devoured them whole.

The bag across his shoulders weighed heavy and it too seemed drawn, almost magnetised, down towards the wound of the earth. For one moment he considered letting it go, letting it fall. Drop. With the weight gone he would be able to climb easily, but without the bag he knew he could climb but then on reaching the top he would reach no further.

The bag was his lifeline. It was his only chance of survival and the weight was his salvation.

Putting himself back into the state of sleepwalking he climbed numbly, unaware of the pain, unaware of the thirst, unaware of anything. He, like Lazarus, pushed beyond unconsciousness and the grave and went in search of life.

Resting on a tiny ledge he drifted between the two realms of death and life, and caught in the balance between the two points, he journeyed.

The journey was initiated by two guides. On his left side the male guide took hold of his arm and on the right side the female guide held him. Together they gently led him to a narrow path which lay between the two worlds.

They supported him, held him in the safety of their presence and they began to walk with him. The narrow path undulated and stretched into the distance. Together they walked this distance.

At the end of the path towered a great and marvellous city, a city like no other. The walker watched in awe as its huge crystal walls radiated waves of pulsating light.

A door opened within the wall. Concerned for his safety, the walker held back. His two guides slowly moved forwards and together they guided the walker inside.

Once inside the walker was mesmerised. The inside of the crystal city was filled with a huge pool of liquid light. He knelt beside the pool and began to drink. He drank until he had quenched the unbearable thirst that he had carried for so long.

Back on the ledge he awoke and in that flash of awareness he knew what he had seen and experienced. He knew with his mind, body, soul and heart that he had seen the New Jerusalem.

Charlie watched as the sunrise filled the land with her light. He loved to sit and watch the tiny droplets of early morning dew being transformed into pearls of light.

His favourite spot was on the edge of the woodland. Here was an abundance of spider webs, catching the dew and the light, becoming living works of art. Charlie was fascinated by their diversity. Each web was different in size and unique in composition. The rainbow pearls of light pinpointed and illuminated the beautiful structures.

Charlie looked towards the distant mountain range. Its form, bathed in moving mists, was ethereal. Pastel shades blended together and touched the land around him.

He placed his hand on the ground and felt the peace of the earth. It connected with the peace within himself, and looking towards the sun he felt connected to the whole structure of life.

Almost silently Maddy walked towards him. When she reached him she sat down next to him. 'I thought I would find you here.'

Charlie smiled at her and then looked back towards the mountains, 'It always looks so special, so pure and clear.'

'Very soon the whole planet will be like that, pure and clear,' adding, 'all of the time.'

Charlie turned to her. 'That was the original intention, wasn't it?'

Maddy nodded, 'We are all here to make sure that it happens this time. We have the experience of the past and insight into the future. These are our gifts and they are also our tools.'

'I sometimes think that we wouldn't have made it if it hadn't been for you.'

Maddy looked puzzled. 'Why?' she asked.

Charlie looked back at the mountains. 'On the night of the midsummer party you triggered something off. It was as if you awoke something inside of us all. You were like a beacon or a lighthouse shining its light into the darkness.' He turned to her. 'We all saw it in our own way.'

Maddy remembered the night of the party. She remembered clearly the moment when she had given reverence to the sun. The sun, she knew, was the true beacon. She was about to explain but Charlie stopped her. 'There's no need to explain.'

'Then let me show you with my mind.'

Charlie closed his eyes, cleared his mind and made space for Maddy. Her pictures formed slowly in the haze within his mind. On the blank hazy screen he saw an image begin to take shape.

Light from the sun formed the image. A whole landscape was being formed and transformed as the light brought to life every part of it.

Charlie watched as a group of trees transformed. The energy within them spilled out. Not contained in trunk or branch, the energy radiated from them. Catkins hanging from the branches became luminous and hung like delicate lanterns.

As snow began to fall, Charlie could see that it too was made up of light. Thousands and thousands of snowflakes were transformed into thousands and thousands of tiny crystals, each one beautiful, each one unique.

Maddy showed Charlie the valley. He watched as it too became crystallised. The intensity of the colours, the blues and the violets, astounded him.

As the image disappeared Charlie opened his eyes and Maddy explained to him, 'Through the transforming ability of the subtle energies, the earth is becoming a crystal planet of light.'

Charlie looked up to the heavens. 'Like the other celestial bodies out there.'

Steve wanted to have a little bit longer in bed. 'It's Sunday,' he said, 'and it's warm and cosy in here.'

Sylvie threw back the covers. 'Come on, get up or I'll go without you.'

'Sylvie!' objected Steve as he pulled the covers back up.

She began to dress. 'Ten minutes,' she said to him, 'or I go on my own.'

'You won't,' said Steve from under the covers.

Sylvie knelt on the bed and pulled the covers down from his face. 'I will!' she exclaimed.

Half an hour later she had washed, eaten breakfast and was on her way across the courtyard with her rucksack.

Steve called from the steps, 'Wait. What's the rush?'

Sylvie stopped, turned and waited for him. 'If we find some we can get back and add them to the pot for lunch.'

Steve walked alongside her. 'Did you bring gloves?' he asked.

'Only one pair,' she said.

'It seems a lot of trouble to go to just to add something green to the soup,' Steve said.

Sylvie carried on walking. 'Nettles are full of vitamins and minerals and the young ones will clear out our systems. Besides, there's not much else right now.'

'It's a pity we didn't get the chance to pick the walnuts or the chestnuts.' He bent down and picked up a chestnut. He opened it with his thumbnail. 'They're all rotten like this one,' he said, throwing it to one side.

'We'll get the chance this autumn,' said Sylvie.

'We can store the walnuts in the cellar, but we'll have to try and dry the chestnuts.'

'Giles was on about that,' said Sylvie. 'He said we need to get organised. I can't take it all in sometimes.'

Steve agreed, 'Neither can I. My thoughts are often with my mum. I keep wondering if she has made it, if she's survived.'

'That's how I feel about my family. I can't bear this not knowing, always wondering and imagining what could have happened to them. I feel gutted inside.' Sylvie began to fill up with tears.

'Let's change the subject,' said Steve. Looking across the valley he said, 'When we can get over to the other side maybe we will find other survivors. There's bound to be some.'

Sylvie walked on in silence. The track narrowed and wound its way around a small spring. Water trickled from between the rocks and filled a tiny pool. Steve bent down. 'Look at these,' he said, pointing to a clump of fresh green leaves.

'What are they?' Sylvie asked.

Steve picked one of the leaves, took a sniff and passed it to Sylvie. 'Wild garlic.'

'It smells wonderful,' said Sylvie, pushing the leaf into her mouth.

Steve picked the rest of the leaves and put them into the rucksack. 'The bulbs will shoot new leaves so we can take these.'

Cupping his hands he took a drink of fresh springwater.

'Should you do that?' Sylvie asked. 'Maurice said we should still filter all drinking water. It might not be safe.'

Steve finished drinking. 'It seems fine and clear to me.'

'I hope so, otherwise you've had it.'

They continued walking along the narrow track. Eventually it wound its way into a small thicket. Here Steve spotted a clump of young nettles. 'Take a look here,' he called to Sylvie.

Sylvie joined him. 'They're perfect, aren't they?'

'We used to treat these with such little respect,' said Steve as he put on the gloves and began to pick the nettles.

Sylvie sat on the ground. 'It's like we are having to learn the old wisdom,' she paused and then added, 'the hard way.'

'Maybe we shouldn't have forgotten it in the first place.' Steve closed the rucksack. 'Come on let's get back and then we can finish having our Sunday rest.'

The horrendous retching sounds from upstairs could be heard clearly in the kitchen. Leo eyed his soup with suspicion.

'What's in this soup?' With his spoon he pulled out a long piece of green vegetable matter. 'What's this?' he asked.

'It's a nettle,' replied Sylvie as she carried on eating.

'It doesn't look like one to me.'

Sylvie looked across at him. 'Oh that, that's wild garlic.'

'Are you sure?' said Leo, showing the piece to his mum. Anita smiled. 'I checked everything that went into the soup.

That bit is definitely wild garlic.'

'Well, what's up with him?' Leo asked.

Sylvie stopped eating and put down her spoon. 'It's the water. He drank the water. He drank from the spring.'

'How far down were you?' asked Maurice.

'Not far. We were near the small thicket.'

Anita got up from the table. 'I'll make him some peppermint and slippery elm tea.'

'I told him he was being stupid but he didn't listen.'

'I'm sure he'll be OK,' said Maddy.

As Anita climbed the stairs the retching sounds ceased and Steve came out of the bathroom. 'Are you all right?' she asked.

'I feel a bit better now,' he replied, 'but my legs feel like jelly.'

Anita opened the bedroom door for him. 'Come and sit on the bed, you look ever so pale.'

Steve sat down. 'I feel pale.'

Anita passed him the cup of herb tea. 'Here, this will ease things.'

Steve took hold of the cup and began to take small sips. 'I should never have gone out. I felt ill as soon as I woke up.'

'You mean you were ill before you left home?' Steve nodded. 'Could it be a bug?'

'Probably, we have all been waiting for one to appear. But in future if you feel ill say something and then we can treat it straight away.'

Steve looked at her. 'I'm sorry, I've put you all at risk, I should have said something.'

'Drink that up and then get into bed. Do you still feel sick?'

Steve shook his head. 'Just very tired, that's all.'

Anita went over to the door. 'I'll bring you another drink in a little while. Just keep warm.'

Returning to the kitchen, Anita explained to everyone that it seemed like Steve had picked up a bug and that he had felt ill before leaving the house. 'We are all at risk of catching it,' she said.

'So what do you suggest we do?' asked Charlie.

'We can take some precautions.' Anita sat at the table. 'We can wash our hands regularly and we can also take cups of peppermint tea to help ward it off.'

'I thought that was for wind,' said Giles.

'It is good for wind, but it is also anti-viral,' she explained.

'You've lost me,' said Giles.

'It will help hit the bug on the head,' said Anita, 'but if any of you get gastric symptoms let me know straight away, and you can have some slippery elm bark.'

'When you strip a tree of its bark does the tree actually survive?' asked Charlie.

Giles answered, 'If you are very careful and make sure that you don't strip the bark in a ring around the trunk, the tree will survive.'

'How many elms did you plant?' asked Charlie.

'We planted ten, seven have survived, the other three were damaged in the storms.'

'Have the other trees survived?'

'It looks like we have lost some of the junipers, we'll just have to wait and see, they may pick up.'

'I had a good look at the fruit bushes,' said Charlie, 'they look worse for wear.'

'Any sign of lambs?' asked Giles.

Charlie shook his head, 'I didn't really expect any this year, the sheep have had too many shocks.'

'Haven't we all,' said Sylvie. 'It's left us all feeling...'

'Bleak,' said Leo. He washed his hands and went outside.

Sylvie followed him. 'Wait,' she called as she ran down the steps. 'Leo, wait for me.'

Leo stopped walking and turned around. 'Leave me alone Sylvie.' He paused and then added, 'Please.'

Sylvie walked up to him, 'Leo, it's hard for us all.'

'Do you think I don't know that?' he said, and then carried on walking.

Sylvie kept pace with him. 'Let me finish. It's hard for us all but we have got each other.'

Leo stopped walking. 'You have got Steve, Charlie's got Maddy, Mum's got Giles, Maurice has got God, who have I got?'

'You've got all of us,' she answered.

'That's not what I mean and you know it.'

'Talk about it.'

'For the first time in my life I not only found myself but I found my true love. This situation has taken it all away from me.'

Sylvie stood in silence and then said, 'It won't be long until we can all get out and about again and then you'll be able to go and look for him.'

'And what do you think I'll find?' When Sylvie didn't answer Leo continued, 'Get real Sylvie, it's not fairy land out there, it's hell.'

'Leo, don't, we all have loved ones out there, all of us.' Leo wrapped his arms around her. 'I shouldn't have said that, I'm so sorry, I was being completely selfish.'

Sylvie looked up at him. 'Why don't you ask Maurice? He'll know if Sion's still alive.'

Leo knocked twice on the bedroom door. 'Maurice, can I come in?'

Maurice opened the door. 'I thought it might be you. There's a chair by the window, come and sit down.'

Maurice sat on the edge of the bed and looked at Leo. 'I know why you are here, I was expecting you sooner.'

'Can you help?' Leo asked.

'I will help you access the information you want but you must help me in return.'

'Help you? I can't even help myself. Some days I'm on cloud nine and other days I'm in the depths.'

'You are adjusting, it will take time, be patient.'

'How can I help you in return?' Leo asked.

'Your vision, Leo, your complete vision of the future, share it with me.'

Leo looked down and studied his hands. 'The view of the completed new world, that's what you mean, isn't it?'

'Share it with me,' asked Maurice.

Leo became deep in thought. 'I will share it with you after you have shown me Sion.'

Maurice walked over to the table and lit a small piece of candle. Standing behind Leo, he placed his hands at either side of his head.

Maurice began to breathe slowly and deeply. His breath took him to the threshold. Here, familiar to the passage beyond the threshold, he waited.

He waited and with every endless breath he slowly moved Leo towards the threshold.

As the threshold opened, Maurice guided Leo into the realm where journey was possible. Light illuminated the passage. In the safety of that light Leo travelled onwards.

Far across and beyond the barriers of time and space he gravitated towards his love. Here he found Sion. Sion was alive. He was alive and he was waiting for Leo.

Love feeds. It nourishes. It brings life. It is life. As Leo and Sion renewed themselves, regenerated themselves, they made themselves whole.

Maurice sat back on the bed and waited. Slowly Leo returned. He opened his eyes and watched as the tiny remains of the candle burned away.

Unable to sleep, Leo tossed and turned in bed. His restless mind, filled with a multitude of images, could not find the peaceful space where sleep dwells.

He got out of bed, pulled on a jumper and went over to the window.

The clearness of the night had transformed the sky. The stars and the planets, known and unknown, filled the vast and endless night sky.

Through the telescope he searched for the constellations but they eluded him. He was instead fascinated by the shapes and forms which remained nameless. Man had not claimed these.

He wondered how many true constellations were out there, how many pinpoints of light to influence us?

'And we influence them,' he said to himself.

Then he realised the importance of the survival of the planet. He realised why the great cleansing and healing had been necessary. He realised that, without doubt, his new world view was in reality something far bigger and far greater than his own mind could ever imagine.

CHAPTER 23

'We need to get moving.' Anita looked at her list. 'There's a lot to be done. The greenhouse needs finishing, so that we can sow tomatoes, lettuce, cucumbers and celery.' She looked at Charlie. 'We're falling behind, and if we're going to be successful and grow our own food then we need to get the timing right.'

Charlie looked at the list. 'The garlic's in and so are the early potatoes.'

'Turn the page over,' Anita told him.

Charlie read the list aloud. 'Outdoors we need to sow beetroot, beans, cauliflowers, leeks, lettuce, onions and shallots, spinach and turnips.'

'Not turnips,' groaned Leo.

Charlie grinned and carried on reading, 'We need to sow parsley, lovage, rosemary and thyme.' He looked at Anita.

'Haven't we got enough thyme?'

'They form an important medicine,' she replied.

'Well, we'll split the list up, who wants to do what?' he asked.

'Just tell us what you want us to do,' suggested Giles.

'I'm not being director.' Charlie pushed the list over to Giles. 'You have a go.'

Giles looked at the list and began to designate the work.

'I'll finish the green house,' he added.

Anita told everyone, 'When you sow the seed, keep to the garden plan, you know where it is.'

'Is the ground ready now?' asked Maddy.

'More or less,' Anita answered.

'You haven't given me anything to do,' Leo said to Giles. Giles smiled and pointed to the list, 'Turnips.'

'Can I make a suggestion?' Sylvie asked. 'Can we move the compost bin nearer to the house? It's a heck of a walk.'

'It's not the best spot,' agreed Charlie, 'but the second bin will be closer.'

Giles began to get up. 'Not so fast,' said Anita, 'we need to think about protecting the fruit crops.'

'We haven't got any,' commented Leo.

'We will have and they will need protecting.'

'You want me to make a framework, don't you?' Giles said to her.

Anita smiled and then nodded. 'Have we got enough netting?' she asked Charlie.

'We have two rolls plus the stuff you brought with you.' Anita looked around the group and said, 'Bear in mind that these seeds are important. The plants they produce will not just feed us this year but hopefully they'll produce the seed we will need for the following year. Don't plant them too deep or too shallow.'

Charlie stood and watched as Maddy planted her seeds. Each seed was given both time and consideration. The task of placing the seed into the earth seemed endless.

Without looking around she said, 'I know you're watching me, Charlie.'

Charlie moved along the line of the seed drill and stood beside her, 'Do you always know?'

Maddy looked up at him, 'Most of the time, and so do you.' She smiled and then asked, 'Have you finished your seeds?'

'I finished them ages ago. You are taking forever.'

Maddy stopped planting. 'The seed is a living thing,' she looked at the tiny seed in the palm of her hand, 'it is linked to the higher forces and the seed mirrors those forces.'

Charlie knelt beside her, 'Can you teach me to see those forces?'

Maddy moved a small section of earth, planted the seed and then carefully covered it. 'You do see them, we all do.' She looked at him. 'Just take time to notice them. Slow yourself down and quieten your mind. Move your chattering thoughts to one side and you will then have the space. The sacred space. Find the sacred space within you and you will then find the higher forces.' She kissed him and added, 'It's in there!'

After planting his seeds in record time, Leo went to sit near the hives.

The bees seemed more active than usual, more industrious. Leo wondered where they were finding the early spring pollen.

Their flight paths did not seem any different, yet the bees were definitely finding a greater quantity of nectar and pollen.

The main flight path headed into the woods and it was here that Leo decided to take a look. He knew that their flight could take them a couple of miles from home but he didn't have to go very far to find what the bees had discovered.

As he entered the wood, he saw that the shady floor before him had become home to a carpet of early flowering violets and primroses. The bees had made this discovery long before anyone else.

With Steve's help, Giles completed the work on the greenhouse. Anita called to them from the garden, 'Don't forget the potting bench.'

'It looks like we're not quite finished here,' said Giles.

'Where does she want the bench?' Steve asked.

'The far end of the greenhouse, I think.' Giles picked up one end of the bench, and as Steve picked up the other end he said, 'Oh, let's leave it here.'

'She won't be happy with that, come on, let's put it where she wants it.'

Together they moved the bench to the far end of the greenhouse. When they had finished, Giles asked, 'Do you fancy giving me a hand with the fruit cage?'

Steve pulled a packet of beetroot seed from his pocket, 'I've got these to plant.'

'I'll give you a hand with those later.'

The fruit bushes formed a square in the corner of the garden. The bushes, blackcurrant, redcurrant and gooseberry, needed to be protected from the birds.

'What's wrong with a good old-fashioned scarecrow?' asked Steve, as he helped Giles to carry the posts and supports.

'They don't work,' replied Giles. 'The birds get used to them and there's nothing more frustrating than seeing the birds ignore the scarecrow and completely strip the bushes of their ripening fruit.'

'This alternative,' said Steve, 'looks like a big job to me.'

'If we can get the frame in place, we can cover it with the netting tomorrow and I'll sort a door out later.'

Steve helped Giles to measure the fruit bed and together they knocked the tall posts into place. 'This is the crucial bit,' said Giles, 'we need to make sure that the posts have a firm footing so that they don't keel over.'

'This is really not my forte,' said Steve.

'And cooking isn't mine,' laughed Giles. 'In fact I detest it.'

'Do you?' asked Steve in surprise.

Giles nodded. 'It's everyone to their own. We all have our own skills and they are all important in their own way.'

'The education system didn't think like that,' said Steve. Giles walloped a post with his mallet. 'Thankfully that part of the system has gone and hopefully it will never come back.'

'You sound like you didn't enjoy your school days.'

'I didn't,' said Giles. 'They seemed a waste of time.'

'They taught you how to measure your wood,' said Steve.

Giles stopped what he was doing. 'I reckon I could have worked that out by myself.'

'I detested school too,' admitted Steve. 'I found it very humiliating. A rough school in a rough area doesn't bestow you with much self-esteem.'

Giles passed the mallet to Steve. 'You don't have to use it, just hold it for a minute.'

Steve continued, 'Mind you, Charlie's top-class school didn't provide him with much better.'

Giles inspected the posts. 'Kids need to learn from what is around them. Nature, growing veggies, learning how to use tools, learning how to look after things and make them last. I'm glad the education system has gone. It's the end of a mistake.'

'Well let's hope we get it right this time,' said Steve.

Having left Maddy to her painstakingly slow method of planting, Charlie went to survey the field of pasture.

It was here that the wheat had failed and it was here that it would have to survive if they were going to have fresh grain to store.

The thought and prospect of preparing the land again by hand filled Charlie with dismay. Here he was, Charlie the luddite, wishing for a machine.

The regret at not having some kind of mechanical assistance troubled him, and the solution troubled him even more.

A small voice inside his head spoke to him, the voice he had heard many times before. The voice was never wrong. It said to him, 'Go and find a working animal.'

The thought of wandering around the barely recognisable countryside, on foot, searching for a working beast, not only troubled him, it dominated him, yet he knew it was something that he had to do.

He put the idea to Steve and Giles.

'You are completely mad,' said Giles. 'It wouldn't just be like looking for a needle in haystack, it would be like trying to find a haystack to start with.'

Charlie asked Steve, 'What do you think?'

Steve gave it some thought, 'It does sound a crazy idea, but it also sounds like it might be a good idea.'

Giles shook his head. 'Madness,' he said.

Steve pointed out to him, 'We wouldn't be here if he...' Steve pointed at Charlie, '...hadn't believed in and followed those thoughts of his.'

Charlie looked at Steve. 'Will you come with me?' he asked.

'Don't I always?' said Steve.

The house, once the happy home of many generations, now housed no one. Shutters and roof slates lay broken amongst the debris from the storm. The walker stepped over them.

As the door pushed open, the room exhaled a stale and rancid air. The walker dropped his bag and walked over to the sink. He turned on the tap and began to drink.

With impaired vision he then began his urgent search for food. Mice had eaten all that they possibly could, but they had left behind the untouchables, a small stock of tinned food.

Relying on his touch more than his vision, he found an opener, opened one of the tins and using his torn and blood-stained fingers, began to eat.

He pulled from the tin small pieces of pate, pushed them into his mouth and swallowed hard. Being unused to solid food, the pate formed a lump in his throat and would not budge.

He walked over to the sink, turned on the tap and drank again. Within seconds the mixture of water and solid food began to rise from his stomach. Suddenly the contents of his stomach were violently expelled.

Through the haze of everything he had seen, everything he had heard and everything he had done, he searched his mind for anything that could help him. Then he remembered.

He remembered the faces in the book. The faces had survived their own hell and like he, they too had been unable to eat solid food. To save them, they had been given very small but regular amounts of semi-liquid food.

In the tin, he mixed together water and the pate. Then slowly, very, very slowly, he took tiny sips of the precious semi-liquid food. Then closing his eyes, he slept.

In the depths of his sleep he heard the footsteps. He heard them tread on the broken slates, but the sound became diffused, stretched out and altered. He no longer heard the footsteps, for they were now a different sound.

That altered sound entered his dream and punctuated the endless miles that his sleeping mind had walked.

Never reaching the point where the sleepwalking ended, he continued over and across the miles of abstract earth searching for the one thing that had once made sense of his waking life.

As the footsteps faded into the distance the sleepwalker was left alone in the endless search for himself.

Steve caught Charlie up. 'How many abandoned places are there?'

'Your guess is as good as mine, but there's an awful lot down there,' he said, pointing into the valley. 'Some are still submerged.'

'Lost forever,' said Steve. He then pointed to the deep cleft to the side of the valley bottom. 'That's weird. I've never seen anything like it before.'

Charlie stood next to him and looked down. 'I wonder how deep it is.'

'I don't want to find out,' said Steve. 'There's an emptiness here, a sadness.'

'It's depressing,' said Charlie. 'Let's go further on.'

They walked until the narrow track came to an abrupt end. A huge landslide had completely transformed the land in front of them. The landslide had pushed into the valley a large chunk of mountainside and along with it the main access route.

'There's no way that we can get over there,' said Steve. Charlie looked across. 'We've got to get over there somehow. There's a good chance that the farm over there will still have their mules.'

'You don't know that. They could have packed up and gone, mules and all.' Steve surveyed the land. 'How on earth would you get a stubborn mule to cross this?'

'There'll be a way,' said Charlie. 'It's persuading you to cross it that's my immediate problem.'

Steve looked at him, 'You never give up, do you?'

Charlie studied the ground in front of him and worked out a possible route across. 'There is a way,' he said.

'What if the ground under our feet decides to move into the valley and take us with it?' Steve shook his head. 'No way. It's foolish.'

'That's your logical mind telling you that. I'm not following logic, I'm following intuition and my intuition is telling me that it's safe to cross.'

'You are telling me to ignore my logic and listen to your intuition?'

'All I am saying is that I will follow my intuition, it's up to you what you listen to.'

Charlie scrambled onwards, climbing slowly and carefully across the fallen boulders and freshly moved earth. Steve followed gingerly behind.

A mound of loose stones fell away and plummeted into the valley below. 'This is unstable,' said Steve.

'It was only a few loose stones,' Charlie replied as he carried on.

When they had eventually reached the other side of the landslide, both men sat on a grassy bank and rested. Steve was badly out of breath. 'We are not fit,' he complained.

'I feel OK,' said Charlie. Looking at Steve he added, 'You need to build up those lungs.'

'I'll never manage to repair the damage that I've done.' Charlie looked at him and then back into the valley. So much had changed. So much had been damaged and so much was in need of repair. 'They'll get better,' he said to Steve.

'Is that logic or intuition?' asked Steve.

'Both,' Charlie answered, 'and that's as good as it gets.'

It was dusk when they returned home. Maddy ran down the steps to greet them. 'We've been worried about you. You should have said how long you were going to be.'

'We didn't think we'd be this long. But we have come home with wonderful news.'

Steve walked through the door and kicked off his shoes. 'It is pretty good,' he said.

Leo, asleep in front of the range, woke up when he heard Steve's voice, 'Do you have to make so much noise?'

'Where are the others?' Charlie asked as he took off his shoes.

'Playing cards in the living room,' Maddy answered.

'Come on,' said Charlie, taking hold of her hand. 'I want you all to hear this news.'

'Come on, Leo,' said Steve.

Charlie began to explain to everyone, 'As you know, we went in search of an animal to help us plough and what we found is pretty incredible,' he smiled and then continued, 'We made our way...'

'Precariously,' chipped in Steve.

Charlie continued, '... to the large farm near the lake. We had a difficult time getting there because a landslide has taken a large chunk of the mountain with it as well as the main access route. But we made it. When we got to the farm we were greeted by other survivors, six of them, including the farmer and his wife.'

'They survived!' said Giles in amazement.

Charlie nodded, 'And they are doing well. They have a good stock of provisions, a brilliant store of wood and plenty of hand tools.'

'And like us,' said Steve, 'they have their own supply of water.' He added, 'It was amazing actually to see other human beings! We stared speechless at each other for ages.'

'It was disbelief,' said Charlie.

'Who are the other four survivors?' asked Maddy.

'Neighbours from the far side of the farm,' answered Charlie.

'There are others too,' said Steve. 'They've been trading eggs with survivors who live on the other side of the lake.'

'So we are not alone!' said Giles.

'And now for the other news,' said Steve. 'They still have their mules, which we can borrow in exchange for some wheat.'

'Brilliant!' exclaimed Sylvie.

'It all seemed so unreal,' said Steve, 'and it still does.'

'What did you expect?' said Leo. 'Did you think that we were the only people left on the planet?'

'No,' said Steve, 'but it's been such a long time, a long time of wondering and never really knowing if there are others out there who are surviving like us.'

Leo asked, 'Is it safe to go out now?'

'The danger is not what you can see, although that is bad enough, it's the unseen things like infection. If we pick up an infection it could easily wipe us all out,' said Charlie.

'You should have a shower,' said Anita, 'and change your clothes.'

In the twilight kaleidoscope world within his head, the walker heard, for the first time in many months, music.

It came from a deep recess in his mind, formless at first, it drifted. Then, weaving itself into a discernible pattern, it became recognisable.

As the walker listened, the form carried with it solid waves of sound. The sound was a memory. Uncaptured, it breezed through and beyond his conscious waking mind.

As it faded it left behind one single reverberation. It left behind the vague recollection of who he was.

He was PJ.

CHAPTER 24

The bee and the sun were powerful symbols of life regenerating itself, and the new life was linked to both.

As fecundity began to bathe the earth, the shadow of its darker self began to fade. Healing had begun.

What had been lost was beginning to be replaced with something totally new and completely unique. There was magic in the air and the bees noticed the magic before anyone else.

The veil which normally separated the different dimensions was slowly being removed. A new reality was being born.

Maddy prepared for the midsummer celebration. She didn't need to check the perpetual calendar for the date, she could feel the solstice with every cell of her body.

She walked into the garden and called out to Charlie, 'Will you help me collect the salad?'

Charlie, deeply engrossed in weeding the young carrots, didn't hear her. Giles, who was walking close by, did.

'Maddy's shouting for you,' he said.

Charlie looked across the garden and gave Maddy a wave.

'Two minutes,' he called and then went back to weeding. 'This job is sending me loopy,' he said to Giles. 'The young carrots look just like the weeds. I've already pulled up a handful by mistake.' Looking at Giles he asked, 'You wouldn't finish off here would you?'

Giles walked over to the bed of carrots and knelt down.

'You owe me one.'

Charlie picked up the bundle of young carrots and made his way down towards Maddy. 'Here,' he said to her, 'put these in the salad.'

Maddy smiled and put them into her basket. 'Will you help me to collect the salad?' she asked.

'What's ready?' Charlie asked.

'Tomatoes, lots of lettuce, tons of radish and two cucumbers.' Charlie walked beside her to the greenhouse. 'No peppers?'

Maddy shook her head. 'They're too tiny yet,' she added.

'Anita's collecting the leaves from the herb garden. She says there's an abundance of chives and plenty of spring onions.'

'What are spring onions doing in with the herbs?'

Maddy put down her basket next to the door. 'She had some empty space and so she has filled it with a variety of things.'

'That's clever,' said Charlie, opening the greenhouse door.

'It's less room for the weeds,' he inhaled deeply, 'I love the smell in here.'

'Tomatoes,' said Maddy. 'Come and look at them.' She led him to the rows of ripe and ripening tomatoes. 'This one is perfect,' she said picking a small but perfectly ripe tomato. She put it into Charlie's mouth. 'Is it good?' she asked.

Charlie closed his eyes and savoured the taste, 'It's wonderful, it really is.'

Together they picked the ripe tomatoes, the two cucumbers and the lettuce. Maddy showed Charlie the radishes. 'Look at this lot,' she said. 'They are all ready at once. If we leave some they'll go woody and taste too hot, so we'll have to use them all.'

Charlie thought and then said, 'We need to stagger the sowing and then we won't get a glut like this.' As he helped to pull the radish he asked, 'What are we having for our meal?'

'A bean salad, a huge one. Steve's picking the beans. We've got an abundance of French beans and lots of broad beans.'

'It's a pity about the peas,' said Charlie. 'They were full of mildew.'

'We are bound to have some losses,' said Maddy.

When they had finished collecting all the produce for the salad, Maddy turned to him and said, 'Can I ask you something?'

Charlie looked at her and waited. 'Have you noticed a different energy around the place?' she asked.

'We've all noticed it, perhaps not as strongly as you or Maurice, but we've been aware of it.'

Maddy took Charlie's arm and they began to walk back to the house. 'We are moving towards something sacred,' she said.

The imminent need to find food was pushing him closer and closer to his greatest fear, the outdoors. Hostage to his own fear, he had not ventured outside since arriving at the cottage.

His memory of the outside world was a memory filled with pain, confusion and disbelief. The jagged scenes of destruction haunted him, they filled his days and his nights, and the torment which he endured he linked to the outside world.

The final tin of food had been eaten. His food supply had come to an end and intensive searching by misty eye and damaged hand revealed nothing more.

He drank the water, but the pang of hunger would not be satisfied by water alone.

He walked over to the window. All was quiet now, but the quiet could not be trusted, for it harboured the chaos.

He paced to and from the window, walking, walking the miles again. He clawed at the wall, climbing, climbing again, and he submitted himself to the pain, the grief and the loss.

Curled upon the floor, he wept. Then, clutching at the root of his driving hunger, he transformed his weeping into one single raging howl. The sheer force of that animal need to survive blasted open a doorway within his mind. The doorway let in the light, and the light dissolved his fear.

Battered, broken and beyond recognition, PJ grabbed his bag as a talisman, left the house and began a new search for life.

Giles showed Anita the young trees. 'Every single one of the willows has rooted.'

Anita examined the saplings, each one had come to life and had produced leaf. 'They'll make beautiful trees.'

'Useful,' Giles corrected her, and pointing to the row on his right he said, 'These are the ones most suitable for basketry.'

'That won't be an easy skill to learn,' said Anita, 'and I'm not sure that we will have the time, there's so much to do.'

Giles looked at her. 'You are being negative.'

'I can't help it. Making sure we have food is hard enough and then there's the herbs, we can't survive without them.'

Giles tried to reassure her, 'We are doing OK. Bit by bit, day by day, we are getting organised.' He pointed to the willows.

'When they are in their second year we will be organised.'

'It's the fibre problem that is defeating me,' said Anita.

'I may have a solution,' said Giles. 'It's possible to produce fibre from nettles. I don't know how easy or difficult it would be but we could experiment and find a way. So stop worrying.' He pointed to the hillside. 'There are plenty of nettles up there.'

Anita held his hand as they walked towards the house. Giles squeezed it. 'Anita,' he announced, 'you have one hell of an amazing washing machine,' he pointed to the newly completed working model of the bicycle-powered washing machine.

Leo waited until his mum and Giles had gone into the house, then grabbing his rucksack from behind the bushes, he made his way quickly along the edge of the garden.

This was not a premeditated act, it was an action based on an impulsive decision, fuelled by Leo's overwhelming need to see Sion.

As long as he kept to the far edge of the garden he knew that he would remain out of sight, even so, he felt eyes burning into his back. He shrugged off the feeling of being watched and continued to walk quickly towards the track.

As the land sloped downwards Leo's optimism renewed itself, from now onwards he was definitely out of sight.

Stopping momentarily he searched in his rucksack. He searched amongst the clothes, the food and under the bottle of water. He searched through everything twice, three times and then the realisation sank in, he had forgotten one important thing, he had forgotten to pack the map.

He had taken the map from the bookcase, he remembered that clearly. He then remembered clearly what he had done with it, he had put it on top of the settee while he had gone to get his clothes.

He could see the map lying there, stating an obvious fact, and that fact was that he had left home. It also stated that he had not only left home but that he had placed himself in a dangerous situation. To travel beyond the local and familiar land unaccompanied and without a map was lunacy.

Leo sat down on a pile of rocks and reviewed his situation. He had two options, to turn back or carry on.

He looked out across the valley. The great storm had changed the landscape, it had altered the valley and Leo wondered just how much detail remained unchanged.

He considered going home but something deep inside himself refused to accept this option. A voice inside his head told him, 'Wait.'

'Wait for what?' he asked himself. 'What is the point of that?'

Still the voice inside his head said, 'Wait.' Then he remembered. He remembered hearing the same voice as he crouched down outside Sylvie's cottage.

Leo turned around, half expecting to see Maurice standing only inches away, but Maurice was not there, he was alone.

A mixture of indecision and incapacity triggered by the voice in his head caused Leo to sit on the rocks for quite some time.

He rummaged in his rucksack and pulled out the bottle of water. He was about to take a drink when a movement in the distance distracted him.

He put down the bottle, shielded his eyes from the sun and focused on the moving dot in the distance.

He knew almost immediately that the moving dot was another human being.

Leo watched the slow moving dot meander along the narrow track. It stopped and then continued. As it came within a closer range Leo could see that the figure was stumbling and its stiff gait made him realise that this survivor, this other human being, was injured.

Leo pushed the water bottle back into his bag, slung the rucksack across his shoulders and began to make his way down the mountainside towards the figure.

Anita knew where he was and she didn't want or need Giles or anyone else to tell her any different. 'He's gone to see Sion,' she said, throwing the map to the floor. 'That's where he is.'

'Maybe he's with his bees,' suggested Sylvie. 'He follows them all over the place.'

Giles walked up to Anita. 'He'll be home soon, he's an adult, he needs some freedom.'

Anita swung around. 'You know what it's like out there, the earth hasn't settled yet. There are landslides all the time. It's not safe.'

'I'll go and have a look for him,' said Giles. 'Who'll come with me?'

Steve made his way to the door, saying, 'Let's get going.'

Sylvie sat down on the settee with Anita. 'He'll be OK, he's no fool.'

Anita looked at her. 'He's my son, and there are times when he is definitely a fool, and this is one of them.'

The heat from the midsummer sun felt unbearable, and the mixture of that intense heat and of hunger pushed PJ into a world beyond normal endurance.

Waves of dislocated thought made movement difficult and at times the simple action of walking seemed impossible.

As PJ fell to the ground, the ground itself seemed to rise up and swallow him. In that belly of the earth, he lay completely still.

He opened his eyes and the sun, like one huge, all-seeing eye, looked down on him.

PJ's words, barely audible and semi-incoherent, were spoken to that towering glaring entity. 'I am nothing,' he said. 'I am no more. Take me, take me now. Don't leave me here. Let me rise up.' PJ wiped his dirty and bleeding hand across his eyes. When his eyes had closed he whispered faintly, 'Take me.'

'There's no need to hold onto me,' Leo snatched his arm away.

'I'm not running from you, there's someone down there.'

'If you're not running away then why have you got a rucksack full of stuff?' asked

Giles.

Leo became agitated. 'There's someone down there.' He pointed frantically into the distance.

'Well, I can't see anyone,' said Giles. 'It all sounds like a cock-and-bull story to me.'

'For fuck's sake!' said Leo turning to Steve. 'Will you listen to me? There IS someone somewhere down there. I saw them.'

'OK,' said Steve. 'Let's go and have a look,' he said to Giles. 'He seems fairly sure that he's seen someone.'

Leo didn't wait, he threw down his rucksack and scrambled down the steep slope towards the narrow track.

When he reached the track, Leo realised that the figure was nowhere to be seen. He turned and called to Steve. 'He was down here.'

Steve caught him up. 'Exactly where did you last see him?'

Leo pointed. 'He was just about to reach the bend when you two showed up.'

Steve carried on walking. 'Let's take a better look,' he said. Leo followed and as he did his eyes searched beyond the edge of the track and down to the valley bottom. 'You don't think he could have fallen down there?' he asked, pointing to the deep cleft in the floor of the valley.

Steve looked down. 'I suppose it's possible. Let's go to where you last saw him and then take a look.'

When they reached the bend Giles peered over the edge and said, 'If he's down there then he's lucky, it's the shallow section.'

'How do you know?' asked Leo.

'I've been down there and had a look. The section further along is really deep, it's like a deep cave and he wouldn't have survived that fall. But here,' Giles pointed below them, 'it's quite shallow.'

Steve tried to work out a way down. 'Which way did you go?'

'There's a ledge back there. It's easy to climb down from there and then walk along the side of the cleft. But take care, some of the stones are loose.'

Leo was the last to climb down. The sight of the large gaping crevice, only inches away from him, worried him. 'Is this safe?' he asked.

Giles turned around. 'Look ahead, not down.'

Leo continued to look down. The seemingly bottomless pit was hypnotic and strangely luring, he turned his head away and focused on the ledge in front of him.

'Are you OK?' Steve asked.

'It's weird,' replied Leo. 'It's the magnetic pull of the earth.'

Giles came to a stop and pointed above. 'The bend is just above here. This is the shallow bit,' he looked down, 'we can climb in here.'

As Leo looked up towards the track something bright blue resting in a clump of bracken caught his eye. 'There's something up there,' he said.

Steve looked up to where Leo was pointing. 'It's a bag,' he said, 'and recently dropped there by the look of it.'

'Let's climb in here and take a look,' said Giles as he began to make his way down into the cleft.

Steve and Leo followed carefully. 'We'll lose the sunlight in around half an hour,' said Steve.

'It'll be enough time to check this section,' Giles said.

They didn't need half an hour of sunlight, it only took five minutes to find him.

Lying unconscious and barely breathing, PJ was completely unaware of anything. He didn't hear the voices around him. He didn't feel their touch. In his own silent limbo world, PJ didn't feel, hear or see anything.

Maddy sat on the edge of Maurice's bed and watched as PJ slept. Now clean and with his wounds dressed, he had been partially restored and he slightly resembled someone Charlie had known well. 'He resembles PJ,' said Charlie, standing by Maddy, 'but it could be someone else, I can't tell. I would have recognised him by his hands but they are damaged.'

'Charlie, when he wakes up you'll know if it's him, so let's not worry about that now. The main thing is to try and get some nourishment into him.'

'Anita's taking forever,' said Charlie anxiously. 'What is she doing?'

'She'll have to blend the soup by hand but I'm sure she won't be long. Why don't you go and help Maurice?' Maddy turned and looked up at him. 'It's upsetting you in here, isn't it?'

Charlie looked down at the figure lying so still and deathly. He nodded. 'I'll be in Leo's room if you need me.'

Maurice had placed his campbed behind a makeshift curtain. Leo had moved his own bed as far away as possible.

'Will you be all right in here?' Charlie asked.

'Well it's not ideal is it?' said Leo, as he pushed his bed up against the wall.

'It won't be for long,' Charlie reassured him.

Maurice appeared from behind the curtain. 'I could convert one of the goat sheds into a temporary bedroom, would you give me a hand tomorrow?'

'Sounds like a good idea,' said Leo.

'Are you asleep?'

Maurice's voice appeared from behind the curtain, 'No, but I should be.'

'Can we talk?' Leo asked.

'What's on your mind?'

'I feel really terrible. I can't believe that I was going to leave here without saying a word to any of you, especially my mum. How could I have done that?'

'Perhaps it was impulse.'

'I certainly didn't plan it. It was like some sudden overwhelming urge or desire and I was swept away with it. It was stupid of me, absolutely stupid, and I've really hurt mum.'

'If you hadn't gone when you did, no one would have discovered that person lying through there. He would have died. I'm not saying that it was right of you to up and leave, I'm saying that some good came from it. Perhaps it was meant to be.'

'The strange thing is that I have no real wish to leave here. I want to see Sion but that need is not great enough for me to leave everything that we have got here. I don't want to leave you lot and I certainly don't want to leave the bees.'

'Maybe it was midsummer madness!' said Maurice. 'It can affect us all.'

'Can I ask you something?'

'Go ahead,' said Maurice.

'Does not having a partner bother you?'

Maurice thought about Leo's question and then answered, 'I have enough love in my life. It's all around me and it's in everything. When you look for it you find that it is everywhere and that it is limitless. Vast amounts of love are waiting to be discovered by us all.' Maurice paused and then continued, 'True love is in all things. Experiencing love and giving love are the reasons why we are here, and that is the real meaning of true love. So no, being without a partner doesn't bother me at all.'

CHAPTER 25

Charlie moved the chair closer to the bed and sat down. The sleeping body lay lifeless, as it had done for the past six weeks. Charlie gently lifted the fragile hand and held it between his hands, he spoke quietly, 'PJ, it's me, Charlie. Wherever you are I hope that you can hear me. You are all right here, you are safe with us.' Charlie looked down at the pale hand and stroked it gently. 'Come back now, it's safe here, come back to us.'

He waited for a response, any response, but the lifeless body did not respond. He continued to speak quietly, 'The garden's looking good, PJ, you'd love it. We've got rows and rows of healthy haricots, we've got beautiful tomatoes which smell and taste divine. The cucumbers are taking over! The plants are like triffids and you have to battle your way into the greenhouse. We've got melons too, and courgettes, and we have enough turnips to last for the next ten years.

I want you to see it, PJ. I don't just want you to see it, I want you to be a part of it all. Leo has put a little seat near the beehives, when you feel better we can go and sit there. It's a shady spot to sit and it's surrounded by lavender and thyme, the smell is quite amazing. You'd love it there.' Charlie looked towards the window and then back at the sleeping body. 'You've got to come back, PJ. Find your way back.' Charlie lowered the hand back onto the bed and sat in silence.

Maddy opened the bedroom door and walked over to Charlie. 'I'll take over for a while, you go and get some sun on your face.' She bent and kissed Charlie's cheek.

'But I like hearing you sing.'

Maddy walked over to the window and opened it wide.

'You'll be able to hear me, now go and get some sunshine.' When Charlie had left the room, Maddy began to sing to PJ. She sang softly and sweetly. She sang all the things she wanted to share. She sang love songs, she sang songs of joy and she sang the simple uncomplicated songs from the heart.

Her prayers and her songs flowed together and filled the air with healing sound.

Charlie went to see how Maurice was getting on with the goat shed. He found him perched at the top of the ladder. 'It really needs re-roofing,' he called down to Charlie, 'but it will make do with being patched up.'

'Do you want any help?' Charlie asked.

'No, not now, I've nearly finished,' Maurice hammered the tin sheet into place.

'I didn't think this was your kind of thing.'

'It isn't,' replied Maurice.

Charlie poked his head into the goat shed. 'Will you be OK in here? It looks austere.'

Maurice climbed down from the ladder. 'It will be fine for me and it will allow Leo to have his room back.'

Charlie rubbed his head in thought. 'We need more bedroom space,' he said.

Maurice shook his head. 'No, we've got enough bedroom space, it's not a problem.'

Leaving Maurice to continue, Charlie walked into the garden. Here, everything had not only come to life but it had produced a bumper harvest.

He stood amidst the rows of beans and looked around. Every plant seemed vital and robust. He walked through the rows of beans and into Anita's herb garden. With its random planting, the herb garden was a delight to the eye.

Height, colour and fragrance mingled. The beds, unable to contain all of the growth, allowed the herbs to tumble and sprawl naturally. The bees were in their element in this the magical heart of the garden.

Charlie stood and watched them at work. Their constant labour was more than just labour alone, it was, he thought, an intense labour of love. Just then he remembered the words of an old saying, and it gave him an idea, an idea that involved Leo.

Leo was sat in the kitchen behind a huge pile of blackcurrants. He was deeply engrossed in the task of stripping the currants from their stalks when Charlie walked in. 'Have you come to take over?' Leo asked.

'No,' replied Charlie, 'but I'll do you a deal.' Leo sat back in his chair and waited. 'I'll do that job,' said Charlie, 'if you will paint a small sign for the herb garden.'

Leo looked puzzled, 'What do we want a sign for? We all know where it is.'

'Not that kind of sign,' said Charlie, 'I'd like you to paint a picture on a small piece of wood. I'd like you to put the bees, the herbs and the words, "Nothing Without Labour".'

Leo got up from the table. 'It'll take me much longer to do that than it's going to take you to finish this lot.' With a smile he added, 'It's a deal.'

Leo sat with his paints on the bench near the beehives and began to paint. He painted the hive, the bees and the lavender, and in a semicircle at the bottom of the painting, he painted the words 'Nothing Without Labour'.

When it was almost finished he sat back and closed his eyes. He could hear Maddy's song in the distance and when the song was over, he added one more thing to the painting. He added in the top left corner a golden orb surrounded by seven golden petals.

With sight, sound and senses unaware, PJ lay dormant. His body existed in a state of waiting, neither a part of this earthly world nor a part of that transient celestial space.

The body, an empty shell, continued its bodily functions. It breathed, it drank, it spewed, it defecated, and all the time it waited.

The cord linking spirit to body had unfurled and it had extended far into the outer reaches. The cord had not severed, it had not separated spirit from its mortal case, it had allowed the spirit to wander.

In a timeless abstract reality, and drifting in endless space, the spirit searched for the one thing that would draw itself back into its rightful place. It searched for the root of its existence.

The healing sound of love reverberated and wrapped itself around and within the lifeless body. It pulsed. It pulsed constantly and like a lighthouse it sent out its continual message.

The beam and the message radiated from the sound. The sound, the light and the love were not separate, they were inextricably linked. They were the one. They were the sacred complete and balanced whole that held the power and that power was calling PJ home.

'It doesn't seem right to me.' Steve looked away and then looked at Charlie. 'What do you think?'

Charlie pushed his hands into his pockets. 'It doesn't seem right to leave everything either. I think Giles may have a point.'

Giles spoke to Steve, 'Look at all these abandoned places, some are completely empty but some have things we could use. You can't just leave those things to rot.'

Steve looked him in the eye. 'Those things and those houses belong to someone and who knows, they might return here one day.'

Giles sighed, 'Come on, Steve, it's more than likely that they are never going to return, if they have survived, that is.'

'If they have survived,' said Charlie, 'it's doubtful that they'll be able to make their way back, the roads have all but gone.'

Steve looked around. 'It doesn't seem right to go into one of these places and ransack it, never knowing if the owners are dead or if they may return one day.'

Giles pointed to Steve's feet. 'What will you do when those shoes you are wearing wear out?'

Steve shrugged and then said, 'I wouldn't want to wear a dead man's shoes, that's for sure.'

'You might have to one day,' said Charlie.

'I think we should at least go inside and have a look around,' said Giles, heading down the path. 'You wait there if you can't bring yourself to join me.'

Charlie grabbed hold of Steve's arm. 'Come on,' he said.

Steve pulled his arm away. 'You go Charlie, but I'm not, because I don't agree with it. It doesn't feel right. I'll wait for you here.'

Charlie and Giles went from room to room downstairs. The smell left behind by the flood filled each room and mingled with the smell of decay. 'What is that terrible smell?' asked Charlie.

Giles made his way upstairs. 'Something decomposing, and it's worse up here.'

Charlie followed upstairs and as the two men stood on the landing Charlie said, 'I don't want to find out, I'll wait for you downstairs.'

'I'll be with you in a few minutes. I want to check in here,' Giles said as he opened one of the bedroom doors.

'That was quick,' said Steve as Charlie came out of the house.

'There's an awful smell of decay in there, I had to get out, but Giles is investigating.'

'Can he not leave things alone?' Steve asked. 'We aren't in such a desperate need for things to stoop to this.'

'You might be right,' agreed Charlie, 'but on the other hand, there will come a day when we will need to replace our things and we may regret not having...'

'...pillaged,' added Steve.

'We face a moral dilemma,' said Charlie, 'and I think it's something we all need to discuss.'

Giles slowly and gently closed the front door behind him. Walking up to Charlie he said quietly, 'Don't ask.'

Steve confronted him. 'You knew it didn't feel right to go in there, but you still went. Why couldn't you have left them in peace?'

Giles stared at him. 'How did you know it was "them" and not just a he or a she?'

'All three of us felt the atmosphere of the place,' said Steve.

'You chose to overide it, ignore it. I didn't, I acknowledged it but as a result of your insensitivity you completely missed what the place was saying.'

'And what was it saying?' Giles asked sarcastically.

'It was asking to be left alone.' Steve turned away and then added, 'They were both calling out to be left in peace.'

'I was aware of them too,' added Charlie quietly.

Giles looked at him. 'You didn't say anything.'

'You wouldn't have listened to me if I had, would you?' Charlie turned to Steve. 'I heard them when I was on the landing. They both called out the same thing. They called out the word "leave".'

'That's rubbish,' said Giles, 'there wasn't a sound in that house.'

Both Steve and Charlie looked at him but didn't say anything. Giles continued, 'I know what you're really telling me. You are telling me that I'm an insensitive bastard.' He marched out of the gate and then called back, 'But save your breath, I've heard it all before!'

Charlie went after him. 'Hold on,' he said, 'that's not what we are saying.'

Giles stood and waited, 'That's what it sounded like to me.' Steve caught them up. 'Don't take it personally. We all need to be a bit more sensitive to what lies around us, all of us.'

Charlie stood quiet for a moment and then said, 'If we could be more sensitive and aware it would help solve this awful moral dilemma.'

Steve asked Giles, 'What do you want to do now? Go home or carry on searching?'

'We've managed to get across here,' said Giles. 'We might as well carry on. But let's clarify, we are searching primarily for other survivors, but if we should come across anything that could be of use to us, we collect it, is that right?'

Charlie nodded in agreement, 'But we don't invade.'

'Come on, let's get going,' said Steve, checking the map.

'We've wasted enough time.'

Giles looked over his shoulder at the map. 'Are you sure you know where we are?'

Steve pointed to the map. 'We are here. No road or signs to guide us and the river has altered course but I think that there should be a church and a hamlet over there,' Steve pointed to an area of woodland in the distance, 'It should be behind those trees.'

'Are you keeping a record of where we have searched?' Charlie asked.

Steve showed him the map. 'We've covered the areas coloured red.'

'We haven't covered much have we?' said Charlie, picking up his rucksack. 'Let's get a move on.'

'Here,' Anita passed Leo the small feeding cup, 'it's your turn.'

Leo pulled a face. 'I hate this job. I'm not good at it, I either drench him or I choke him. Can you do it?'

Anita shook her head. 'It's your turn. Tiny sips and you won't choke him. Don't forget to lift his head slightly.'

Leo took hold of the cup and went upstairs. PJ lay oblivious to Leo entering the room, and oblivious to his mumbling. 'I hate this job,' Leo mumbled. 'It's awful.' He dragged a chair alongside the bed and sat down.

'I'm sorry PJ, I know that you need a drink but I'm no good at this. I never wanted to be a nurse, I'm not sure what I wanted to be. I thought I wanted to be an artist but then I found out that I really wanted to be a beekeeper. I suppose I enjoy being both. Did you have that problem?' Leo stared out of the window, 'Or did you always want to be a piano teacher? I bet you did. I bet you knew at an early age what you wanted to do and who you really were. They say insight is a gift, don't they?' Leo looked down at the sleeping PJ. 'I wonder who decides and who bestows these gifts? Do you think about things like that?' PJ continued to sleep. 'I sometimes can't switch my mind off, it goes rambling on, always asking questions and looking for the answers. I don't always find the answers, sometimes I do and sometimes they come like a flash of light. They are the best ones.'

Leo lifted PJ's head slightly. 'A little sip now. Don't choke, PJ, I can't stand it.' From the feeder Leo poured a little of the drink into PJ's mouth, waited for him to swallow and then gently let his head rest back on the pillow.

Leo sat back down on the chair. 'I bet that was good,' he said, and continued, 'Anyway, I was telling you about my thoughts. I think about God, you know, and sometimes I can hear him speaking. Last night he was telling me about love, not that lovey-dovey love but real love. It's a vibration, you know.' PJ continued to sleep. 'God made this planet out of love and it's in everything, the birds, the fishes, plants, rocks, the sea, clouds, the night sky, the mountains, you and me, all made out of love. It must be one amazing creative impulse. He made mother earth out of love and she IS his love. She is the queen and he is the king and that is why it has been so important to save her.' Leo looked away. 'She was dying and love saved her.' He looked back at PJ. 'I wonder if it will save you?'

Leo leant over and gently lifted PJ's head. 'Remember, no choking.' He gave PJ a sip from the feeder and then explained, 'I once saw God as an enormous spider made out of light. I couldn't see all of its body, just its head and two front legs. It held one leg outwards and opened the very end of its leg like a pincer. It actually looked like the two points of a compass and it astounded me because it resembled the Masonic symbol. God was showing me that he was the master builder and he was also showing me that the cosmic web was his.'

Leo leant over PJ. 'Come on let's have another sip. No choking.' He lifted PJ's head and began to tip the feeder into PJ's mouth. Suddenly PJ began to cough and splutter, the liquid splattered everywhere. 'Oh I'm sorry, PJ, I'm really sorry. I choked you and I've drenched you too. I am so sorry.' As Leo began to wipe the side of PJ's face with the sheet, PJ very slowly opened his lips and in a hoarse whisper he said, 'It's all right.'

'Tell me in a minute,' said Charlie to Leo as he put the rucksack on a chair next to the table. He said excitedly, 'The first group, ten altogether, live...'

Charlie pulled out the map and passed it to Steve. 'You show them while I unpack this lot.'

Steve opened out the map and found the hamlet marked in red. Leo interrupted again, 'Charlie I've got some wonderful news.'

'So have we,' said Charlie, pulling a bundle of plants from the rucksack. 'These are for you,' he said to Anita, 'but in exchange you have to take them some wheat, they've hardly any left.'

Anita unwrapped the bundle. 'What are they?' she asked.

'Perennial flax!' Charlie announced with delight. As he was about to pull another bundle from the bag, Leo grabbed his wrists and stopped him. 'Watch my lips. We have wonderful news, PJ has spoken.'

Charlie stopped what he was doing. At first the words would not fully register and then the impact hit home. 'Spoken?' he said in disbelief.

Leo explained, 'I accidentally choked him again and when I apologised he said, "It's all right." He hasn't said anything since but he isn't lying flat on his back, he's turned himself over onto his side and he looks alive.'

'Maddy's with him,' said Sylvie.

Charlie didn't finish emptying the bag, he left it by the table and rushed upstairs.

Giles pulled a parcel from the bag. 'The second lot of survivors we came across were a family of four, they gave us this lot.' He put the box of eggs and large wedge of cheese onto the table. 'In exchange they want medicinal herbs.'

'How amazing to know that people are surviving,' said Sylvie.

'They are getting on with life,' said Steve. 'Although they have had their share of problems they are enthusiastic.'

'The first group we came across,' explained Giles, 'have some really useful skills. The old guy can make clogs and he said he will teach us.' He said to Leo, 'If you need any beekeeping advice, he's your man, he's been keeping bees all his life.'

Anita took the bundle of plants over to the sink and soaked the moss around them, 'I can't believe this,' she said.

'Perennial flax!'

'The family we met have some cows and hens, they used to run a working farm and offered to help Charlie with lambing if ever need be.' Giles examined the cheese. 'There's enough here for us all to have a piece.'

'Can I have mine now?' asked Leo.

'That's up to you,' said Giles, cutting the cheese into equal pieces. 'I'm having mine on bread with spring onions.'

'I'll have that too,' said Leo. He then opened up the box of eggs. 'There's not enough to go round.'

'No,' said Steve, 'but they'll make a good-sized omelette, a cheese and onion one!'

'I'll have that,' said Leo. 'Are you making it?'

Steve smiled. 'Pass me the eggs.'

CHAPTER 26

Another wave of new energy entered the atmosphere, and it entered every cell throughout the whole living structure of the planet.

The new energies transformed the living structure. They pushed the barriers outwards, augmented every cell and strengthened their core with wave after wave of healing energy.

The energy transformed degeneration, changed it into rejuvenation, and as a result the ageing process began to slow down.

The higher frequencies flooded through and into the electrical circuitry of all life, causing a sudden and undeniable change. The change brought about a fuller, greater awareness of the higher forces.

This realm was now integrating closely with the earth energies, and the earth energies were magnetised by this strong, undeniable pull.

Man, being linked to both the higher forces and the earth energies, experienced a shift as the huge wave passing between heaven and earth swept through him. It moved him. It took him from the stale static energy of the past and placed him within the dynamic and constant coil of living light.

The inner spark of life within the heart of every living creature received one almighty pulse.

The pulse rang through the whole cosmos and it vibrated every structure within the creative realm.

This was God's powerful wave of thought and this thought was entwined with the equally powerful wave of his love.

Within the group a new and harmonious level of thought developed. It created a closer, clearer and more precise way of being, and enabled each individual to function and respond with greater ease. A sense of peace embraced the group.

Together they experienced a new kind of happiness and this happiness flowed through their daily lives. It cemented and sealed the cracks and fissures of old. It brought strength and durability. It nourished, fed and healed.

It gave to each individual another aspect of God's beauty, another facet of his holy and divine grace.

The seasons and man moved together as they had done in the very distant past. It was no longer possible to ignore the call and cry of nature, for it clearly lived within the heart of man and all living creatures.

Shifting levels re-established the relationship between man and fellow creatures. The power of man over beast dissolved as he became able to communicate on a greater level with the real world around him.

The illusion was fading as truth, once battered, torn and bruised, now stood renewed, healed and strong.

For Leo, the message was clear. It was, after all, the message he had been carrying inside himself for a long time, and the bees, an intricate part of his life, carried the same message.

On days when he tended his forest garden, the bees would follow and they would work around him and with him.

His garden had grown from the single thought that nature is natural, and so he had planted the seeds and allowed nature to take over.

Vegetables, herbs, fruit and nut trees grew happily together amidst the wild flowers, wild plants, bushes and trees. Areas of sun, shade, light, dappled light and darkness provided a wealth of opportunity for the diversity of those plants.

Leo collected water from a spring high in the forest. He had diverted the water to a pond close by the garden. The outer edge of the pond was home to a variety of moisture-loving plants and insects.

Here Leo filled buckets with the cool crystal water and began to water the dry areas of his garden. When he had finished, he sat down at the edge of the pond. From this spot he could see down and across to the other side of the valley.

The valley, once wounded and violated, was now fertile. The river and its close lying lines of energy flowed together and fertilised the deep earth.

Leo tried to spot the perimeter of his garden but there wasn't one. As the plants grew naturally, the garden, like life itself, had no beginning and it had no end.

The colours of the garden fused together and made whole a living picture, they radiated natural beauty and harmony. Leo studied the colours in the way that The Magpie had taught him to see. The subtle transient colours that had remained obscured for so long were now clearly visible.

Leo watched as a bee, loaded with pollen, located its flight path and began its journey home. Leo picked up his buckets and made his way down through the garden. The real journey, he mused, was like his garden, it had no beginning and it was without end.

As the handle of the old sewing machine turned, the child's dress began to take shape. The fair-haired child, bored with watching her mother work the machine, wandered off in search of her father. Her tiny feet padded into the kitchen. Dad bent down and picked her up.

From the lofty height she could see everyone and everything. Leaning to one side she outstretched her arm and reached into the bowl of fruit. Her tiny hand, too small to grab anything big, retreated empty.

Charlie picked out a small section of plum from the dish and passed it to her. Before pushing the fruit into her mouth she offered it to him. 'Bite now,' she said.

Charlie placed his lips to the fruit and in make-believe he momentarily devoured the whole piece. Wide-eyed, the child watched as the fruit disappeared and then giggled as the piece of fruit miraculously reappeared in his hand. Quickly she grabbed the fruit from him and pushed it into her mouth.

Steve wiped his daughter's smiling mouth and then gave it a quick kiss. The child wiped the kiss from her lips and said, 'Let's go, Daddy, let's go.'

Maddy walked up and asked, 'Where are you going today?'

In reply the little girl closed her eyes, stretched out both arms and said loudly, 'EVERYWHERE!'

As Steve made his way down the outside steps, the little girl spotted the man with the buckets. She wriggled and squealed, 'LEO!'

Leo put down his buckets and ran towards her. He took her from Steve, twizzed her around and received one very wet kiss. 'I don't like that bit,' he said, wiping his face with his sleeve.

'She takes after her mother,' said Steve.

The little girl, soon bored with Leo, toddled towards the buckets and began to fill them with stones.

'Are you in for lunch?' Steve asked.

Leo shook his head. 'No, and I won't be here tomorrow either.' Watching the little girl, he asked, 'Where are you two off to?'

'Everywhere, apparently,' Steve replied.

'So you'll be quite some time!' said Leo.

Maurice pushed the thick liquid into the rectangular tray, stood back and waited. Nothing happened.

'You haven't got it right,' said PJ, squinting.

'I followed the instructions,' said Maurice, gently shaking the tray.

PJ looked under the tray. 'There's nothing coming out. I think the bits are too big.'

'That's not possible,' objected Maurice.

Leo walked up and looked over PJ's shoulder. 'How's it going?'

'It's not,' answered Maurice, giving the tray another shake. Leo looked under the tray and then into it. 'I reckon the bits are too big.'

'That's what I thought,' said PJ. 'The liquid can't escape.'

Maurice held up his hands. 'Back to the beginning!' He said to Leo, 'You should be making paper, you're the arty type.'

'I can't do everything,' said Leo, putting his rucksack onto his shoulder, 'and besides, we all need to have a go at everything.'

PJ picked up the tray. 'I'll put this attempt onto the compost heap.'

Maurice shifted his gaze towards Leo. 'I'd like to come and listen to you sometime. I'd really like to hear you put your vision into words.'

'You don't need to,' replied Leo, 'you can see the complete picture.'

On his way back along the path, PJ stumbled, fell onto his knees and then picked himself up. Leo looked at Maurice, 'I wish I could find him some glasses.'

'His eyesight is improving,' said Maurice. 'It gets better each day.'

Shifting his rucksack to a comfortable spot, Leo said, 'I'd better get a move on, I've got a long walk ahead of me.'

As the first speaker moved aside, Leo took his place in front of the gathering and began to speak.

'It is synergy and it is how nature provides. It is a diverse and balanced living entity, not external to ourselves but a part of the fibre of which we are also a part.

That fibre connects all living things, it is within us.' Leo placed the palm of his hand upon his chest. 'It is in here and it is also external to us. It is all around us. It is underneath us and above us. It moves. It vibrates. It is alive.

When we damage the fibre, we damage our connection to and with nature. We damage ourselves.

Our new life has its fibre intact, it is undamaged. It is whole and it is fertile. We can live with and in that bursting fertility both as creator and as a part of creation.'

Leo stopped speaking for a moment and crouching down, he stroked a hand over the tiny plants covering the ground. He continued, 'Mother earth covers herself. She protects the delicate fragile structure of the surface of the earth, never leaving vulnerable even the smallest of living organisms.'

He stood up, paused for thought, then continued to speak,

'When we prepare the land for planting we can work with this natural structure, observe and respect its presence and realise its true value.

The seeds we plant can grow in harmony amidst and with the diversity of nature. Held and protected by the natural structure they are able to resonate fully and accurately and they will be healthy.

The edible garden we create, we can co-create. We can work with and alongside nature and allow nature to be our teacher. We can observe her principles and we can listen to what she is saying. We can learn from her.

We are not external to her, we are a part of her, and like the seeds I hold in my hand,' Leo held out his hand, 'each of us contains a living spark of life which connects us to the earth, the sun and to the heavens.'

He closed his eyes for a moment. 'The planets move within their destined journey and are connected to and by the great cosmic web. That web, or fibre, is made up of the same living, pulsating beads which connect all living things.

Within this structure the plants are alive, our planet is alive and this seed in my hand is alive. It absorbs and reflects the pulsating energy from above and below and it is influenced by both realms, the heavenly and the earthly.

We too live in both spheres. During the day our waking minds move with the earth and at night our sleeping minds move with the heavens.

In a state of balance between the two, we rest, grow, flourish and develop. Like the seed we experience fertility.

Fertile energy lives within our hearts, our minds and our spirits. It lives in all forms of life. It lives in the heavens and in the outer reaches of the imagination. It nourishes the crystal clear waters and provides us with the vital element, living water.'

Leo walked over to the small spring, cupped his hands and filled them with the clear water, and said, 'The earth is abundant with sources of living water.' After drinking the water from his hands he continued, 'It flows and moves on its journey throughout the structure of the earth and it absorbs and carries with it fertile energy from above and below.

It is a vital part of our natural edible garden. It provides not only moisture but also valuable nutrients and it provides support for the varied wildlife, who like us, depend on water for their survival.'

Moving away from the spring he went on, 'The insects and the animals experience, like we do, the whole gamut of experience that nature provides. When we respect this we begin to understand the true relationship of ourselves with fellow creatures.'

Leo distributed the seeds amongst the people. 'Study the forest and see how it grows, let it be your teacher, then plant your seeds as nature would have planted them.

Collect your water with care from the living sources and bring to your seeds life from the heavens, the sun and from the earth. When the plants have grown allow them to establish their own natural rhythm. Let them seed and let them fertilise the earth. Allow your garden not to mirror nature but to be a complete and whole part of it.'

Leo became quiet for a few moments and then closed his speech. 'A complete part of nature has no beginning and it has no end. Every person here contains within them the blueprint for that complete fertile life. A life without beginning and a life without end. We have all been invited to share this sacred journey.'

As the next speaker moved to the front of the gathering, Leo picked up his rucksack and made his way to the back of the crowd. Here he found an empty space to sit and as he rested back against the trunk of a tree he looked around.

The speeches in celebration of nature had been organised by word of mouth and the gatherings had become not only an important place to share knowledge, they had become a place where people could share resources.

Leo watched as the variety of seeds, seedlings, saplings, herbs, yeasts and garden implements changed hands. No one went home empty-handed. In exchange for his words Leo had been given a small parcel of offerings.

Towards the end of the day, when the crowd began to disperse, Leo picked up his rucksack, slung it across his shoulders and went on his way.

EPILOGUE

The sacred time revealed itself. It touched every element of life on and within the planet. Every part of existence was touched by the hand of the sacred.

Moments of deep silence occurred and became a part of everyday life. These moments contained the pulse of the life- giver. The reverberation sounded within the silence and linked together all that was new. It brought harmony and it brought peace as it filtered into the hearts and the minds of man, and it forged a new divine link.

Fear was dissolving and being replaced by something new, the light of the pulse. Everywhere the seeds of harmony were germinating and pushing thought forwards.

Man was no longer bound by fear, he was elevated by the pulse of the sacred which sounded within his own heart. He shared the pulse with all animals and all creatures. He shared the pulse with every living and growing thing within nature. Mother nature had not only reclaimed her child but she had given birth to the new.

The rules and confines of man were being replaced by an order that was natural, pure and whole. It had no limits. It was linked to and by the waves of celestial thought. This was truth radiating and illuminating itself.

Those moments of deep silence contained the blueprint of the present and they contained the passage into the future. Within the silence man discovered a part of himself that had been lost for so long and this discovery was the greatest of all discoveries, for it was the bridge which linked not only man to his higher self, but also linked the earth to heaven.

This wasn't just a passing thought or a glimpse, it was a living and dynamic experience and it was being shared by every living thing on and within the planet.

Animals roamed free, for like man, their old confines had dissolved and had been replaced by the limitless divine order. They too experienced the full gamut of the sacred.

The plants, the herbs and the trees all expressed the fullness of their link with the sacred. They breathed the holy breath and the air was pure again.

The sun once more bathed the land and all its inhabitants with gentle healing light. It caressed the very fibre of being and brought joy. It sounded the celebration of life but it did not sound time, for time could not be counted, it had ceased to be.

To be limitless, boundless and free, this was the gift from the heavens to the earth. Just as the earth was holy again, so too were all the components that were connected to the earth.

The bee, the messenger of the higher realms, connected and collected the nectar of the new life. Their honey, containing all the precious sacred elements of the new life, was not harvested. The bees' precious work was respected and this respect was rewarded. Nature became productive, balanced and healthy. The tiny unseen particles, fertile impulses scattered by the bees, linked together and formed a perpetual, regenerating and completely whole union within nature.

The ebb and flow of the celestial tide could be felt clearly. It moved man and it moved all things into their rightful place. Here man could live in harmony with the earth and he could live in harmony with himself. He was no longer alien to his surroundings nor alien to his own mind. He had become part of the structure encompassing the whole cosmos.

Limitless, he was able to transcend his material form. By the nature of thought he was able to discover and re-discover others like him. He was able to share and to give love and he was able to receive love.

This love was boundless. It would not be held in a strangle hold, for it was free. Forever floating on the waves of sacred thought, it was rich, life-giving, unsoiled and filled with grace. It lived in hearts and minds.

This love was the core of the new life.

Lightning Source UK Ltd.
Milton Keynes UK
UKHW050953100822
407113UK00007B/1482